PRIME RIP

PRIME RIP

WAYNE SWANSON
and GEORGE SCHULTZ
introduction by DAN RATHER

PRENTICE-HALL, INC.
Englewood Cliffs, New Jersey 07632

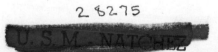

Prime Rip by Wayne Swanson and George Schultz
© 1982 by Wayne Swanson and George Schultz
All rights reserved. No part of this book may be
reproduced in any form or by any means, except
for the inclusion of brief quotations in a review,
without permission in writing from the publisher.
Address inquiries to Prentice-Hall, Inc.,
Englewood Cliffs, N.J. 07632
Printed in the United States of America
Prentice-Hall International, Inc., London
Prentice-Hall of Australia, Pty. Ltd., Sydney
Prentice-Hall of Canada, Ltd., Toronto
Prentice-Hall of India Private Ltd., New Delhi
Prentice-Hall of Japan, Inc., Tokyo
Prentice-Hall of Southeast Asia Pte. Ltd., Singapore
Whitehall Books Limited, Wellington, New Zealand

10   9   8   7   6   5   4   3   2   1

Library of Congress Cataloging in Publication Data
Swanson, Wayne, date
Prime rip.
Includes index.
1. Meat industry and trade—Government policy—United
States.   2. Meat industry and trade—United States—
Corrupt practices. I. Schultz, George, date.
II. Title.
HD9416.S96   364.1'68   81-8635
                         AACR2
ISBN 0-13-700351-X

For our parents

Introduction
by Dan Rather

In the American classic *Streetcar Named Desire,* playwright Tennessee Williams has Blanche Dubois say, "I have always depended upon the kindness of strangers." So do journalists. Many major news stories result from leads and information provided not by the highly visible public officials or renowned celebrities but from lesser known and unknown people: government employees who do all of the work and get none of the recognition; scientists and engineers who discover safety or health problems with products of their corporate employers but whose warnings are ignored; consumers angered by paying good money for bad goods and then getting no satisfaction after justly complaining to retailers and manufacturers; executives' assistants and secretaries who help prepare and type documents which contain lies and cover-ups; and blue-collar workers who help manufacture materials containing obvious faults. When these people contact journalists, we listen. Carefully.

Because of its audience and reputation, *60 Minutes* receives its share of such contacts. Most 'leads' do not lead anywhere. Many writers simply bear grudges while others see evil and mendacity and corruption in places where goodness and innocence prevail. Still other correspondents provide good leads which simply cannot be proved to the satisfaction of responsible investigative reporters—or at least not within budgetary and time parameters. But occasionally *60 Minutes* receives information from strangers that is treasured by its staff with as much enthusiasm and delight as excavators finding gold.

One of the fine nuggets that arrived unsolicited at *60 Minutes'* doors was a letter from Frank Hogya—a gentleman profiled in this book. Succinctly, he outlined a pattern of alleged abuse in the meat business and invited us to contact him or his attorney, William Bauer, who had recently hired a law school graduate named George Schultz. This is what we did. Mr. Hogya and Mr. Schultz provided us with solid information and further leads that eventually resulted several months later as a *60 Minutes* story entitled, "Bum Steer."

Viewers called it one of the best pieces of investigative journalism they had seen. Government officials called it lots of things: Some stung by charges of government inefficiency called it unfortunate reporting while others applauded it and used it to initiate administrative changes to help protect consumers and encourage fairer competition.

Mr. Hogya got us started but Mr. Schultz helped take us most of the way thereafter. Unlike some attorneys who rotate their thumbs, lean back in their stuffed chairs, and tell you what you already know, Mr. Schultz helped his client by being as much a reporter as an attorney. He helped us comb neighborhoods to look for people who knew what was going on—not uncaring government bureaucrats or callous businessmen but knowledgeable meat-packers, butchers, truckdrivers, low paid government meat inspectors, and graders—anyone and everyone who had firsthand knowledge about practices and mispractices in the meat business. Since our *60 Minutes* broadcast, Mr. Schultz and Wayne Swanson have continued the investigation, which has resulted in this book. By helping publicize his client's concerns, Mr. Schultz not only served his client but the general public. If Mr. Schultz ever decides to leave the law, I will try to have him hired by CBS News.

So let us praise strangers—and everyone else—who know the public is getting a raw deal and, despite all the hurdles placed in their paths, do something about it.

Contents

PRIME RIP

1
The Case Against the Meat Industry

Frank Hogya has a word for much of the meat Americans buy. "It's crap." He has a saying about many of the people who produce meat. "They're trying to make a silk purse out of a sow's ear." He has an opinion about some of the people who are supposed to police the meat industry. "They don't know a rump from a stump." Hogya is an old Navy man, a retired chief petty officer. Like any CPO, he's not about to let anybody jack him around. He was a hard-nosed veteran at Pearl Harbor, serving on the USS *Nevada,* and he's hard-nosed these days in a new battle. Frank Hogya knows consumers are buying inferior meat at inflated prices, and something damn well better be done about it.

"When I enlisted in the Navy, I took an oath to protect the nation from its enemies, both foreign and domestic," he says in his firm, deep voice. "We took care of the foreign ones. Now we've got to get some of the domestic ones." He has been going after his new national enemies since 1973. That was when he started to see second-rate meat at the counters of the Navy commissaries in San Diego where he shopped—"meat I wouldn't feed my dog." At first, he couldn't convince people to listen to his complaints. They said he was a crackpot. They said he didn't know what he was talking about. But now there can be little doubt that Hogya knows his enemies. Bribery, price-fixing, and other forms of corruption have inflated meat prices in California and throughout the country, sometimes pushing up the prices of meat by as much as 20 per cent. And Hogya has set out to get some justice.

Glenn Freie's combine broke. Fixing it will shoot another day, so it will be still longer before Freie can get back to the task of bringing in the crops. The cornstalks have turned golden brown and the groves of trees that dot the gentle rise and fall of the north central Iowa farmland have turned brilliant reds and oranges. Some say it is the most beautiful time the Midwest has to offer, but for a farmer it can be the most hectic. The harvesting must be completed before the bitter cold comes, and Glenn Freie has gotten a late start. For the past few months, he has worked the fields only on weekends, sometimes staying at it until midnight. But at three-thirty Monday morning he'd be up again, heading for the airport to start another week in Washington, D.C. There, he walked the corridors of Capitol Hill, talking strategy with Ted Kennedy; getting signals straight with the Senate majority leader and the speaker of the House; rounding up support from the powers of Capitol Hill. It has been a long, hard task, and it may be years before Freie sees results. But he is laying a strong foundation.

Once Congress adjourned, Freie would head back to the farm and try to catch up as best he can. He owns some four hundred acres near Latimer, Iowa, eighty-eight miles due north of Des Moines. It's not a large operation, and now that the kids are grown, he only plants about two hundred acres and raises about 125 head of cattle and a like number of hogs a year. Still, it's more than enough to keep a man and wife busy, and come October, Freie finds himself behind. He's behind because of his 125 head of cattle. Thanks to them, Glenn Freie has spent the past six years crisscrossing the nation in something of a one-man crusade to clean up the American meat industry. His goal is nothing less than to expose a conspiracy by the dominant supermarket chains and the largest meat-packers to shortchange both the farmers and the consumers of the nation by manipulating and fixing prices. Along the way, he is laying bare corruption, fraud, and incompetence in every aspect of the American meat industry.

Frank Hogya says he's nobody important. Glenn Freie says he's just an old country boy. But these two men, from opposite ends of the food chain, are rocking the foundations of the meat industry. They have hauled the giants of the industry into court and are making them answer for years of abuses. They are uncovering evidence that consumers pay for an insidious combination of corruption, fraud, collusion, and incompetence every time we buy a steak, or roast, or even a hot dog. The rip-off extends from the farms to the feedlots, to the packinghouses, to the supermarkets, to the upper levels of the government bureaucracy. And it is costing Americans upward of $8 billion a year.

Americans love their meat with a passion. Many of us would not think of letting a meal go by, let alone a day, without our fix of meat. Burgers on the grill. Chuck roasts, rib roasts, pot roasts. Lamb chops and pork chops. Ham on rye, BLTs, salami and bologna sandwiches. Big Macs, Whoppers, and Arby-Qs. Filet mignon in an elegant dining room, rib eye at the Sizzler. For every man, woman, and child in America, 181.3 pounds of meat was consumed in 1979—39.6 billion pounds in all. Meat is a major source of protein, iron, and many essential vitamins, and it has become accepted as a virtually indispensable ingredient for a healthful diet. Medical and nutritional experts have begun to voice serious doubts about whether meat deserves its place at the absolute center of the American diet, but the fact remains that many Americans would sooner give up their freedom than give up their meat.

We consume all the meat industry provides us, almost without question. And for too long, the American meat industry has taken advantage of us. It sells us products without really telling us what we're getting. And it charges us prices without really justifying why we should pay so much. The meat industry is the second largest manufacturing and processing industry in the nation, behind only the automobile industry, yet few people would ever guess it. Everyone has heard of General Motors, but who has heard of Iowa Beef Processors, a company that may have a tighter hold on its industry than GM? Meat is a $50-billion-a-year industry, but few people even within the industry understand its workings. As a result, consumers know more about what they're getting for their money when they pick out a new Chevy than when they pick out a porterhouse steak. Sadly, it is meat, not cars, that consumers purchase daily.

The crooks in the meat industry have made the most of this ignorance. The abuses uncovered by Freie and other critics run the gamut from unfair pricing to inferior quality, to fraud, mob influence, and governmental corruption. Now Congress, the courts, and a variety of governmental agencies are being forced to confront the problems. They can no longer ignore the evidence that the meat industry is overburdened with archaic practices, which it has tried to cover up through bribery and fraud. They can no longer ignore evidence that even the government has been the industry's partner in crime. They can no longer ignore the simple fact that while other industries have become more sophisticated with the times, the meat industry has mainly become more corrupt.

The modest white farmhouse where Glenn Freie lives stands off a gravel road four miles from Interstate 35 on its way from Des Moines to Minneapolis. The smell of manure is heavy in the driveway separating the house from the red barns and the pigpens behind them, while dogs roam the yard and barns. Freie is a squat, barrel-chested man in his mid-forties with sandy brown hair that is beginning to turn gray at the temples. A smile crosses his open, round face when he meets strangers, revealing a gold-capped filling that dominates the lower row of teeth. An easy, friendly laugh punctuates his flat, midwestern voice, and he speaks in a matter-of-fact conversational tone. The words aren't charged with emotion, but the message is disturbing. Quite simply, he is convinced the giants of the food industry are behind a massive conspiracy aimed at cheating both the farmers and the consumers. He has no doubt about it. He says he has proof, and over the next few years it will all come out. He reaches into a battered cardboard La Choy Chow Mein Noodles box and pulls out some reports and some statistics sheets to back up his claims. Then he calmly continues his narrative of how consumers and farmers are being taken for a ride. He feels strongly about his crusade, but he is not strident in presenting his position. His opponents would like to dismiss his charges as the wild ravings of some paranoid conspiracy freak, but they have not succeeded in discrediting him even though the battle has raged for years. Glenn Freie is a man of tremendous energy and drive who has taken to heart the perennial complaints of cattlemen that they aren't getting enough money for their livestock. On those complaints he has built a vigorous assault on the power structure of the American meat industry.

It began in 1975, when Freie got together with five other central Iowa farmers and decided it was time to do something about the pitiful prices they were being paid for their cattle. "We had all followed the markets and knew it didn't make any difference what the total amount of supply was on the market at any given day," Freie recalls. "That didn't seem to affect the market at all." It was something that had bothered midwestern farmers for years, but no one had been able to do anything about it. The Iowa farmers had, however, heard of Irvin Bray, a California rancher who, with a group of other ranchers, took on the Great Atlantic & Pacific Tea Co.* Bray and his partners charged the supermarket giant with manipulating beef prices, and 1975 was the year a federal court jury in San Francisco found A&P liable for $32.7 million in damages for conspiring to fix high retail prices and low wholesale prices for meat. The judgment was later reduced to $9 million in an out-of-court settlement, but the Bray case had proven to the Iowa farmers that some strange things were indeed going on in the marketplace. What they needed was a plan of attack.

A year before, five farmers in nearby Durant, Iowa, had filed suit charging three supermarket chains with manipulating prices, but the farmers were short on financing and attorneys, so when they were hit with a barrage of corporate legal work from the supermarkets, they dropped their case. Freie and his friends picked up the challenge only after they had mapped out a different strategy. "Us six guys sat down and decided, hey, if you're going to do it right, you're going to need the kind of talent that will be able to do the things necessary to insure success. And that means economists, lawyers, top-notch talent. You see, these boys in Durant started out with somebody who was a

---

*Bray v. Safeway *et al.*, U.S. District Court, San Francisco, 1975.

small-town lawyer who didn't really realize, I don't think, what he was going to get himself into."

Freie and his partners first went shopping for a lawyer with a national reputation and background in antitrust litigation. They came up with Lex Hawkins, the attorney with the biggest name in Iowa. He built the Democratic party in Iowa and ran it for years. Some of his court settlements have been spectacular— $5.8 million for one company in an industrial secrets case, $4.2 million for one man who charged his employer lured him into a job and then didn't live up to its promises.* Hawkins' law office is a historic English Tudor mansion furnished at the cost of nearly a million dollars—about what he can make in one year. The Des Moines *Register* has described him as "an extremist—a man who will settle for nothing less than the biggest, the best, the most in whatever he does." Lex Hawkins takes only the cases that intrigue him, and Freie and his partners presented him a challenge he couldn't pass up.

Hawkins told the farmers when they first approached him that it would take $10,000 to start, just to cover his expenses. And the farmers agreed. "Then, we went from February to the first of July doing nothing but finding, first, is there price fixing going on? Is there monopolization going on? And then what kind of staff can we put together?" Freie says. "We did a great deal of traveling just to talk to top-notch people and try to get them on our staff." They interviewed agricultural economists, and came up with two who shared their concerns and weren't afraid to risk their reputations and their university tenures to challenge the very people who supported their research. They signed up computer experts who could analyze meat prices and find out how they are manipulated and who is doing the manipulating. "After we put these people together, and after we did our preliminary investigation, one, we knew we had a case, and two, we thought we had the kind of people that if anybody was going to get the job done, we were going to get the job done."

That first year Freie logged two hundred thousand miles, traveling to meet with people in every aspect of the meat

---

*"Man Awarded $4 Million Over Firm's Promises," Des Moines *Tribune*, Oct. 23, 1978.

industry, lining up his experts, and trying to convince farmers to support his campaign. He put together five hundred backers in fourteen states, mostly small farmers, who donated $300,000 to finance the operations of Meat Price Investigators Association, a nonprofit corporation. "We're only five hundred of us in this group, we're not a large group, you know, but look at the thousands and thousands of dollars that a lot of these people put in," Freie says. "And they put this in at a time when they were financially in dire straits because of the economic conditions they faced for two or three years." The commitment of the farmers gave Freie the confidence to mount the fight, even though he knew it would take years before the group would see results. "I guess you're never assured success at anything in life, but it's always been my belief that if you've got the right cause, and put together the right kind of people, you have a chance for success."

The risks to the farmers supporting Meat Price Investigators were very real. They were alienating the people they depended upon to buy and slaughter their cattle. Most of the farmers Freie talked to when he was rounding up his support weren't willing to take that risk. Some told Freie he was on the right track, but they feared the power of the packers and the supermarkets was too much to buck. Their feeling was, you'd better take what you can get for your cattle and shut up. Some farmers wouldn't believe the abuses Freie talked about were possible, but Freie gathered enough support to move ahead. In late 1975 and in 1976, Meat Price Investigators Association filed suits against the eighteen largest supermarket chains, the four largest packing companies, and the price-reporting service for the meat industry. The suits charged that all were partners in a conspiracy to depress the price farmers are paid for their livestock, and to raise the price consumers pay for meat. The suits were consolidated with more than a dozen similar suits filed by farmers throughout the country, forming an unwieldy collection of charges likely to be in the courts for years. Freie and his group have gone on to investigate other abuses, and while the legal maneuvering continues, Freie has turned his attention to Washington. He has worked closely with Ted Kennedy on legislation to help his cause, and he is pushing hard on Congress and the government bureaucracy to take notice of the sorry state of the meat industry. Freie is aiming much of his criticism at the U.S. Department of Agriculture, which has allowed scandalous conditions to fester and, Freie contends, is under the thumb of the industry giants.

At first the meat industry powers took the suits and all the other activities of Freie and his small band of disgruntled farmers lightly, but six years later, neither Freie nor his supporters have gone away. They have fought all the way up to the Supreme Court on countless procedural issues, and they have beaten back numerous attempts to have their suits dismissed. The fighting has become as bitter as it has been protracted. Lawyers on both sides have charged their opponents with dirty tricks and unethical behavior, and even after all the cases are settled, the attorneys could be in court for years, fighting each other. For the farmers, the pressures have been more subtle. Early on, a few MPIA members charged that the buyers for the major packers wouldn't pay them as high a price for their livestock as they paid other farmers. For other members, there was just the nagging feeling that maybe buyers wouldn't give them the benefit of the doubt like they would other farmers. Then, in the fall of 1978, Freie says Iowa Beef Processors, Inc., the nation's dominant packer, sent its buyers out to western Iowa with a message for the 122 MPIA members there. Iowa Beef's management wanted them to know that if their suits failed, the company would countersue, charging that the suits were brought only to harass Iowa Beef. If that happened, the buyers warned, the farmers could be in for severe financial penalties. It was just a friendly warning to the farmers. Just something for them to think about. Freie says the court had already ruled the suits were not "frivolous," so the farmers had nothing to worry about. And Freie went to court to make sure Iowa Beef stopped its friendly warnings. The warnings ceased, Freie says, but Iowa Beef's message was the kind of thing that could work on a farmer who was struggling to get by. It was the kind of thing that could make him think twice about continuing his support.

As the campaign dragged into the 1980's, some MPIA members started to get discouraged. "I remember Mr. Hawkins, our lead lawyer, told me when we started this thing, 'You think you're going to have trouble fighting the defendants, but you're going to have a lot more problems keeping your people happy.'" Freie says there's really no way to keep everyone informed on the complex issues they are dealing with, but he has always been able to show enough indications of progress to keep the crusade going. Money, however, has been a problem. "We're not talking thousands of dollars, we're talking hundreds of thousands and millions to keep it going. It's a battle all the time. There have been times when we probably would have moved even faster if we had a bigger war chest. But like other things in life, sometimes you have to move a little bit slower."

All along the way, however, there has been pressure from other farmers to slow down even more—preferably to a complete stop. "After we'd been in this thing about a year," Freie says, "I started getting a fair amount of phone calls from producers who were begging me to drop the suits, stating there were people in the industry who were saying if these suits were dropped, they'd bring the price of beef up." These farmers would tell Freie he was only hurting the relationship between the farmers and the packers and the retailers. He was making it hard for all farmers to get along with the people they needed to process and market their livestock. Freie would tell the callers, "You're telling me that they do have the power to manipulate the market."

"Oh, yeah, we believe that," they replied. "We believe that, but we've got to stay on the good side of them. Maybe if you drop the suits they'll bring the price up four to five dollars a hundred, and maybe we can survive."

The effect on Freie was more overt. Once he started to speak out, the cattle buyers stopped coming to his farm. For the first two and a half years of his campaign, no one would come to look at his cattle. "I would then take my product to an auction where it was bought, maybe at a lower price, who knows, but what difference does it make to me now? I realized what I was facing when I got into this thing." The situation changed after two and a half years when Freie found that not everyone in the packing industry was against him. He was contacted by a group of California packinghouse officials who complained they, like the farmers, were the victims of the market dominance of a few large packers and supermarket chains. They were upset enough to want to join Freie's suits. Ironically, these were the same packers Frank Hogya was learning to know. These were the packers who were being charged with price-fixing and bribery. They later explained they had to bribe and fix prices to have any chance at competing with the industry giants. It was hardly a noble motivation, or a noble justification for joining the Meat Price Investigators' suits, and the idea fell through. But Freie knew then that it wasn't only the farmers who were being squeezed. The small and medium-sized packers were telling him they were in the same fix. They too were at the mercy of a few giants. Freie began to talk to the small and medium-sized packers scattered throughout the Midwest, and once he did, he soon had cattle buyers coming out to his farm again. The packers he talked to told him they were behind him 100 per cent. They said they wanted to support him publicly, but they too were afraid of the power of the market giants. In private, these small packers would give Freie all their support, but publicly they couldn't say a thing.

If Freie had had any doubts about his case, they now had been dispelled. He knew his enemy—the corporate giants who are taking over the meat industry. A handful of firms with the power to control the market in various sections of the country are squeezing the farmers. They are pushing out the smaller packers. They want complete control, and they will push until they have it. "I think we've been oversold on bigness in this country," Freie says. "We've been told it's the answer to everything, and I have too much documented evidence to show that in most enterprises, the saturation point for being efficient is a lot lower than a lot of us have been led to believe." The giants are a threat to what he calls the "private enterprisers," those independent farmers and businessmen who once were the backbone of the American economy. Now they face extinction at the hands of these new corporate powers. The force these corporations can muster is shocking, Freie says, and their tactics surpass even the worst imagination.

Freie says they have devised a broad web of corruption. It involves government—from elected officials under the thumb of industry groups to the USDA, an agency riddled with ineptitude and bent toward special interests. It has perverted the mechanisms that determine the prices of meat products. It has tainted the relationships among farmers, packers, processors, and consumers. And it has driven up the cost of all meat products. "We can document these things. We have proof," Freie says, his voice rising. "We don't smoke pot all day, we aren't making this up. I've been all over this country. I've talked to thousands and thousands of people. I've put together document after document on what's really happening. We've got a heck of a battle ahead of us. We've gone through a lot, but we've got a lot ahead of us."

Frank Hogya is an old-fashioned man with old-fashioned values. A tall, rumpled figure nearing sixty, his Hungarian heritage is reflected in his face. He's proud of the years he served his country in the Navy. There's an American flag pin on his lapel, and you'd better believe he's serious about his patriotism. And about his conservatism. He doesn't want anything to do with "lefties" or "fruits" or "women's libbers." He grouses about "fruits and muggers and bums taking over the parks." He gripes about "elected prostitutes who get in office and screw you into the ground." To some, he is just a kook, and when he goes off on one of his tangents it can be difficult to take him seriously. But behind the raving is one central ideal: Frank Hogya wants fair treatment. He wants people to get what they pay for. He doesn't want anybody trying to take advantage of people. Because of that ideal, Hogya has spent much of the last six years in court. Dressed in the formless blue suit that has served him for years and the faded floral tie with the script *H* across its center that may have been stylish in the McCarthy era, Hogya has stood with his attorneys, challenging the American meat industry. He has been thrust into the forefront of the consumer revolution, but he hardly fits in with the young liberals and radicals leading the consumer movement. In this case, however, he shares their goals, and he brings to the cause a special expertise: Frank Hogya knows all about meat.

"Hardly a day goes by that I don't read something about

meat," Hogya says. "I have friends in the business, and I talk to them a lot. It's sort of a hobby of mine." He carries with him a large briefcase overflowing with printed material about meat. Technical studies, trade journal reports, and newspaper articles, all classified by subject, are neatly folded and tucked into compartments in an exact order. He grew up around cattle. He has studied farming and cattle breeding, and for a while he thought he'd like to raise cattle when he retired from the Navy. That didn't work out, but he still takes a headful of knowledge with him every time he approaches the meat counter. And often, he doesn't like what he sees.

Hogya appreciates the lusty aroma of a fine T-bone on the grill. He prizes the delicate flavor and tenderness of a steak that seems to melt off the fork. But he usually doesn't see the kind of meat that will give him that pleasure when he goes to the supermarket. And he knows why. Hogya knows about beef breeds, beef grading, and beef marketing. He knows that different cattle breeds are being used today to produce meat, and federal grading standards have been relaxed, so beef that is leaner, tougher, and less tasty is finding its way to the dinner table. And consumers are paying ever-higher prices for this inferior beef. The problem starts with the cattle. All cattle are not created equal, and neither are the steaks that come from them. There are standard beef breeds, such as the Hereford and Angus, that have been developed for their fine eating qualities. But increasingly, they are being crossbred with other animals whose strong quality is their ability to survive in more varied climates. In the South and Southwest in particular, the beef breeds are being crossbred with the Brahman bull, a scrawny, humpbacked animal from India. It can withstand heat and rough treatment, but its meat is equally tough. "There's a place for these cattle," Hogya says, "but I personally think that place is on the hamburger and rodeo circuit." Instead, they are making their way into the breeding stock, and Hogya says they are reducing the quality of beef.

It's a problem that has been building for years. As the quality of the cattle has decreased, so has the quality of the meat, and less of it has qualified for the federal grade choice— the grade most consumers prefer. But Hogya kept seeing just as much beef marked choice at the counters of the commissaries in San Diego where he shopped. "I first noticed this to where it bothered me in 1973," he says. "The beef at the commissaries looked just awful. Nothing like the pictures in the booklets shown by the Department of Agriculture to tell the difference between choice and good meat. So I complained to the commissary people about it, and nothing was done." Hogya didn't let the matter drop. He started writing letters to officials in the USDA and the Department of the Navy. Eventually, the USDA and the Navy agreed to meet with him so he could present his case. "We discussed this, and nothing much was gained. They insisted everything was fine. So I invited them to come over and I'd show them what kind of crap they had over there. But they refused to come with me." All he got was a "seagull salute"— "You know, they just threw their arms in the air like it was nothing."

It all fit the pattern Hogya kept encountering. Every time he complained to someone, the response was the same. First he was told he must be mistaken, because government procedures ensured that only the finest-quality meat was reaching the public. Then he was told, politely, that he simply didn't understand the meat industry. He was dismissed as a kook, an uninformed meddler unable to understand the complexities of the meat industry. Today, those who have taken the time to hear Hogya out have a different view. Many have told his attorneys, "This Hogya sure is strange, but he knows what he's talking about."

When Hogya was convinced governmental agencies would not investigate his complaints, he decided to do it on his own. In 1976, he went to an attorney who had helped him out once before when his outspoken views had gotten him in trouble. In that instance, Hogya had taken on the San Diego public school system, charging it with violating his freedom of speech. Hogya had worked as a school gardener after retiring from the Navy, and one day he gave the principal some free advice. He told the principal that the schools shouldn't give in to the demands of Mexican pupils to be taught in Spanish; Hogya said the Mexicans should be like the Japanese, who make it a point to learn in English. The principal didn't appreciate the advice, and instead had Hogya transferred to a school out in the boondocks. Hogya's attorney, William Bauer, succeeded in getting him his old job back, so Hogya decided to try Bauer again. This time, Bauer considered giving him the brush-off. But he took a chance. Bauer had just hired a law clerk, so he figured they could afford to spend a couple of days looking into Hogya's claims. What they found was staggering. They found evidence that federal meat graders were accepting bribes of up to four hundred dollars a week to mark beef USDA choice that was of inferior quality. They found that supermarket buyers who accepted this inferior meat were the recipients of lavish gifts from packinghouses. They found numerous abuses within packinghouses involving mislabeling and relabeling of beef. They found evidence that many Southern California packers would literally sit together around a table once a week to fix the price of beef.* And while the investigation was snowballing, Hogya's earlier complaints to federal officials finally brought results. In 1974 and 1975, sixty-five packinghouse officials, packing firms, and federal meat graders in Southern California pleaded guilty to bribery and gratuity violations in a scandal that dated back to at least 1960. And in 1978, thirteen packers were fined a total of $640,000 and nine company officials were sentenced to jail terms for their part in a price-fixing conspiracy that had gone on for at least ten years.

Hogya began to see that the corruption was not limited to Southern California: the abuses were nationwide. He found evidence of the same problems Glenn Freie was fighting in Iowa. And he, like Freie, began to shake the foundations of the meat industry. First, in 1977, Hogya filed a class action suit on behalf of the patrons who had bought illegally upgraded meat at the San Diego commissaries. † The result was a three-hundred-thousand-dollar settlement paid by the packers to the commissaries. It allowed the commissaries to lower beef prices 10 per cent for three months to repay patrons for the inferior meat they had bought. Then Hogya, along with the California Public

---

*U.S. v. Reuben Krasn, U.S. District Court, Los Angeles, 1978. Also in U.S. v. Acme Meat et al., U.S. District Court, Los Angeles, 1978.

†Hogya v. National Meat Packers et al., San Diego Superior Court, 1975.

Interest Group, a Ralph Nader-founded consumer group, filed the largest class action suit in California history on behalf of all the beef-eating consumers in Southern California. It demanded $6 billion in damages from meat-packers and supermarkets for price-fixing, bribery, and other irregularities. That case was later dismissed, but Hogya is still on the offensive.

He has moved up to Los Angeles to be with his children and grandchildren, but he still rails against the inferior-quality meat he finds. He has developed a running battle with his commissary in Los Angeles. "I bought some porterhouse steaks there," he says, "and they looked pretty in the case, but they weren't right. They're tender, but there's no flavor to them. It's just crap." And he is still on the back of government to do its job. "The Department of Agriculture is the main bastard responsible for all of this. As I told them, there can't be a crooked grader without there being a crooked packer, because the grader ain't going to be crooked for nothing." The USDA must start doing a better job, Hogya says, to make sure nobody is crooked.

Frank Hogya's obsession with the poor taste of meat, Glenn Freie's complaints about the low return to farmers raising cattle, and the gripes of a handful of other individuals throughout the country are now being translated into a wide-ranging collection of suits and inquiries into the operations of the American meat industry. Hogya is telling us the quality of our meat is deteriorating, yet we are paying ever-increasing prices for it. Glenn Freie is telling us every time we buy a piece of meat we are paying a nickel or dime per pound more than we should, yet the farmer who raised the livestock is getting a dime or quarter less than he should. Both are saying government has sat idly by while these problems have festered.

Neither man had any idea he was stumbling onto abuses of such massive proportions when he made his first complaints. And each man tries to be modest about his role. "I'm not so important to this whole deal," Hogya tells people, although he is proud to display the Navy Meritorious Service Citation he was awarded for his efforts. Freie says, "I never got to college, and I feel inferior lots of times, but I just keep on pushing ahead. I'm just a country boy, that's the theme I like to use. My English isn't that good, my wife tells me. And I know it isn't. But I sometimes think in some of these offices they get tired of hearing highfalutin lawyers in there all the time, and somebody different, sometimes they'll listen more."

They are starting to listen, in Washington and throughout the country, to the Glenn Freies and Frank Hogyas who are finally blowing the whistle on the prime rip that is costing Americans billions of dollars each year.

2

The Declining
Quality of Meat

*You can feed them any goddamn thing you want, but you ain't
going to make Hereford or Angus beef out of one of them water
buffaloes.*

—*Frank Hogya*

Frank Hogya has been around. "In my travels over the world,
I've eaten what they call caribou out in Guam, I've eaten
monkey meat, and I've eaten even dog meat. Not that I liked it
or would eat it again, but I guess you can eat anything, if you
really want to." What Hogya really likes to eat is a good steak.
But he says consumers might just as well eat monkey meat as
some of the "crap" passed off as steak today.

Hogya, the self-styled California meat expert, knows what
meat should be like. He was born and raised in the cattle
country outside of Omaha, Nebraska. Even when he joined the
Navy he took courses in ranching and dairying at the U.S.
Armed Forces Institute, and in scientific breeding at the Grange
School for Cattlemen. He had a friend who ran a dairy, so he'd
help him out whenever he could. He will still occasionally head
out to stockyards to watch the operations. He talks shop with
packers and rancher friends when he gets the chance. He's a
faithful subscriber to agricultural bibles like *Farm Journal* and
Successful Farming, and he keeps his portable briefcase library
stocked with the latest stories, studies, and government publi-
cations about cattle. He dreamed about going into ranching or

dairying when he retired from the Navy, but when the time came, he found out it had become too expensive. "My interest is still there, though," he says. "You might say it's my hobby."

These days it's a frustrating hobby, because every time he goes to the supermarket, he sees what has gone wrong with the American meat industry. And he sees how shoppers are being ripped off. Every day, as the Muzak pumps out of the brightly lit supermarket ceilings, the shoppers wheel their carts up to the refrigerated meat cases. They pick and choose among the steaks and chops and roasts that all look so enticing in their tight plastic wrappers. But increasingly, shoppers find the meat beneath the plastic wrappers is as bland as the supermarket Muzak. The steaks are tough, the chops are dry, and the roasts are tasteless. Quite simply, the quality of meat is deteriorating. Hogya knows why, and his findings are backed by the research of experts nationwide. Hogya and the experts have found that federal quality standards have been lowered; breeding and feeding practices have become geared toward producing quantity, not quality; and consumers are being misled by confusing federal regulations and by commercial hype. The bottom line is that making an intelligent selection at the meat counter has become a chancy proposition.

The problems begin with one fundamental distinction: the difference between federal inspection and federal grading of meat. Some supermarkets, butcher shops, and even manufacturers try to impress shoppers by proudly advertising, "We Sell Only USDA Inspected Meat!" As Hogya points out, the only proper response to that is, "So what? The Alpo I buy is inspected too!" The U.S. Department of Agriculture has been inspecting meat since 1906. That was one year after Upton Sinclair exposed unsanitary packinghouse conditions in *The Jungle,* and the public became outraged at the thought of rats in the sausage meat and human bodies in the "pure leaf lard" they bought. As a result, all beef, lamb, veal, and pork—even if it's intended just for dog food—is inspected by the USDA or state agencies to make sure the meat isn't diseased, spoiled, or contaminated. But the "USDA Inspected & Passed" seal is no guarantee that the meat won't taste like shoe leather.

The USDA set up a separate meat-grading service in 1927,

and it is the meat grade that gives the consumer a clue about the quality of the meat—the flavor, tenderness, and juiciness of the cuts. There are eight federal grades for beef, six for veal, and five for lamb. Prime is the highest in quality and the highest in price. It is usually found in the top restaurants and the gourmet butcher shops. Choice meat is second, found in many supermarkets. It is the grade desired by most shoppers because it is supposed to combine a large degree of flavor and tenderness with a slightly lower price. Good meat is third, a lean and less expensive grade. But it is seldom found in supermarkets because there is little consumer demand for it. The remaining grades denote meat of decreasing quality, and are almost never seen on meat in retail stores. The meat is used primarily for institutional food services and processed meats like hot dogs, sausages, and lunch meats. Pork grading is slightly different. Grades U.S. No. 1, No. 2, and No. 3 are roughly comparable to prime, choice, and good, but they are not widely used, since brand names have long been more important in the sale of pork than in other meats.

It all sounds as if it should be a very efficient system, but meat grading has never been as useful as it could be. Meat grading is admittedly an inexact science, but it is one that is practiced with amazing speed. With beef, for example, long rows of carcasses, split in half, are suspended from hooks on rails in the ceiling of the packinghouse cooler. One side from each carcass is slit open between the twelfth and thirteenth ribs to reveal the rib-eye muscle. A federal meat grader, dressed in hard hat and white freezer coat to protect himself against the 35-degree chill, makes his way down the line. He checks the marbling, the small flecks of fat interspersed through the red meat. He checks the color and the texture. He studies the cartilage on the carcass to determine its age. Sometimes, he puts a grid over the rib eye to calculate how much meat the carcass will yield. This entire process takes all of fifteen seconds. The grader inks a metal shield with his identification number on it, and he records his grading decision by the dull slap of his metal stamp against the chilled side of beef—three slaps for prime, two slaps for choice, one slap for good. He inks another stamp that indicates how much meat the carcass will yield, slaps the carcass again, and moves down the line. The grader will pass judgment on hundreds of carcasses every hour. In some packinghouses, the carcasses are hung from motorized chains and pass by the grader at dizzying rates of up to 330 carcasses each hour.

The system is obviously open to many errors. In 1978, the General Accounting Office, the investigative arm of Congress, confirmed just how error-prone the grading system really is. The GAO found that one out of every five carcasses is misgraded. The majority of the errors favor the packer, so the consumer buys an inferior piece of meat at an inflated price. And the packer makes a nice profit on the mistake. On just one carcass graded choice that should be only good, the packer makes about $47, or about 6.7 cents per pound. At the supermarket, the consumer pays 15 to 20 cents per pound more, and the yearly overcharge to consumers runs to the hundreds of thousands of dollars.

Inaccuracy isn't the only problem. The grades themselves are not something consumers can depend on. They were originally established to give packers uniform guidelines to help market their cattle, not necessarily to give consumers guidelines to help determine the quality of the meat. So the correlation between grades and quality has always left something to be desired. And considering the way grade standards have been changed during the past fifty years, they seem to have been constructed on quicksand. The government has shifted the grades for a variety of policy reasons that have seldom shown much concern for the quality of the meat. The latest change came in 1976. In a cruel fraud on consumers, grading standards were relaxed so now some beef that used to be marked choice qualifies for the prime grade and sells for as much as twenty cents per pound more. And the choice grade was expanded to include meat that used to be just good. In fact, 80 per cent of the beef graded today qualifies for the choice stamp, so the grade has become virtually meaningless. The difference in quality between meat at the top and meat at the bottom of the grade has become so profound that meat buyers for supermarkets, butcher shops, and restaurants now must specify to their suppliers whether they want "high" choice, "mid" choice, or "low" choice, and pay a premium if they want the better meat. But shoppers, who see only the choice label, have no way of knowing which end of the spectrum they are buying from. And most likely they are buying meat that just barely made it to the bottom end of the choice grade. As a matter of economics, most cattle are bred and fed so they will produce beef just good enough to slip into the choice grade, and no better.

The USDA cited many reasons for the grading change, but none of the reasons showed any concern for safeguarding the quality of the meat. One consideration was that the government had agreed to a grain sale with Russia that would raise grain prices in the United States. The higher grain prices would mean higher feed prices, and thus higher meat prices, so the government needed to find a way to keep prices from going out of sight. Their solution was to cheapen the choice grade, allowing cattle that had been fed high-quality feed a shorter period of time to qualify as choice, the grade consumers want to buy. Consumer groups criticized the change, while initially it was enthusiastically received by the meat industry. But soon many packers began complaining about the change too. The packers who were producing a quality product found the change actually worked against them: the grading change was a boon only to the packers producing marginal beef.

People like Frank Hogya complain that the grading change was pushed through by these packers because they were finding that an increasing amount of their beef wouldn't qualify for the choice grade. "There's nothing wrong with the meat, but the packers don't pay as much for it, so why should the public?" Hogya asks. He says the public should have the opportunity to buy the meat for what it really is—USDA good quality meat. "There's nothing wrong with USDA good. But it's like comparing two cars. A Ford is a Ford, but you don't want to pay Lincoln Continental prices for it. Likewise with meat. You don't want to pay choice prices for good meat." Before the grading change in 1976, packers were forced to bribe graders if they wanted to make this inferior meat choice, and it was the widespread bribery of graders in Southern California that initially got Hogya involved in the fight against the meat industry. Now, the packers can save themselves the cost of the bribe because some of this same inferior meat is now legally choice, thanks to the grading change.

These problems are compounded by the fact that many people just don't understand grading anyway. Numerous studies have found that many consumers are unfamiliar with the grading terminology. Some confuse grading and inspection, some don't know which grades are better than which, and some don't know the grade names, period. If that weren't bad enough, federal grading is not mandatory, so not all supermarkets carry graded beef. In fact, in some areas of the country, the majority of the supermarkets don't. Instead, these supermarkets invent their own store brands, such as Bonded, or Preferred, or Supreme Cut. Some are even devious enough to use names such as Butcher's Choice or Gourmet Choice in an attempt to dupe shoppers into thinking they are getting USDA choice. All the fancy names may sound impressive, but generally the quality is not: the vast majority of the meat does not qualify for the choice grade. When a USDA meat grader walks into the cooler, he is generally directed by the packer to grade only those carcasses that qualify for prime or choice stamps. Beef marked with only a supermarket house brand carries no government assurance of quality. For this house name the consumer usually pays a price roughly comparable to what choice beef sells for—sometimes even higher. Yet most of this ungraded beef would only qualify for the good grade. The difference in price between choice and good can be as much as sixty cents per pound on some cuts, so on a large roast a shopper can end up paying a few dollars too much while the supermarket makes some extra profit.

Some of the ungraded meat sold by supermarkets is choice meat, but the shopper doesn't know which piece. And the supermarkets and the packing industry have fought efforts to give the consumer more of a clue. In 1978 they blocked a proposed USDA policy that would have required meat that was not federally graded to be marked "U.S. Ungraded." The proposal was developed by Carol Tucker Foreman, assistant secretary of agriculture during the Carter administration, one of the few champions for the consumer to be found in the USDA in recent years. The intent was to cut down on opportunities for deception in the sale of meat. "Unfortunately, the present system lends itself to practices which are confusing and mis-leading to consumers," Foreman said when she proposed the ungraded policy. "Without accurate grade information, con-sumers may pay choice prices for meat of lesser quality." The meat industry ridiculed her ungraded proposal, complaining that it was yet another intrusion of the bureaucracy that would raise prices and confuse consumers. Industry spokesmen said the proposal would undermine confidence in their products because consumers would assume "ungraded" somehow meant uninspected or unwholesome or unsanitary. But Foreman and other consumer advocates are convinced the meat industry was mostly afraid consumers would catch on to its game of selling low-quality meat with fancy names at fancy prices. Foreman concedes, however, that the ungraded proposal as drafted did cause confusion, with some people assuming it meant unin-spected. She adamantly maintains that the USDA must continue to search for ways to make grading more useful to consumers. That leads to yet another problem with grading meat.

Health and nutrition research increasingly indicates that the best-tasting meat may not be the best meat to eat. The choice and prime cuts that are the most tender, juicy, and flavorful are also the most heavily laden with fat. One of the best indicators of top-quality meat is the marbling—the little flecks of fat interspersed through the red meat. A piece of meat with a delicate spider web of fat laced through the muscle will be more flavorful than a piece with little or no marbling, and it will command a higher federal grade. But researchers are also linking this fat to heart disease and cancer, and suggesting that Americans eat leaner meat. That means eating good-grade meat, the meat packers don't want to produce and consumers don't want to buy. The USDA is faced with a dilemma: should its grading system continue to bestow the highest marks on the best-tasting meat, or should the system be changed to promote meat that may be more healthful, even if it doesn't taste as good?

The USDA is trying to sort out these concerns, and it could once again attempt to change the grading system. But for now, confusion reigns, and supermarkets all too often play on this confusion. They speak in glowing terms of their lean meat.

They say it has the bright red color housewives want; they say it has "sizzle," and they say it isn't fatty. But there is one thing they don't say: lean meat just doesn't taste as good. It would be one thing to promote lean meat as a product that is healthful for Americans, but instead they try to imply that the lean meat tastes the same as the more heavily marbled choice and prime meat. After all, health doesn't really sell, and without hyping its taste, supermarkets would be faced with promoting a product that should cost less and doesn't taste as good—hardly a favorable marketing idea. Supermarket officials argue that their lean meat is what consumers want. Yet at the same time they admit shoppers generally won't buy meat graded good—the lean grade—because shoppers don't think the quality is high enough. So what the supermarkets are really saying is that consumers will buy their lean, ungraded meat as long as they don't know what it really is.

Even the supermarkets, however, are victims to a certain extent, because there is one more reason why they try to promote lean meat: sometimes it is the only kind of meat they can get. Visions of prizewinning steers at the country fair, cared for lovingly and fattened leisurely, have little to do with meat production today. The meat industry is a high-volume, low-profit-margin business, and it is structured to raise, fatten, slaughter, and merchandise its product as quickly and cheaply as possible.

The sirloins, rump roasts, hamburgers, and all the other beef cuts at the meat counter today are as much as two and a half years in the making. And each link in the chain of events leading from ranch to supermarket has an impact on the ultimate quality and price of the meat consumers buy. The process begins with the birth of a group of wet, wobbly calves. Usually, these calves are raised by a farmer who keeps them just about nine months, until they have grown to a weight of about 450 pounds. Then they are sold to a "backgrounder," a farmer who begins the process of rapid weight gain that will see the calves grow at the rate of a pound and a quarter to a pound and a half a day. They graze on grass, which is cheap, and then on grain and corn, which are more expensive but fatten animals more quickly. The next step is to the feedlot, a massive collection of pens where the only job for the young cattle is to stand around and eat.

The feedlot has become the key factory for today's mass-produced beef. Dusty pens that in the largest feedlots extend as far as the eye can see are filled with cattle, all segregated according to age, weight, and general condition. The cattle wear color-coded tags on their ears, indicating just how far along in the fattening process they are, and just what they should be fed. For each group, mountains of corn and other grains are mixed with protein, minerals, and chemical additives for a specific ration that will give the animals the "finish" that will make them marketable, and the feed is distributed in the feeding troughs that line each pen. Corn used to be the most important element for producing the most flavorful meat, but since it is also the most expensive, it is increasingly being replaced by barley and other less expensive grains. A variety of chemicals and drugs are added to the feed or injected or implanted into the animals to guard against disease and help them gain weight quickly. It is a common practice to feed livestock "subtherapeutic" levels of drugs as a preventative measure to eliminate the chance of disease before it starts. But there are growing questions about whether the chemical residues in the resulting meat are harmful, and whether the continued use of these drugs will result in the development of drug-resistant disease strains that in the long run could pose more serious health hazards to the livestock and to humans.

Other drugs are used specifically to make the animals put on weight quickly. Until 1979, the most important drug in this process was diethystilbestrol, or DES, which was considered one of the most effective growth stimulants. It also causes cancer. DES first came under attack a decade ago when it was used in another form—as a drug used by women to prevent miscarriages. It was banned for use by humans as a result, and many other countries banned its use in livestock. But it wasn't until November 1979 that DES was outlawed in the United States. Even a year after the ban, the Food and Drug Administration charged that illegal use of the drug in livestock continued, calling it the most widespread violation of a drug ban in the administration's history. Other drugs, however, have been developed to take the place of DES, and while they are not quite as effective in stimulating growth, they come close. "God only knows what they put in that feed," Hogya says. "I guess that's why they call it hot-shot feeding, because the protein content is so high it pushes the animal past its normal capacity." But as a consequence, the feed is not fully assimilated, and the quality of the meat suffers. The marbling to be found in much of today's meat is coarse—flecks and globs of fat within the red meat, not a fine, delicate webbing.

At the feedlot, cattle put on weight at a rate of two to two and a half pounds per day, reaching a weight of more than a thousand pounds. Now they are ready for market. In the old days they were loaded on trucks and trains and transported to one of the major stockyards, most prominently the Chicago stockyards. But the cattle market today is decentralized, and the massive stockyards are a thing of the past. Many packers buy their cattle directly from the feedlots, or rely on smaller regional stockyards closer to the feedlots.

The brief life for beef cattle ends some one and a half to two and a half years after birth when a slaughterhouse employee fires a gunlike device, sending an eight-inch-long pin into each animal's forehead. Within twenty-five minutes, the hide is stripped, the head removed, and the young animal is reduced to a carcass and its by-products. In addition to the meat, the animal provides the makings for fertilizers, soap, pharmaceuticals, and other products. The old industry saying is that they use everything but the moo.

The carcass may be shipped to a butcher shop or a supermarket chain's distribution center, where it is cut into manageable pieces. Then to the supermarket, where it is carved into retail cuts. But increasingly, this last step is being removed as the industry turns to a concept known as "boxed beef." Packers are finding it cheaper and more efficient to chop the carcass into wholesale or even retail cuts at the packinghouse, rather than shipping carcasses cross-country with the excess weight of fat and bones that must be discarded eventually anyway. Instead, packers send out boxes filled with already cut meat, and supermarkets can order just the cuts they want rather than being forced to make use of everything that comes with the carcass.

Efficiency is the key word at each step in the journey from ranch to meat counter, and as profit margins tighten and costs continue to rise, more corners must be cut. What is sacrificed, of course, is the quality of the meat. When Frank Hogya talks about making silk purses out of sows' ears, what disturbs him even more than the production-line mentality is the fact that the meat industry has been tinkering with the animals themselves. "For several hundred years farmers strove to develop good beef breeds, your Angus, your Hereford, your shorthorn, and several other breeds, and then they come along and attempt to destroy what they developed by all this damn crossbreeding," Hogya says. Years ago the pride of the meat industry was corn-fed midwestern beef—Angus and Hereford cattle, raised on corn, the richest feed, and bred to produce the best choice and prime meat. But the meat industry has now become a national industry, and each section of the country has its own cattle-raising areas. The fat, round cattle grazing on the plains of the midwestern corn belt would not survive in some of these other climates, so crossbreeds have been developed that can withstand tougher conditions. Even in the Midwest, crossbreeds that can put on weight more quickly are taking over from the purebred cattle. "I defy you," Hogya says, "to take two cows, one's a regular beef breed and the other's one of these damn crossbreeds, feed them the same, and come up with meat that tastes the same. It can't be done."

He points to studies that show the palatability and taste of meat from the new crossbreeds just doesn't compare with that of meat from the traditional beef breeds. But he also knows that in an industry that is more concerned with quantity than with quality, taste will lose out. He has seen it happen all too graphically where he makes his home now: the beef he finds at the meat counters in Southern California is a perfect example of what goes wrong when people start fooling with Mother Nature.

Most of California's cattle are raised for slaughter out on the hot, dry expanses of the Imperial Valley and Mexico in the south and the San Joaquin Valley in the north central portion of the state. Anyone familiar with the crusty, parched old men swatting flies on their desert front porches can get some idea of the kind of animals that can take the California heat. Many of the cattle entering California slaughterhouses are humpbacked because they have been crossed with the Brahman bull, an animal that can withstand sweltering heat and other harsh climates. In their native India, some Brahmans are sacred, and under the Hindu religion they cannot be killed for food. Maybe the Indians are lucky, because the Brahman meat is about as tender as beef jerky. The Brahman bull must be crossed with other breeds to produce beef that is palatable at all. But even the crossbreeds will not produce beef that can compare in taste to that of the true beef breeds. Or, as Hogya complains, "You can feed them any goddamn thing you want, but you ain't going to make Hereford or Angus beef out of one of them water buffaloes."

Harsh cattle-raising conditions are to be found throughout much of the Southwest and Southeast, which have supplanted the Midwest as the largest cattle-producing region. So cattlemen resorting to these crossbreeds must learn to live with the fact their meat will seldom qualify for the choice and prime grades. As a result, federally graded meat is disappearing from some of these areas. In Southern California, for example, the supermarkets selling choice and prime beef are an ever-shrinking minority. Graded meat started disappearing from the counters of California supermarkets shortly after the meat scandal Hogya helped uncover was cleaned up. Until that time, packers could get their inferior meat graded choice and prime by bribing graders. Afterward, they couldn't provide enough legitimately choice meat. So many supermarkets had to stop selling graded meat altogether.

Even in the Midwest, quality is deteriorating. The buyers for the best butcher shops and the fanciest restaurants lament that they can find less and less of the highest-quality beef. "The whole industry has changed," says one buyer. "Packers aren't interested in quality, they're only after profit." The custom packers who handle only the finest meat are now afraid to expand their businesses, because they find it harder and harder to locate meat that fits their exacting standards. Barney Grayson, owner of the meat company that supplies many of the best restaurants in Los Angeles, gave up on California-raised meat years ago. Now he bemoans the fact that the search in the Midwest for top quality meat gets tougher every year. He agrees with Hogya that the problems nationwide can be linked to the breeding and feeding of beef animals. "You have to start out with good breeding," Grayson says. "It's like racehorses. You've got to have a quality animal to begin with." Then it must be fed right. "There's no substitute for corn. That's what gives beef its flavor." But the meat industry is doing more and more substituting.

People like packer Grayson and consumer Hogya now fear they are seeing the passing—probably forever—of the richest-tasting meat. In its place is meat bearing federal grades that are a poor gauge of quality, or private house brands that are no gauge at all. Whether anything can be done to stem this trend is problematical. Proposals have been developed to tie grading more closely to such considerations as beef breeds and the time animals were fed high-quality feed. And the USDA is working on developing grading tools that would take the guesswork out of grading and make it more uniform. But the root problem is the fact that today's meat is the end result of a mass-production mentality that is robbing meat of its natural flavor. Unfortunately, robbery of meat's flavor is far from the only crime to be found in the American meat industry.

3

The Meat-Grading Scandals

Judge Gordon Thompson, Jr.: *Let me ask you this; did you sell your judgment?*
Hugo Ralph Lueck: *Yes, Your Honor, I sold my judgment.*
Court: *What was the basis upon which the payment was made, was it per carcass?*
Defendant: *No, no. If I got paid per carcass, I'd be a millionaire.*

—U.S. v. *Hugo Ralph Lueck,*
U.S. District Court, San Diego, 1976

Hugo Lueck* is not a millionaire by any means. He is now a heavy-equipment operator, working the night shift, just as he was thirty years ago. He's a hardened, muscular man, starting to grow bald. A beer can is a fixture in his massive hand, and he carries with him a beer drinker's paunch. His voice is low and gruff, and when he speaks his sentences are heavily touched with cynicism. It's a description that fits most of the men who have spent their lives in the meat industry. Lueck is but one of the many tough characters that are its work force. He spent twenty years of his life in packinghouses, most of that time working as a meat grader for the U.S. Department of Agri-

---

*All quotes from sworn depositions in Hogya v. National Meat Packers *et al.,* San Diego Superior Court No. 379573. Deposition taken Nov. 16–18, 1977, at Palm Springs, CA. and from transcript of sentencing in U.S. v. Lueck, U.S. District Court, San Diego, No. 75-2024 Criminal, Feb. 23, 1976.

culture. He was one of the men who judged the quality of the meat produced in Southern California. He gave the meat his stamp of approval so consumers could have confidence in the quality of the cuts they bought. And Hugo Lueck was one of the men who abused that confidence by misgrading meat, causing consumers to be ripped off by several billion dollars.

To look at his record, Lueck was an excellent grader. His supervisors praised his efficiency, offered him promotions, and gave him commendations. "The success enjoyed by the Los Angeles meat grading station is in no small part due to the caliber of our graders," states one letter from R. W. Theobald, assistant main station supervisor, "and you are among the leaders of this group. Keep up the good work, Hugo." The good work of Hugo and the rest of the high-caliber graders was something to behold. Most of them were taking home payoffs of up to four hundred dollars a week from packers in addition to their government salaries. For that money they perverted the federal grading standards by certifying beef USDA choice that was of inferior quality. This beef, sometimes USDA good, sometimes even worse quality, ended up in supermarkets as USDA choice. The result was that consumers paid 30 to 40 cents per pound extra for second-rate meat.

The scandal went undetected in Southern California for at least fifteen years. It's hard to tell exactly when it started, because it's hard to tell if the Southern California meat industry has ever been without corruption. When the grading scandal was finally uncovered in 1975, sixty-five graders and packers were convicted on charges of bribery and gratuity violations. What had once been a close-knit collection of buddies—packers and graders all looking out for each other—degenerated into a vicious band of enemies, each turning against his friends in an attempt to save his own ass.

It was an ugly scene, with scores of lives and careers ruined. But for all those years before the fall, the meat graders of Southern California had a very nice life. "Hell, I got my gratuities, and I got baseball tickets, and life was easy—simple," Lueck recalls. "Eat New York steaks for lunch, two or three double Manhattans, sometimes nice big New York steaks about that thick every day, with mushrooms, fresh bread. Ham and eggs for breakfast . . . Dinners, eat in the best places, see all the nice-looking girls." All was provided by the packers. Every packinghouse had a bar so a grader could go pour himself a drink whenever he felt like it. There were many times when Lueck was undeniably drunk as he set out on his appointed rounds. Breakfast, lunch, dinner, were all paid for by the packers. Lueck can't remember ever paying for a meal.

And there were the parties. It surely must have been a bizarre scene—middle-aged, beer-bellied graders, supermarket buyers, and packers lounging around drinking expensive booze, smoking marijuana, and making time with "the ladies." They got to meet a former *Playboy* centerfold, who became a local celebrity when she posed nude for a Los Angeles packinghouse poster showing the cuts of meat tattooed on her side, under the caption "You can't beat Western meat." And high-class hookers were as much a part of the graders' lives as the payoff. The packer was always ready to pick up the tab for a quick trip to a nearby motel. Or maybe a grader would just find an empty office at the packinghouse, spread his white freezer coat over the desk, and get down to business.

All of it was standard procedure throughout Southern California for at least fifteen years. All but a handful of the federal graders, and even some of their superiors, were living far above what they could expect from their low-grade federal salaries. They had a network of spies in the packinghouses and in the grading-service bureaucracy to tip them off about anybody snooping around. And they had the cooperation of the packers—their friends—who had much to gain by giving out a couple of hundred bucks, a good meal, and a quick screw.

Lueck puts it this way. "One hundred dollars was peanuts compared to what they were getting. That was one of the best business deals that ever was created, the return for that hundred-dollar bill. They were happy to pay me that one hundred dollars. You know why? Just for example, there is a spread of money between good and choice cattle, right? And I've seen it range from a half a cent to five to seven cents per pound [wholesale]. Now, we'll just take one cent. So there is a one-cent spread and the average carcass weighs six hundred pounds. That's six dollars for one carcass, right?"

A grader would need to upgrade just seventeen carcasses a week to pay back the packer for the one-hundred-dollar bribe. Usually, Lueck upgraded that many cattle each day. He recalls days when out of 500 carcasses, he illegally upgraded 450. "Yeah, it is amazing, isn't it," he admits. The windfall profits go even deeper. A packer who knows the grader is going to take care of him can also save some money by buying inferior cattle. Normally, cattle must be fed expensive, high-quality grain for the last 240 days before slaughter to produce meat that will qualify for the choice grade. But why bother feeding cattle that long if the grader is on the take? A packer can get by with feeding high quality grain for only about two hundred days. "So they are making money on the feeding end and money on the slaughter end," Lueck says.

Corruption in the federal grading service is nothing new. Meat has been graded since 1927, and corruption has plagued the grading service since the start. Almost every major city has been rocked by at least one grading scandal, and some places, such as Los Angeles, have been hit repeatedly. But as each scandal is cleaned up another pops up in a different town. In the past eight years the USDA has found bribery and grading violations in more than fifty of the over six hundred packing-houses that use the federal grading service. "These are drops in the bucket," says Sydney J. Butler, deputy assistant secretary of agriculture for food and consumer services during the Carter administration. "I don't think we have the resources to commit to launching a full-scale attack on bribery."* Each time the USDA uncovers a problem, it tries to step in with new safe-guards. But the sad fact remains that the meat industry is prone to corruption. And the grading service is part of a bureaucracy not always dedicated to punishing corruption. As long as the graders and the packers can find ways to make each other a little richer, the scandals must be expected to continue. "I don't think anybody would deny that there is a bribery problem," Butler continues. "I don't know the extent of the bribery and corruption in the industry and I don't think anybody does."

---

*Quoted in "Beef Industry Ripoffs Add to Cost to Consumer," by Terry Atlas, Chicago *Tribune,* Feb. 11, 1979, Section 5, Page 1.

It is easy, though, to see how problems start. The meat industry is a close-knit fraternity of men, many of whom have worked both sides. The grading service is filled with men who got their start working in packinghouses. And the packing industry is filled with former graders—many of whom needed a job after their shady behavior got them in trouble with the government. Day in and day out, the packer and grader work side by side. They get to be friends. They understand each other and they look out for each other. Even if it isn't a conscious attempt to help the other guy out, there can be a tendency to give him the benefit of the doubt. And as the scandal in Southern California dramatized, there have been times when they both have ripped off the consumer mercilessly.

Hugo Lueck had drifted from job to job. He graduated from high school in 1948 and went to work for the Hanna Coal and Ore Company in Crosby, Minnesota, as an oiler and car spotter. Four years later he got tired of the cold Minnesota winters and set out for the West Coast. He got a job in a lumber mill in northern California, worked construction in Oregon, Washington, Utah, and Nevada. He was a truck driver, dredge operator, whatever came along. "And then my wife says, 'No more moving around.' My boy was going to school. She says, 'You're going to get a full-time job, enough moving around.' So I says, 'Okay.' "

Lueck found a steady job as a truck driver for a small packing company outside of Sacramento in 1955. For the next twenty years, the meat industry would be his life. Soon Lueck moved from the trucks into the packinghouse. He was a cooler manager, a tough character typified by the roles played by Burt Young in *Rocky* or Steve McQueen as the Cooler King in *The Great Escape*. His job was to supervise the loading of the trucks, select meat for customers, follow the graders as they did their job, pressure the graders, fight with the graders, cajole the graders—do whatever was necessary to get the best grading for his company. "Every one of the packers puts pressure on the graders," he says. "Every one of them wants to get blood out of a turnip." He learned all about grading, and he learned all about little tricks. He knew how to take a knife to a carcass, cutting off some fat and scratching the red meat to fool the grader into marking it with a higher grade. And he knew how to keep graders happy with an occasional package of meat to take home. He was the kind of man packers liked to have working with the graders—and the kind of man packers liked to see become a grader. Lueck says he never paid out bribes when he worked for the packing company; if it happened, it happened over his head. For Lueck, the money wouldn't come until he switched to the other side.

In 1961, Hugo Lueck became a federal grader. At the urging of Cal Santere, then the main supervisor for the grading service in San Francisco and now the head of the powerful Western States Meat Packers Association, Lueck filled out the proper forms and passed the proper tests to qualify as a federal meat grader. For one year he trained with an established grader, going from packinghouse to packinghouse to learn the trade with a veteran of the service. He says there was no talk by graders or packers of bribes or upgrading, but as soon as the one-year training period was up, and Lueck went out on his own, everything changed. He doesn't remember exactly how it started, but the packers got their message across. "They feel you out, and they give you kind of an idea," he says. "They take you for lunch, or they have a bottle of liquor, you know? They ask you if you want a drink, you know, and that's how they start out, and if you take a drink or if you go to lunch, then they just work it real slow. They ask you whether or not you would like to take home a package of meat, you know, first. If you accept this, well, then they tell you, if you'd like to make a little extra money, you know, that can be arranged too with a little help. That's how they start with you. Then once you get started with one packing-house, well, that just goes like wildfire from one. All the packers, you know, get together and they talk."

It was all so matter-of-fact. It was business as usual. Everyone knew that federal regulations strictly forbade graders from accepting "anything of value," no matter how small, from a packer. And everybody knew those strict federal regulations were a joke. Lunch on the packer's tab was routine. Graders always had as much meat to take home as they wanted. Tickets to ball games, gifts, booze, all flowed freely from the packers.

There were times when the entire Los Angeles packing district closed down so the packers, the graders, and even the grading supervisors could head out for an afternoon of golf. "It was so wide open, I just figured it was part of the job," Lueck says. So taking home a few hundred dollars in cash each week was natural.

For the money—bribes ranging from one hundred to four hundred dollars a week depending on the packer—Lueck's job was to do one thing for the packers: "fill their orders." "They buy cattle, and it doesn't grade out like it's supposed to, and they got these orders to fill, these choice orders to fill. And sometimes they come up short, and that's my job." Every morning, starting at 6 A.M., Lueck would don his white freezer coat and hard hat, walk into the brisk air of the cooler, and begin grading beef carcasses according to the strict standards of the U.S. Department of Agriculture. He'd work his way down the rails of carcasses, each one split in half and sliced open to reveal the rib eye Lueck would examine to determine the grade. Lueck would mark the carcasses that qualified for the federal grades prime or choice with dull slaps of his metal USDA stamp on the chilled sides of beef, two marks for choice, three for prime. He left the remaining beef, the inferior beef, unmarked. "I'd grade the cooler, and then they'd go through it and see how many choice cattle they had and how many choice cattle they needed that day. And then they would tell me, 'Hugo, we're going to be short of choice cattle today. We're going to need some help.' "

So Lueck would put on his freezer coat again, return to the cooler, and toss away his USDA standards. He picked out only the best of the inferior meat to upgrade to choice. And just about every day, these carcasses were shipped from Southern California packinghouses as USDA choice—the grade most consumers prefer. "It could be five [carcasses] one day. It could be twenty one day. It could be fifty one day," Lueck says. Or more—whatever the packer needed. The payoff was the same if he upgraded one or one hundred. Sometimes he didn't even bother to go back through the cooler himself. He just gave his stamp to the packer and let him pick out the carcasses he needed to fill his order.

"It was pretty wide open. Nobody didn't seem to care.

Nobody didn't seem to care who knew," Lueck says. The scandal was so widespread that almost every grader and some supervisors were in on it. The graders had a sophisticated system worked out to make sure they weren't caught by the few honest grading officials around. "Most of the packinghouses had what they called a spotter, a guy looking out for you. All the packers had a pipeline between one another, and they knew just within minutes where all the supervisors were." The pipeline extended into the supervisors' office, where one former grader who had been promoted would get on the phone to warn packers about where each supervisor would be. This former grader wasn't motivated by loyalty to his fellow graders, however. He wanted his own cut from the packers.

The grading supervisors were supposed to make unannounced visits to the packinghouses to check on the graders' work. But by the time they got to a packinghouse, there was usually nothing out of the ordinary to find. If beef had been upgraded, it had also been loaded onto trucks and moved out into the parking lot when the spotter's warning came in. Once the supervisor left, the trucks were wheeled back to the docks and the meat redistributed. The West Coast packers were also big on what became known as GRO grading—Going Right Out. The grader would do his job on the loading dock instead of in the cooler, so the evidence was loaded on the truck and driven out of the lot before anyone had a chance to ask questions.

These precautions, however, were seldom really necessary. The "surprise" visits by the supervisors never seemed to happen more than twice a month, so in between the graders could do as they pleased. And often, the inspections conducted by the supervisors were laughable. "Sometimes they wouldn't even go into the cooler," Lueck says. "Sometimes, just for pure gesture, they'd drive up and make sure I knew they were there. They'd go into the office and talk to the packer for a while." If Lueck had anything to hide, he had plenty of time to do it. Lueck says there was only one time when he was caught misgrading meat. A supervisor walked into the cooler as Lueck was blatantly mislabeling some beef chucks. What happened? "He just kept on walking." Shortly thereafter, Lueck received a commendation for his superior grading. That supervisor was promoted to national technical supervisor—one of four men responsible for monitoring grading throughout the country.

The attitude of the supervisors bred an atmosphere of safety among the graders—a feeling that nobody would do anything about corruption or even cared about corruption. Even if a grader was accused of misconduct, the common procedure was for the supervisor to simply transfer the man out of his jurisdiction. "The worst they did was make you resign," Lueck says. Nobody was afraid of criminal charges—until the indictments finally started coming down. And then, curiously, no supervisors were named in the indictments. As the scandal was exposed, a few supervisors got transferred, and a couple were demoted, but no supervisors had to worry about going to jail. Lueck and other graders say it wasn't because all of the supervisors were innocent. While Lueck knew that some of the supervisors went by the book, he knew that many went to lunch at the expense of the packers, he saw them at the packers' parties, and he has suspicions that they were taking money too. But it's nothing he can prove, and nothing he wants to talk about very much. The supervisors let it be known that as long as they were protected, they would minimize the penalties for the graders. Sure, the graders went to jail, but the supervisors saw to one thing: none of the convicted graders lost his pension.

And so it went. Year in and year out. After Lueck had been a grader five years, he got a transfer that made his life even easier. He left Los Angeles to become the senior grader in San Diego. The manager for one of the packinghouses, a former grader himself who was well acquainted with the graft, encouraged Lueck to come down, and let him know he could expect the same fringe benefits he was accustomed to in Los Angeles. Lueck had to take a pay cut, however: his bribes dropped to only one hundred dollars a week. But Lueck said it was worth it. With fewer packinghouses in San Diego, there was less for him to do. "I never did put in eight hours a day when I was in San Diego," he says. Most days, he was done before lunch. He had the rest of the day to eat and drink and shoot the breeze with the boys hanging around the packinghouses. And there were fewer supervisors on his back. He had developed a reputation as a man who needed little supervision, so he could go about his business with a minimum of interference. In fact, Lueck had been offered a promotion to supervisor, and he took the sun and the easy pace of San Diego, called the Country Club by the graders, instead of the promotion.

For another nine years Lueck enjoyed the easy life, and then it fell apart. First came the rumors from Los Angeles in 1974 that somebody was squealing to federal investigators. Then, over a period of nearly a year, the indictments started coming down. Ironically, the scandal was being broken by a grader just as crooked as the ones who would ultimately go to jail. He was a grader from back East who had been living the same kind of high life enjoyed by the Southern California graders. Then he got a divorce. When his wife examined the financial declarations her husband filed for the divorce, she was amazed: she knew she and her husband had been living like royalty, but the financial declarations said they should have been paupers. She turned her husband in to the USDA Office of Investigation, hoping to get her fair share of her husband's booty. She didn't get a cent, but the Office of Investigation did make a deal with the grader. The USDA told him it would drop its charges if he would move to Los Angeles and repeat his success at taking bribes. He did a fine job, and slowly the happy family of Southern California packers and graders fell apart. One by one the packers and graders were indicted and convicted. In sentencing one Los Angeles packer, federal district court judge Warren J. Ferguson concluded, "There was a cancer in the meat-packing industry. A cancer which was permitted to grow so long it undermined not only the rights of the consumer, but the integrity of the government."

As the list of convictions grew longer, it became evident that some of the indicted men, as well as the USDA's informant, were fingering everyone involved. Lueck heard all about the indictments and the convictions, but he hoped maybe the investigation would not reach down to San Diego. He and the San Diego packers had a talk, though, and agreed the payoffs should stop. But the gratuities continued, the booze, the meals, the parties. Lueck agreed to continue upgrading cattle, and the packers would "take care" of Lueck later. If everything blew over, the payoffs would resume.

But on June 27, 1975, Hugo Ralph Lueck was indicted on seventeen counts of bribery and gratuity violations. He was suspended, effective July 12, and never worked another day for the federal grading service.

His friendly relationship with all his packer buddies had fallen apart. The packers who one day had been his pals were now accusing Lueck of extorting them and threatening them and forcing them to give in to his every demand. They said he demanded booze, or he wouldn't even go into the cooler. They said he demanded money, or he wouldn't grade any meat choice. One of the indicted packers, the manager of one of the largest packinghouses in San Diego, testified that he paid graders bribes "to get the work done. Otherwise, they'd just slow down. They just don't do the work and hold up your production." He contended the packers paid the bribes to get the graders to work quicker, and to get the equitable grading to which they were entitled. "Well, there is borderline decisions [between choice and good grades] that they can take away from you or they can give you, and if you don't help them with their finances, they take the liners away from you."

The manager pleaded guilty to one count of bribing a grader in early 1975. His attorney, who represented several packers convicted in the scandal, engineered a deal with the U.S. attorney's office to drop sixteen other bribery and gratuity charges against his client. And the U.S. attorney's office agreed not to pursue any additional charges against him, his boss, the two packinghouses owned by his boss, or any packinghouse employees. In return, the packer sang to a federal grand jury. As a direct result of his testimony, Lueck was indicted.

Lueck had known the packer-turned-informant ever since they had both been graders back in Los Angeles. He himself had come to San Diego after he was asked to leave the USDA under less than favorable circumstances. He was the man who urged Lueck to come to San Diego. They drank together. They went fishing together. They partied together. Now his former friend was saying Lueck and the other graders had a stranglehold on the Southern California packing industry, and they were scaring these poor packers to death. To which Lueck replies, "Baloney. If they were that upset about my grading, they didn't have to have me there, and it wouldn't have taken but a telephone call." Just a phone call to his supervisors and Lueck would have been replaced. Instead, Lueck worked in his friend's packinghouse for nine years without ever hearing a complaint about his work. "That's just like fighting words, those kind of statements, you know. And if they were that dissatisfied, I can't understand how they let me even stay down there."

"I worked there from sixty-six to seventy-five, and everybody was on friendly terms—everybody. We used to go to lunch or we used to drink at night together. Now, they come up with this stuff like it was dog-eat-dog. I never had those kind of problems there." But the threat of prison does strange things to friends, and now Lueck had to pay the price.

On February 23, 1976, Lueck was sentenced after pleading guilty to one count of accepting a bribe. Judge Gordon Thompson, Jr., said Lueck, as a federal grader, was in a position of trust, and even if he was approached by the packers, "He, representing the United States Government, above all, should have had enough sense to simply deny their request." Even if the bribes were standard operating procedure throughout Southern California, "It's just as wrong whether it's common in the industry or not. He violated the trust and confidence that is placed in him," Thompson said. He sentenced Lueck to two years in prison, although he suspended all but four months of the term, and fined him five thousand dollars.

Lueck was stunned by the sentence: he was just about the only grader or packer to land a jail sentence rather than probation. And he's bitter about the way the judge treated him, compared with the way he treated his friend. Judge Thompson said he pitied the packer, because "I think he was caught in a trap." The judge placed him on probation rather than in jail "because I take the position that the person who is in the position to take the bribe is much more culpable than the person who is in the position that gives the bribe."

Lueck served his time, and when he got out, like most of the convicted graders, he was without a career. He was back to where he had started thirty years before, working heavy construction. Meanwhile, most of the packinghouses went back to business as usual. But they had hardly reformed. In July

1978, many of the same Los Angeles packers were back in court again, pleading no contest to charges they fixed the price of meat sold to Safeway, the largest supermarket chain in Southern California. Down in San Diego, there were problems as well. The packer-turned-informant was forced to resign because the USDA refused to let its graders have anything to do with him. In April 1978, the two firms which had supplied most of the up-graded meat purchased by consumers in San Diego agreed to pay a three-hundred-thousand-dollar settlement to end a class action suit brought by Frank Hogya on behalf of San Diego commissary shoppers. The publicity generated by the suit had caused the packing companies to lose approximately half their business. And around Christmastime in 1978, the two packing-houses were shut down by the USDA. The USDA suspended grading and inspection privileges for forty-five days when the packinghouses were caught giving gratuities to federal graders and inspectors. The graders—the men brought in to clean up after Lueck—and inspectors were fired, but now those same companies are back in business!

Lueck is living out his days in a trailer home out on the desert. He tries not to think about what used to be his liveli-hood, and he says he's not bitter. "Like I said, I was down there from sixty-six to seventy-five, and we were all on friendly terms until the indictments, and then everybody started talking to help themselves. I'm still not mad at anyone, really. I know what I did. I served my time, and I have no bad feelings, you know?"

Hugo Lueck has taken his punishment. He has served his time and paid his fine. But it could have been worse: Lueck could have tried to be an honest grader. Ted Marugg was an honest grader, and what he has to show for it is a lifetime of harassment.

Marugg is over seventy now. In 1980 he finished a career of thirty years in the federal grading service—thirty years as a loner and an outsider. Now, his movements have been slowed by the arthritis in his back and hands and he must walk with a cane. But as he stretches his stiff body, the movements are still those of an athletic man. He was a boxer in his youth, a welterweight, and while his boxer's physique has settled with age, he still looks formidable. He speaks in a high-pitched, scratchy voice. A smile lifts the corners of his trim gray mustache and brightens his broad Germanic face as he talks, and he seems more bemused than upset about the strange experiences he has seen in the federal grading service.

Marugg worked around meat all his life. He started as a meatcutter in Chicago, he owned his own meat business for a while, and he ran the meat operation for the military at the Panama Canal during World War II. He came back to Chicago after the war, and in 1949 he joined the federal grading service. "Well, right off the bat I had the experience of having to reject and reject and reject meat, and people fought with me and I guess I fought back," he recalls. He thought he was just doing his job, applying the federal requirements and making sure the packers did things right. "I began to discover that I wasn't very well liked in general because I was insisting on what I was supposed to do. And I was discovering there was another way of doing things than the government way. Many of them [packers] offered me to, oh, take meat home, or cash. I turned them all down and I developed a very nasty reputation among the packers. And other graders didn't like me either. I was on the bad list."

Chicago in the late 1940's and the 1950's was the way Los Angeles would be a few years later—wide open. "The majority of places I went to, they were all ready to offer me something or in some instances they'd meet me at my car and expect me to hand them my equipment and suggest that I go sit in the office while they take care of things. Well, no, no, no, I held on to my equipment, and I did the grading. I could tell by the way they came with their offers and requests to have control of my equipment that this was nothing new for them." And the weekly payoffs were there for the taking, just as they would be in Los Angeles. Marugg remembers the first time he was sent to grade at one particular Chicago packinghouse. He was told to go into the office because there was an envelope for him. On the desk he found an envelope with "Grader" written on the outside.

"That's not for me, my name isn't on it," Marugg remembers telling the packer.

"Yah, that's for you, the grader. Every grader gets it the first time he comes."

"Well, it's still not for me."

"What's the matter with you, you rich or something? There's a hundred and fifty bucks in there." The packer opened the envelope and showed Marugg the cash. But Marugg still wouldn't take the envelope.

"What do you want, more? I'll get you more." He went upstairs and came back with $150 more. Marugg still wouldn't take it, so they went around again.

"What's the matter, you rich or something? Or are you nuts? You don't need to be afraid to take it. The national techs [national technical supervisors] get a grand a year. So you don't have to be afraid."

Still Marugg refused, and the matter was dropped. The next day, two national technical supervisors came to that same plant while Marugg was grading. He told them the story. One said nothing, and the other asked if Marugg had taken the money. "You've got nothing to worry about then," he told Marugg. When Marugg got to the part where the packer said he paid off the supervisors, he got this response: "Why don't you get yourself a job with the FBI, you don't belong with us."

Marugg was something of a one-man bureau of investigation. While other graders either turned their backs on corruption or jumped right in with it, Marugg liked to explore shady dealings and expose them. He remembers catching one packinghouse slipping spoiled meat into the hamburger it provided for the school lunch program. Another packinghouse was cutting up carcasses and replacing some of the premium cuts with meat from other, inferior carcasses. "It's kind of fun to catch these people, you know," he says. "They may have been angry that they didn't get away with it, but they respected me after that."

Once Marugg even worked undercover, attempting to expose a grading scandal in, of all places, Los Angeles. That assignment came in 1953, but it happened because Marugg had been alert four years earlier. He was working in a plant in Milwaukee, and the owners didn't like the way he graded. "So when I left there, they, in anger, or in a nasty tone, said they were glad to see me go. At that time they were just starting their new plant in California, and they said when they get out there, they don't need guys like me because they can get meat graded without calling the grading office." Marugg asked how they could do it and he was told a man in Los Angeles had his own grading equipment and he would counterfeit graders' stamps. "He just let something slip. So I reported this to my boss in Chicago. These are the kinds of things, even if you don't jump at 'em, you've got to write them down, they're going to fit in sooner or later." It took four years, but finally the grading service acted on Marugg's tip. The Washington office chose him for an under-cover assignment in Los Angeles. "I was sent out there to sneak around and see if I could find meat graded choice that wasn't choice." His plan was to get a job in a Los Angeles packinghouse. "I looked like a bum, had old overalls on, and never shaved while I was there. I figured on getting a job in one of the most likely ones." But on the day he decided to apply for a job, the packinghouse he chose was surrounded by police. California state authorities had raided the packinghouse, looking for the same thing. Unfortunately, the state and federal investigations had not been coordinated, and the state had blown the chance for anyone to catch the crook. "If I got the job in there, I had a chance to know what was going on," Marugg says. "Of course, I could have had the chance of getting killed too, but never worry about that." Marugg's investigation was halted, because "we felt the guy would be scared away for a while," Marugg says. His superiors sent him back to resume his regular grading duties in Chicago. About a year later, he found out that by a fluke the Los Angeles scandal had been uncovered. A white Cadillac was wrecked in a highway collision, and a set of grading tools was found in its trunk. It turned out to be the phony equipment that was being used to improperly grade meat throughout Southern California, earning its owner fees of up to two hundred dollars an hour.

When Marugg first told his boss about the conversation in Milwaukee that ultimately led to the Los Angeles investigation, his boss told him he was having "hallucinations." In fact, most of the time that Marugg passed along tips to his boss, his detective work was unappreciated. Every time Marugg was offered money, or meat, or any kind of favor, he'd report it to his boss. "Always. And the usual answer was, well, as long as you didn't take anything, you've got nothing to worry about.

"Huh," Marugg shrugs. "I wonder if he went back and got it himself."

Marugg was developing quite a reputation. It was a reputation for honesty, but it didn't win him any respect. Instead, it was hard for him to get along with his coworkers and his former friends in the packing business. Marugg recalls going to grade meat at one packinghouse where he had once worked as a meat-cutter. The meat he saw didn't make the grade, and Marugg wasn't about to do his old friends any favors. So the head man, his old boss, came down to have a talk with him. "He says, 'Ted, you know this grading service is only a sham. They're all phonies.' " But Marugg let his old boss know he was "on the legit," and he wasn't about to give anybody a break. "When I worked for you," Marugg said, "I did things your way. Now, I'm working for Uncle Sam, so I do it the way the government wants. So he tells me, 'You're going to wake up someday with an awful bump.' And that was the last time I ever heard from him."

If Marugg's relations were strained with the packers and the other graders in Chicago, he nevertheless was establishing a record as a competent grader and a conscientious employee. And in recognition of his work, the grading-service headquarters in Washington, D.C., promoted him to acting assistant supervisor for the Chicago region. There was only one problem. The Chicago main station supervisor refused to have Marugg working as his assistant. Marugg filed civil service charges against his boss, and although he didn't succeed in keeping his promotion, he did succeed in having his boss demoted. The boss, who had failed to correct some of the problems Marugg kept reporting, was knocked down to being simply a grader, and he was shipped off to work in Michigan. A few months later, he was caught taking a bribe and he was fired.

The reason Marugg's boss had come up with for keeping Marugg out of a supervisory position was his personality. "I couldn't get along with other people. That was the brand they gave me because I rejected stuff all over town. I was a terrible personality." But Marugg knew there was a stronger reason. He knew that his boss and the other graders feared that if he were given some power they would all be in trouble. Marugg knew that corruption ran deep in the Chicago region. He had seen packers load meat, eggs, and butter into the cars of graders. He had been offered bribes so many times it had become routine. And he suspected that even the supervisors were on the take. He had heard rumors that the supervisors were taking home truckloads of meat, or maybe even cash payoffs. He never did find the concrete evidence to nail the supervisors, but events proved one thing: if the supervisors weren't crooked, they were blind.

It all spilled out one day in 1956. Marugg was sent to grade at a meat company in Chicago where he had known the owner for years. The owner called Marugg into his office for a chat. "I was driving an old hack," Marugg recalls, "and he says, 'Why don't you get next to yourself?' "

The owner named off a number of other graders. "Look at these guys. These guys are all driving brand-new cars, and you're driving an old hack. They go to Florida in the winter, when it costs money. You ever been to Florida?"

"No."

"Well, they go, when it costs real money. These are all your friends, your buddies, your working buddies. Why don't you join them?"

"Join them in what?"

"Night grading."

Marugg acted surprised. He knew he had found the core of the corruption that had engulfed Chicago, but he wanted him to spell it out. "I said, 'You're pulling my leg, they had something like that in Detroit a few years ago, but not Chicago.' And I did push it out of him. He says, 'Heck, these are all your buddies. It's nothing to be afraid of. Your boss takes, all your bosses take. They can't do a thing.' Well, this still wasn't enough to switch me over. So he named them. He named names for me. And of course, when he did, they were all the ones I figured to be in it."

Thirteen federal graders were regularly going back to the packinghouses at night to upgrade the meat that didn't meet federal standards during the day. Marugg never did find out how much the graders were paid, but it was made clear to him that they were living a much easier life than he was. Now that Marugg knew, the night graders had to do something about it. "There was one guy out of that thirteen who was a very nice fellow. They were all nice guys, as far as good Joes, good-time Charlies, see, but there was one very superior fellow among them—crooked as hell, but on an open-faced basis." The grader met Marugg in the garage where all the graders parked their cars, and he tried to convince Marugg to join the night graders. "I said to him, nope, no way. I said I started out on this job on the legit, and I want to stay that way. This is the oath I took. No matter what they do to me, when I leave I'm going to be able to sleep nights." The night grader kept pushing, pleading with Marugg to come along. "So I said to him, you know, one of these days you're all going to get nailed, you know that, don't you?" Marugg got the same reply the owner of the meat company had given him: "They can't do a thing." The night graders were convinced the payoffs reached all the way to Washington, so no one could break the chain.

If Marugg's relations with his fellow graders had been strained before, they were now ruined. Soon he was transferred out of Chicago for a while—"To get me out of their hair. They all knew I wasn't the kind of guy who was going to change my mind, that I didn't take any crap from anybody and that was it, see." There was a rumor floating around that the packers had gotten together and sent out word they'd pay a thousand dollars to the supervisor that succeeded in getting Marugg transferred.

Two years later, Marugg's night-grader friend was called into the meat-grading office and accused of illegally upgrading meat for payoffs. He denied the charge, and he was shown infrared photos of himself entering a packinghouse at night. "That was the end of him," Marugg says. He and the twelve other night graders were given the choice of resigning or facing federal bribery charges. Most of them resigned. The packinghouses involved had their federal grading privileges revoked. But as would happen in Los Angeles years later, the supervisors avoided prosecution. Some were even promoted to soft jobs in Washington.

Marugg had reported the ring to his superiors as soon as he found out about it. And, as in the past, no one wanted to believe him at first. But then a new main station supervisor was brought to Chicago who, with the help of the FBI, dismantled the night-grading ring. The new supervisor, John Coplin, reformed the grading service in the Midwest, and then he set about ferreting out corruption elsewhere. His abrasive style and his penchant for harassing the crooks in the meat industry and the grading service made him notorious throughout the industry.

It was a welcome change for Marugg. "This was the first legitimate supervision I ever had, when John Coplin came here," Marugg says. "If the rest of the country was as clean as our area, this thing would be a hundred per cent, as far as I'm concerned." But the rest of the country is not 100 per cent, and Marugg knows it better than most. From 1969 on, Marugg traveled around the country, grading for short stints at a variety of plants. Technically, he was a relief grader—someone sent to fill in when a regular grader was sick or on vacation. His boss, Coplin, placed Marugg in that role so he could share his years of experience with new graders and help the department handle difficult grading jobs on short notice.

The job, however, made Marugg painfully aware of the problems that persisted in the federal grading service to the end of his career. In 1978 he was sent to Rochester, New York, to help grade meat sold to state prisons and mental institutions. He uncovered improper procedures that had allowed four hundred thousand pounds of foul-smelling meat to be sold to the state institutions—after federal graders had approved the meat! He reported the problem to Washington, and by the end of the year he had his reward. Marugg was reassigned perma-nently to a large packing plant in northern Illinois, where every day he was required to grade five thousand carcasses—a work load heavier than most graders ever encounter. The increased physical labor aggravated the arthritis in his hands and back. "It appears that they really want to make it more difficult for me," Marugg said at the time. "Within a week, my hands are doubled in size from the pain."

The order reassigning Marugg came from grading-service headquarters in Washington, and it enraged Marugg's boss in

Chicago, John Coplin. He charged the chief of the grading service with ordering the reassignment in "retaliation" against Marugg for embarrassing federal officials by blowing the whistle on the improper procedures in New York. "You have permitted the graders to be abused by the meat industry for years," Coplin charged. "We believe our record for the past twenty years [in Chicago] is outstanding, when the record of the national management is disgraceful and humiliating for us all."*

The blistering memo failed to bring results, and eventually Marugg's arthritis forced him to go on sick leave. He filed a grievance through the graders' union, however, and his reassignment by the chief of the grading service was ultimately overturned. Marugg went back to his old job of traveling from plant to plant, but his arthritis still bothered him, and in March 1980 he retired.

Marugg is partially disabled now with his arthritis and with sciatica, but that has not kept him from an old hobby. He was always something of an artist, once illustrating a handbook on grading for the USDA, and now he does intricate wood carvings. The bulls he carves out of sections of log are a favorite of his old friends, and some of the bulls fetch prices of up to three hundred dollars. For all he experienced over the years, Marugg says he's not bitter about his career as a meat grader, although bitterness would be more than justified. His car windows have been broken and spikes have been driven through his tires. He's been run off the road on the way home from work. He's lived through years of icy stares from packers and fellow graders. But he has taken it all. "I'm a different nature, there," he says. "I'm seventy years old now, but I was strong, I was a very strong man. I was a good boxer, and I never took crap from anybody. I wouldn't. When you've got a backbone, a lot of this stuff wears right off."

---

*Departmental memorandum dated Dec. 18, 1978.

4

The Packinghouse Scandals

Judge Lawrence Lydick: *I don't understand how they speak of his high character and distinction. Not one calls him what he is by his own admission, a crook.*

—U.S. v. a Los Angeles meat-packer

They stood before the judge, grim-faced. First it was in 1974 and 1975, then in 1978. Some of them were affluent men, well dressed and well coiffured. They were the owners of some of the most successful meat-packing operations in California. For others, tastes ran to leisure suits and combed-back hair. These were the burly, no-necked laborers who had worked their ways up and were now in charge of smaller packinghouses, ones struggling to survive. Their attorneys told the judge that each one was a "man of substance," a pillar of the community, an honorable man who had never before been in trouble with the law. The attorneys submitted letters of praise from civic leaders, community groups, and friends. The Girls Club complimented one packer for donating forty-six pounds of beef for its horse show; Ms. Ritt's junior high health science class thanked him for the donation of a beef heart; an old friend said he "has exceptional talent in the knowledge of hunting and fishing and this could be used to an advantage in teaching the young people the rights and wrongs in these activities." According to the letters, the community could not do without such men.

51

But the packers all wore the same grim expression, and they all mouthed the same penitent apologies to the judge. They all were guilty. In 1974 and 1975, they were guilty of bribing federal meat graders, or giving them illegal gratuities. They said they were sorry and humiliated, and they would never be in court again. But just two years later, many of them stood before a federal court judge, charged this time with price-fixing. They pleaded no contest or were found guilty. They said they were sorry and humiliated, and they promised they'd never be in court again.

It is all part of a continuing game played out in packinghouses across the country. Corruption has been a way of life for a substantial minority of the nation's meat-packers. They are involved in what can be a hotly competitive business, and all but a few giants must get by on profit margins that are paper-thin. So some of them cheat. They bribe graders and inspectors. They switch meat, substituting cheaper cuts for more expensive ones. They short-weight their customers. They counterfeit stamps used by buyers to identify the carcasses they want to buy and by graders to mark carcasses prime, choice, and good. And they fix prices. In the past decade alone, 176 packing and processing firms were indicted on a variety of these charges. Almost all of the indictments led to convictions, although in many cases the packers were able to plea-bargain their way to minor penalties. Nowhere have the abuses been more widespread than in Southern California. The packers of Los Angeles and San Diego have been the targets of state and federal investigations dating back to 1946. Corruption reached its peak in the mid-nineteen-seventies, and few packers avoided the taint of scandal. The experiences of the Southern California packing industry are an object lesson in what can—and does—go wrong throughout the country.

It is a close-knit group that runs the packing industry in Southern California. The leaders are men who have known each other since they were kids growing up in the same Los Angeles neighborhoods. Now they are in their fifties and sixties, and they have the self-assured look of men who have worked hard to build companies that have given them a comfortable life. But the look of comfort, ease, and wealth is deceiving, because in the past decade the packers have become desperate men playing a losing game. They have seen large, modern, efficient midwestern packers take away their business, and they fear it is only a matter of time before their business is all gone. They were slow in recognizing the threat of the midwestern giants, but they could have taken steps to modernize their operations in order to compete. Instead, they chose another course: they chose to cheat. They were caught in 1974 when the grading scandal was exposed. The chastened packers asked for forgiveness, and they vowed to make the Southern California packing industry a model for the rest of the nation. They set up a committee that would clean up the industry, headed by the president of the largest packer in Southern California. A smooth, dapper, distinguished man, he could project an air of authority and integrity that was good for the packers' image. And he worked well with government, helping out the FBI on some of its meat cases, and consulting with the State Department on some international trade matters.

Two years later, however, he was standing in court. He looked dignified in his expensive cream-colored suit, his graying temples set off against his deeply tanned face. But when he turned to leave, he was shaken and upset, and he slammed the courtroom door on the way out. He had just been sentenced to thirty days in jail and his company had been fined fifty thousand dollars.

Even as the packers had been making their pronouncements about how they would clean up their industry after the first round of convictions, another investigation was under way. Back when the FBI agents were gathering evidence for the bribery and gratuity cases, they were hearing other rumors as well. At the time, they just let them pass, but in 1976 and 1977, they had time to follow up on them. Soon, a federal grand jury was impaneled, and in 1978, thirteen of the same packers were hauled into court once again. This time the charge was price-fixing. For at least ten years these thirteen packers, the backbone of the Southern California meat industry, had been meeting nearly once a week to decide what the price of meat would be. It was known as the "salesmen's meeting" at 9 A.M. Wednesday morning, and its impact was reflected in the price of just about every piece of beef bought at just about every supermarket in Southern California.

The packers are all rather vague about how it started. But they seem to agree that "sometime" in the early 1960's "someone" in the Los Angeles packing industry got on the phone to his brethren and suggested they get together. The president and general manager of one large meat company remembers that the voice said something like "Why don't you come over. We'll discuss some of the problems that we have. We'll discuss marketing."

The Southern California meat industry is centered along a mile-long stretch of Vernon Avenue in the heart of the Los Angeles County warehouse and manufacturing district. Here, the smoky smells of heavy industry give way to the more pungent odors of live cattle and hogs on their way to slaughter. The firms that line this strip produce half of the beef slaughtered in the state. And they've been responsible for a large share of the corruption as well.

Every Wednesday morning, the packers met in a non-descript white building just off Vernon Avenue that contained the office for their local trade association. Other tenants of the building say that on those mornings it was impossible to find a place to park because the lot was jammed with the Cadillacs and Mercedeses of the packers. The packers would like people to believe that they just sat around and chewed the fat about all the various conditions and problems that affect any industry. They talked about new equipment and new regulations. They talked about labor problems and grading and inspection problems. They talked about livestock prices nationally. They talked about the availability of cattle. Whatever came up. Sure, as competitors, they were curious about what they each might be charging for their meat that week, and one purpose of the meetings was to get a general idea of the going prices. "We would just generally try to establish some guidelines as to where we thought the market should be," recalls a packer. After all, once the meeting was over, each packer would go back to his plant and figure out his own variables before deciding what to sell his meat for.

But as the federal investigation revealed, it was hardly that innocent. First of all, the timing was suspicious. Wednesday, the day of the meeting, was the day Safeway Stores, Inc., made its purchases. Safeway, the largest buyer of carcass beef in the state, solicited bids from all the packers, and bought from the lowest bidders. Additionally, because Safeway's buying power was so great, it was an established fact that when other supermarket chains bought their meat later in the week, they ended up paying the price that had been set by Safeway. Obviously, if the packers could control the price paid by Safeway, they could control the price paid by everyone else. And that's precisely what they did.

Meat Packers, Inc., the trade association for the Southern California packers, was a small-time operation. It was run by "Bert," Elberta Butler, a tough older woman originally hired as a secretary. She took charge when her boss died, and she performed all the routine functions required of a trade association head. Each week she put out the calls to the packers, reminding them of the salesmen's meeting, and each Wednesday she sat in her little office while outside, in the cavernous main room of the Meat Packers, Inc. office, the packers gathered around a long conference table.

It was all rather informal, they say. Here were Southern California's major packers, kicking around prices for half an hour or so, until they all agreed. Sometimes they even took a vote, with each man raising his hand to show his preference for what Safeway should pay. One way or another, when the packers returned to their plants they had the price they would charge Safeway well in mind. If a packer missed the meeting, he would just call one of his buddies to find out the new price. And if market conditions changed in the few hours between the time the meeting broke up and the bids had to be submitted to Safeway, the packers would confer by phone to set a new bid price.*

The packers would like people to believe that they didn't always go along with prices set at the meeting. A few contend

---

*Derived from testimony in U.S. v. Reuben Krasn, U.S. District Court, Los Angeles, 1978.

they only went along about half the time. But most admit it was at least 70 percent to 80 per cent of the time. And they don't deny there were serious arguments when it was discovered a packer was using the information to undercut his brothers. At the next meeting the offending packer might be confronted with a pointed question like "What's the matter with you guys? You stealing your livestock or something? How come you can sell so cheap?" From there, it would degenerate to more vicious accusations and threats. One packer remembers being blackballed from the meetings for a while because he didn't go along with the price often enough. And occasionally the meetings broke down completely. Charles Pilch, president of Delta Meat Packing, remembers there was little honor among the thieves, and every so often "people became disgusted and wouldn't come." In that case, why did the meetings always start up again? "Oh, I don't know," Pilch says. "Things may have been getting a little bit tough in the industry. . . ."*

The packers did find one way of keeping each other honest about being crooked. At the end of one meeting in 1974, a packer opened the door to Elberta Butler's office and said, "Bert, next week the boys are going to bring in their Safeway confirmation slips for you to check." When Safeway accepted a packer's bid, the packer was issued an invoice confirming the number of carcasses to be bought and the price. To make sure no packers were cheating on the price, Bert would tabulate the confirmation slips and report any discrepancies in the packers' bids. This she did for roughly six weeks; every price was identical.

The FBI found similar results. In a computer study of Safeway's buying patterns, the FBI came up with a week-by-week printout of Safeway's prices that showed a "general uniformity" in bids by the packers. That's a rather dry way of saying that the FBI had the packers dead to rights. For one five-week period in 1972, the printout showed every bid from every packer was the same. In early 1973, the federal price freeze was in effect, so the FBI disregarded those results. But once the freeze was lifted, the uniform bids remained. For five weeks in

*U.S. v. Krasn, U.S. District Court, Los Angeles, 1978.

February and March of 1974, every bid was the same. For ten weeks from October to December, every bid was the same. One of the FBI agents said later that if he ever wanted to write a primer on price-fixing, all he would have to do is type up his notes from this case.

The end of 1974 was a bad time for the country and for the packers. The President, after trying to convince America, "I am not a crook,"* had been forced to resign. The packers were finding out they were in serious trouble for bribing meat graders, so to avoid additional headaches they decided to end the price-fixing meetings as well. But like the President, they found out it was too late for a cover-up. The FBI was already onto the price-fixing scam, and once the bribery-and-gratuity investigation was wrapped up, the new investigation began. On April 13, 1978, thirteen packing companies and eleven company officials were indicated. They were charged with conspiring to fix, maintain, and stabilize the price of carcass beef in violation of the Sherman Antitrust Act. It has been alleged that the conspiracy may have cost consumers as much as ten cents per pound in inflated beef prices.

As for the conspirators, they had operated a scam marked by mistrust and bad faith, and their attempt to mount a defense was no different. Initially, all the packers banded together. They would present a united front led by some of Los Angeles' highest-paid and highest-powered attorneys. Heading the team was a man with a name as imposing as his reputation, Julian Von Kalinowsky, a leading authority on antitrust law. The attorneys divided up the work load, with the big names handling the key issues and the attorneys for the smaller packers researching the peripheral legal points. Then, on the Friday before the trial was to begin, the united front crumbled. One by one the major packers, the ones who had attracted the high-powered attorneys, went before the judge to change their not-guilty pleas. Instead, they pleaded *nolo contendere*. The "no contest" plea would allow the packers to avoid the stigma of a guilty plea, but not the punishment. As each man stood, grim-

---

*Nov. 17, 1973, Associated Press Managing Editors Association press conference, Disney World, near Orlando, FL.

faced, before the court, Federal Judge Malcolm Lucas, a stern, imposing figure (one packer waiting his turn commented, "He's like ice"), warned the packers that they would be sentenced just as if they had pleaded guilty. While the big packers paraded before the judge, the attorneys for the smaller packers held hurried conferences out in the hall with their clients, explaining what their big brothers were trying to pull off. Basically, they were covering themselves for civil suits that would follow demanding that the packers repay suppliers and consumers overcharged because of the conspiracy. The no-contest plea was a legal maneuver that would deny plaintiffs in the civil suits the use of evidence that the packers were technically guilty of anything. With that in mind, the smaller packers began to follow, and by the day of the trial there was only one packer left.

"My client, Mr. Krasn, and I are virtually alone now, and stand before this court totally abandoned and almost naked," attorney William Katz told the judge. Katz, a short, rumpled old man representing Reuben Krasn, president of Globe Packing Co., pleaded to the judge that he had been "low man on the totem pole" and that he was depending on the high-priced legal talent to lead the defense. "I am a lone practitioner. I have just one single secretary, and she's been with me for thirty-five years and pretty much comes in when she wants to and leaves that way." Judge Lucas, however, was not much moved. "Well, should we ask your secretary when you will actually be ready for trial in this matter, Mr. Katz?" Lucas granted Katz one week to prepare a case that more than a dozen attorneys had been struggling over for months.

Katz and his client might have been justified in feeling deserted by the other packers. But those packers had reason to feel betrayed as well. Although Katz provided a strong defense for Krasn after his hapless start, the fact remained that the packers had been caught with their pants down. And because one packer had forced a trial rather than hiding behind a no contest plea, all the abuses were now placed on the record. The other packers were granted immunity and required to testify, spelling out the conspiracy and the weekly meetings in detail. Reuben Krasn was found guilty and joined the other packers in jail. They were all sentenced by Judge Lucas to terms ranging from ten to thirty days, and their companies were fined a total of $640,000. In addition, they faced sanctions from the USDA. Worse, all the damning evidence was on the record for use in the civil trials hanging over the packers' heads. Suits were filed on behalf of the supermarkets that had bought meat at the illegally fixed prices, and on behalf of consumers who had bought their steaks and roasts at inflated prices.

There's one more loose end. Allegations have been made that Safeway and the other supermarket chains were not merely innocent victims, although no charges have ever been proven in court. After all, if a supermarket's meat buyer kept seeing the same bids week after week, it wouldn't take a genius to figure out something fishy was going on. Yet for at least ten years the Los Angeles packers held their weekly meetings, and no one was willing to say a thing until the FBI stumbled onto the conspiracy while investigating the bribery scandal.

As if the price-fixing conspiracy weren't sordid enough, it turns out the packers had found one more way to screw thy neighbor during this time: a commercial bribery scheme. The principals in the scheme were one of the top meat buyers employed by Safeway and a top meat broker, who arranged sales between supermarkets and packers. According to a complaint filed by the USDA's Packers and Stockyards Administration, the Safeway buyer received weekly payoffs of from one hundred to three hundred dollars for working with a meat broker (at least they found a creative way of covering up the payoffs—the money was funneled through the meat buyer's wife). The meat broker, in turn, accepted illegal brokerage commissions from packers totaling more than $260,000 in less than two years for services he never performed. The packers paid him the commissions in order to sell Safeway more meat than other packers.

It would at least be comforting to think that once the evidence of abuses began to pile up, the packers finally cleaned up their act for good. But sadly, that was not the case. It is a tribute to the arrogance of the Southern California packers that they still believed they had the right to rip off the consumer.

Here, self-styled consumer meat expert Frank Hogya comes into the picture again. His earlier complaints had helped force the federal investigation of the bribery scandal, but once it was exposed, he was not satisfied. He was still upset about the "crap" he found at the supermarket meat counters in San Diego, so he wrote a letter to CBS's *60 Minutes.* The result was a 1977 investigation by Dan Rather proving that even after the fines, jail terms, and consent decrees, the Southern California meat industry wasn't ready for reform.

Rather and his *60 Minutes* team, led by producer Steve Glauber, came to San Diego to check the meat grading. They arranged with top USDA management in Washington to bring in an impartial grading expert. John Coplin, grading-service supervisor in Chicago, accompanied the *60 Minutes* team to take a look at the meat offered for sale at several local supermarkets. At the first two supermarkets, the meat was fine, but at the third, Fed Mart, Coplin discovered obviously misgraded meat—twenty to twenty-five forequarters and hindquarters marked choice that were only good. The meat had been supplied by C&M Packing Corp., one of the packers involved in the earlier bribery scandal. The following excerpt is taken from the transcript of a segment of *60 Minutes,* entitled "Bum Steer."*

Rather went into a Fed Mart store to interview the chain's meat buyer. Standing in front of the meat counter, Rather asked, "When one of your employees calls you or says to you, 'Hey, I don't think this meat is really choice, although it's stamped choice,' do you come and take a look at it?"

> [Reply]: *Absolutely.*
> Rather: *How often does that happen?*
> [Reply]: *I've probably had one call in the last three years.*
> Rather: *Did you have one this week?*
> [Reply]: *Yes.*
> Rather: *Did you check it out?*
> [Reply]: *Yes.*
> Rather: *And what was the outcome?*

Originally broadcast September 11, 1977, over the CBS Television Network as part of the *60 Minutes* program series.

[Reply]: *I was of the opinion the beef was a legitimate choice cattle.*

Rather: *And that's based on your experience and—*

[Reply]: *Yes, that's correct.*

Rather: *You're aware that accusations have been made that, one, that you attend parties with people who work for C&M, grade for C&M?*

[Reply]: *No.*

Rather: *That C&M contributes to a yacht of yours, for example?*

[Reply]: *No. I'm not going to answer your questions.*

Rather: *Could you tell me why?*

[Reply]: *Because I don't like the way you've conducted this.*

Rather: *Could you tell me why?*

[Reply]: *Take that off.*

The meat buyer walked past Rather and the cameraman back to the butchering area behind the employees-only door.

"What we knew about ... [him] ... came not only as a surprise to him but also to his bosses," Rather told his 25 million *60 Minutes* viewers. The meat buyer admitted to Fed Mart officials that C&M Packing had given him an engine and trailer for his boat. But of course that in no way affected ... his ... judgment, as Fed Mart explained in a press conference two days after Rather's interview. "Based on the information that we have now, ... [the meat buyer] ... did nothing to help the vendor in any way," said Fed Mart spokesman Larry Sherman. "According to the information that we have been provided, this was solely a gift from—from the vendor in recognition of ... [his] ... love for fishing, and was not intended in any way to influence any decision that he—he made."

Apparently love of fishing is a serious offense at Fed Mart, however, because ... he ... was also forced to resign. A few months later he was on the payroll of C&M.

The buyer's relationship with the packers was nothing unique. Buyers for most supermarket chains and meat markets were given the royal treatment. "It was one big happy family, the packers, the buyers, and the graders," says one former meat market owner. Just like the graders, the buyers were the recipients of free booze, women, meals, and entertainment. If a buyer needed anything, say, tickets to a big football game, the packer would run right out and buy the tickets to keep the buyer happy. "It's common knowledge that the buyers are on the take," one meat market owner told *60 Minutes.* "They're treated like they're kings."

Knowingly or unknowingly, however, the buyers were also duped. After they picked out their meat in the packer's cooler, they didn't always get what they paid for. Buyers learned early on to do their own weighing of carcasses to make sure they weren't overcharged. They knew the packers sometimes tipped the scales when they weren't watching, or tried to sell them "hot beef," meat that had just been killed and was still heavy from the blood and moisture that would run off before the meat was delivered. And they learned to be very careful about how they marked the carcasses they wanted to buy. At first, some buyers would just stick tags on the carcasses they wanted and leave it up to the packer to load and deliver the carcasses. But eventually they would figure out that the meat that was delivered was not always the meat they had picked out: someone switched the tags. So the buyers would wise up and get metal stamps to mark the carcasses they wanted. That didn't upset the packer, though. The men at the packinghouse were very friendly about the whole process. They'd shoot the breeze for a while, offer the buyer a drink, make him feel right at home. After he stamped his meat, they'd even offer to wash off the stamp for him. They'd take the stamp into a back room, make a copy of it in a block of clay, wash it off, and return it to the buyer with a smile. From now on, the buyer could mark whatever he wanted, but the packer could give him whatever he pleased. It was simple to cut the buyer's stamp off a choice carcass and then use the counterfeit stamp to mark an inferior carcass that would be shipped out in its place. And if the packer had several different counterfeit stamps, he could "sell" the same carcass to several buyers and ship out something less than they all had bargained for.

Dan Rather went into the meat cooler of C&M Packing to

ask one of the company's officers about this practice. "You mentioned earlier to me that over the past few years you'd had—had some problems," Rather said as the two men stood in their freezer coats and hard hats among the beef carcasses, "Could you describe for me briefly what those problems were? Were those problems dealing with the—with the marking of choice, prime, standard? Or were—were they problems dealing with this—this—the store buying stamps?"

"Well, I don't know what you mean by problems," he answered. "We haven't had any great problems of any nature that I—that I understand what you're talking about."

> Rather: *Well, I thought there had been some accusations— now, mind you, I'm saying what's been said to me—that, for example, some of the buyers were not getting what they had stamped as theirs, and that was a continuing problem.*
> [Reply]: *I don't know what you mean, really.*
> Rather: *Well, could—could you explain to me what—what this stamp is?*

From his pocket, Rather pulled out a counterfeit stamp from the Mayfair supermarket chain, one of C&M's customers. He handed it to him.

> [Reply]: *I think probably what you guys ought to do is leave.*
> Rather: *I don't understand.*
> [Reply]: *Well, I—I don't think it's fair. I don't believe that that's at all fair.*
> Rather: *Well, I'm going to give you an opportunity to tell me how you think it's unfair.*
> [Reply]: *Well, I—I cer—I certainly would take the opportunity—*

With the stamp in his hand, he began to wander among the carcasses, moving away from Rather.

> Rather: *May I have that back?*
> [Reply]: *I don't know. Does it belong to you?*
> Rather: *Yes, it does.*

[Reply]: *Where did you get it?*
Rather: *I got it from someone who told me that you used that to put a different kind of stamp on the meat than the store buyer put on his own meat.*
[Reply]: *Is that right? Certainly, I am disappointed in you. Really I am.*
Rather: *Yeah, and I'd like to have back that stamp, if you don't mind.*
[Reply]: *Come on, I'll give it to you.*

He handed the stamp back to Rather.

Rather: *Well, now, could you tell me what it is? This is a phony stamp, isn't it?*
[Reply]: *I don't know what it is. And I'm—I'm—*
Rather: *It isn't made out of metal. It doesn't have a handle on the back.*

The officer of the packing company wasn't really listening anymore. He just wandered off into the carcasses muttering, "Boy, oh boy, what a disgusting deal!"

A disgusting deal it was, and continues to be. The *60 Minutes* report prompted a USDA investigation, and one year later the USDA suspended grading and inspection services from C&M and its sister company, National, for forty-five days because the packers had given gratuities to federal inspectors and graders.* But the problems of C&M, National, and all the other Southern California packers are hardly unique. Every year there are new scandals in new towns, and there's not much hope that they will end. "I wish that somehow, someplace, we had a really definitive idea of how much corruption was taking place," says Tom Grumbly, associate administrator of the USDA's Food Safety and Quality Service during the Carter administration. "I suppose that's wishful thinking. We'll never get to that point."

---

*"Meat Packers End 45-Day Shut Down," *San Diego Daily Transcript*, Jan. 1, 1979.

5

The Inspection Scandals

The President of Our Company, Harvey Nathan, Dared to Question the Ability of Certain Government Personnel. He Dared to Request Better Government People to Supervise Those That Were Available. He Questioned the System. He Dared to Bring Suit Against the Government. He is Questioning the Various Abuses of Authority, and His Enemies Don't Like it. . . .

> —*Newspaper advertisement,*
> *Reading, PA, Eagle and Times,*
> *quoted as Government Exhibit G-7 in*
> *U.S. v. Harvey Nathan, U.S. District Court,*
> *Reading, PA Jan. 30–Feb. 2, 1978*

On August 10, 1977, three officials of the USDA Meat and Poultry Inspection Service drove out to Shillington, Pennsylvania, a small town outside of Reading in the southereastern portion of the state, to pay a call on the owner of Salsburg Quality Meats. The three men, area supervisor Dr. Jonas Detweiler, inspector Stephen Marzen, and compliance officer Frederico Talley, walked up to the house that served as the office for this meat-processing and retail sales firm. They went through the open doorway, past the spice room where the sausage ingredients were stored, and on down the hall toward the office of owner Harvey Nathan and his secretary, Betsy.

Harvey Nathan was a slightly balding man in his late

thirties, short and slim but solidly built. He was a self-assured, winning fellow with a ready smile. But he was also known to have quite a temper. On this day, as inspector Marzen remembers it, Nathan saw Dr. Detweiler walking toward his office first. The two men cordially shook hands and said hello. Then Nathan saw Marzen and Talley. "Mr. Talley, you are trespassing," Nathan said. "Betsy, get me my gun."

Marzen continues his account: "Well, before she could get the gun, he went over to the closet, got a gun out, and said, 'Betsy, get me the bullets.'

"All I saw was a gun, and I seen him reaching for a bunch of bullets, and I saw him put one in the chamber, and he said 'When I get this gun loaded, I am going to start shooting.' "

That was enough to convince the inspectors it was time to leave. Later, Dr. Detweiler was asked how they left. "Well, golly. I—fast. I know that Fred Talley was the first one. I remember seeing his heels. And I was as fast after him as I could go. He was running, and I was doing the same thing." Talley ran down the driveway to Grossman's Lumber Co. next door. Detweiler ran to the government car, got in, closed the windows, and locked the doors. Marzen wasn't as fast.

"As soon as I got outside the building, Mr. Nathan was right behind me and he said, 'Mr. Marzen, stay where you are. Don't move. You and Dr. Cavanaugh were warned.' Then he told me to get against the wall, the wall of the house, the building where his office was."

Nathan stood about fifteen feet away, his Remington 514 .22-caliber rifle at the ready. He waved it back and forth, occasionally pointing the barrel at Marzen. He stood guard, pacing back and forth in the parking lot. Eventually he walked over and sat down on the stoop of the house, still keeping an eye on Marzen, up against the wall. When the police arrived about fifteen minutes later, Nathan unloaded the rifle, leaned it up against the side of the house, and walked over to the officer to turn in the trespassers he had caught.*

---

*U.S. v. Harvey Nathan, U.S. District Court, Reading, PA, Jan. 30–Feb. 2, 1978.

Harvey Nathan's showdown with the USDA was the culmination of a three-year-long running battle. Nathan and the inspectors clashed continually during that time, giving a graphic demonstration of what can go wrong in the relationship between a regulatory agency and the people it is supposed to regulate.

The relationship between inspectors and packers is particularly delicate because inspectors wield a wide range of discretionary powers. Singlehandedly they can make a serious dent in a packer's profits, or even put him out of business. They can condemn individual carcasses or cuts of meat, they can temporarily halt production for unsanitary conditions or mislabeled products, and they can set in motion procedures that can close down a plant completely. The USDA inspection service is similar to the grading service, but there is one important difference. Grading is voluntary; a packer requests federal graders and pays the USDA for their services. Inspection is mandatory; all meat intended for interstate commerce must be inspected for health and sanitation by the USDA, and the service is paid for by the USDA. Even meat that is not intended for interstate commerce must be inspected by state inspectors with similar powers. Inspectors are in the packinghouses, making sure conditions are sanitary and checking for diseased and spoiled meat. And they are in the processing plants, checking again on sanitation, disease, and spoilage, and also making sure the sausages, hot dogs, luncheon meats, hams, and other processed meats are made with the right chemicals, additives, and meat by-products. The inspectors are basically blue-collar workers, but they must make use of a sophisticated knowledge of food chemistry, bacteriology, animal pathology, industrial hygiene, and numerous other highly specialized disciplines while working in a noisy, high-pressure environment.

The inspector's powers give him a good deal of leverage, but they also make him a prime target for the packer. "Inherent in inspection are attempts to influence inspection," says former assistant secretary of agriculture Carol Tucker Foreman, who had ultimate authority over the inspection service. "If management is hostile, the inspector can be involved all day long in a battle of wills. He has to continually punch the button to stop the line, and in the process he makes everyone hate him. The flip side of that is some inspectors out of spite, or for extortion, will push the button and stop the line to get their way."*

Packers and inspectors sometimes do a tango, one leading the other in a subtle back-and-forth game of bribery and extortion. It can start with little favors, a cup of coffee, a lunch, a bundle of meat, offered or requested in such a way that they are clearly something more than friendly gestures. Minor inspection violations can be either ignored or strictly enforced to get a point across. One of the most common tools used in tangoing is overtime pay, which comes out of the pocket of the packer, not the USDA. A packer can bribe an inspector with the offer of some easy overtime work. And on the other hand, the inspector can extort money from the packer by slowing down production and forcing the packer to pay him some overtime. There are many other subtle tricks, and then there are some that are not so subtle.

Outright bribery and gratuity scandals just like the ones uncovered in the grading service have plagued the meat inspection service as well. In 1976, thirty-one Manhattan and Brooklyn inspectors were indicted for accepting $125,000 in payoffs from packers. In 1971, thirty Boston inspectors were indicted in a similar scandal. And every year individual inspectors who have been on the take are exposed. But like the grading scandals, the inspection scandals work both ways. The packer making a payoff stands to gain much more than the cost of the bribe if the inspector then turns his back on minor rule violations and lets the packer move his meat quickly. In fact, there is more of an incentive for a packer to try to take advantage of a grader than the other way around. According to the Wholesome Meat Act, a packer is guilty of a felony only if he offers something to an inspector "with the intent to influence" the inspector. An inspector, however, is guilty of a felony if he accepts "anything of value" from the packer, no matter what the intent. The difference in the burden of proof usually means that inspectors go to jail, while packers go free or pay minor fines.

Not all inspectors and packers want to tango, however, and

---

*From interview with Foreman by author, July 17, 1980, Washington, D.C.

sometimes the relationship turns ugly. An inspector can harass a packer by continually halting production for violation of obscure regulations. And a packer can intimidate the inspector by continually questioning his judgment, or threatening him, or filing complaints with his supervisors. In one particularly vicious ongoing feud, inspectors and the owner of the nation's largest pork-processing plant have been at each other's throats for more than a decade. The plant owner contends the inspectors arbitrarily slow down carcass-processing lines and otherwise foul up production. The inspectors, who charge they are regularly faced with grossly unsanitary conditions at the plant, say the owner has tried to smear them with charges they are members of the Ku Klux Klan, and on at least two occasions has threatened to have inspectors killed.

The USDA has placed a major emphasis on upgrading the inspection service. The agency is also trying to develop equipment that can be used to analyze meat and make some of the critical decisions for inspectors. "Ultimately we need better, more objective tools," former assistant secretary Foreman says, "so the employee's judgment is not so much the determining factor." Until that time, the pressures that lead to corruption will remain. And inspection will continue to be prone to individual conflicts that border on the homicidal.

As far as the federal meat inspectors in eastern Pennsylvania were concerned, Harvey Nathan had a Dr.-Jekyll-and-Mr.-Hyde personality. He could be a friendly, personable man one moment. But he could be hot-tempered, sarcastic, profane, and irrational the next. All too often, it was the Mr. Hyde that the inspectors had to deal with. He threw a telephone at a meat grader once. He threatened inspectors, once telling an inspector who had accidentally scraped some machinery with a scissors that he would stick the scissors in the inspector's ear if he ever did it again, and another time offering to flatten an inspector's nose all over his face. He ridiculed them, once calling a supervisor an "incompetent and a Yo-Yo," another time asking if inspectors were required to go to "Dumb School."* One of

*Trial transcript U.S. v. Harvey Nathan, op. cit.

Nathan's former employees says the inspectors "bent over backward, I think, to please him or try to make it easy, you know, smooth running." And how did Nathan treat the inspectors in return? "Not like a gentleman."

He was always complaining about the inspectors and contesting their judgment. "He made every effort to do exactly the opposite of what should be done and what he knew should be done," says inspector Marzen. If Nathan disagreed with an inspector, he'd take his complaint all the way up the chain of command to Washington if necessary. He even publicly embarrassed the inspectors. Once, the inspection service ruled that twenty thousand dollars' worth of hams had been contaminated, and then reversed the ruling. Instead of selling the hams, however, Nathan called in a local television news crew to film as he destroyed them. He implied that Harvey Nathan was more concerned about protecting consumers against contaminated meat than the inspection service was. Later, when his run-ins with the USDA had won him a large degree of local notoriety, he ran newspaper ads patting himself on the back because he "dared" to challenge the government. Included in the ads were coupons for ten cents per pound off on any purchase in recognition of this man who "*Dared* to Question the Ability of Certain Government Personnel."

It dug at the inspectors that Nathan tried to make himself out to be a hero, because they contend that Nathan was a frequent and heavy violator of meat inspection regulations. They claim he mislabeled products and he hid things from inspectors. Sometimes, when meat was returned to him because it was spoiled or adulterated, they claim he sent that same product right back out again to someone else—or even to the same customer.*

The inspection service had cited Nathan for a long list of violations during the three years his company operated under its supervision. His meat was sent to schools, hospitals, mental institutions, and prisons, and many times it was sent back. On two occasions, eight hundred pounds of frankfurters sent to the South Mountain Geriatric Center were rejected because they

---

*U.S. v. Harvey Nathan, op. cit.

were slimy. Same for sixteen hundred pounds of franks sent to the Philadelphia State Hospital. Six hundred fifteen pounds of hams sent to the Hamburg State Hospital had green streaks through them. Eight hundred pounds of chicken frankfurters sent to the same place contained beef and pork, not chicken.*

Daniel Kozik, a former Nathan employee who quit once and was fired once, contends it was common practice to mis-label products and deceive inspectors. "There were times when making a product, there was something that wasn't supposed to have in, beef lips or chicken or something like that. If the inspector was around, we didn't grind it. We sort of worked around it until the inspector was in another room or something like that." He recalls there was one order for five hundred pounds of chicken franks, but they only had three hundred pounds on hand so they added some regular franks to the order. They at least tried to take the regular franks' labels off the packages, but when the labels wouldn't come off, they just slapped chicken-franks labels on top of the old labels. In general, they weren't very careful about what they put into their products, Kozik says. "We made basically one kind of Polish sausage, which was labeled beef and pork, and pork and beef, all beef, all pork. What we needed is what we labeled."

It was for all these reasons that the inspectors felt they had to keep a close eye on Nathan. They felt if they turned their backs for a minute, he would try to slip something past them. They had battled ever since the first inspector entered the plant in 1974, but the conflict escalated during the summer of 1977. In June and the early part of July, inspector Marzen kept finding problems at Nathan's plant. It wasn't sanitary enough. Ingredients were being contaminated. Meat was spoiled. Finally, on July 8, he found that the processing room was "filthy dirty," and the decision was made to temporarily withhold inspection privileges. Heated negotiations followed, and attorneys had to be called in to work out an agreement under which everyone agreed to try to get along. But on August 2 there was another confrontation.

Inspector Marzen, a tall, handsome, well-built man with

---

*U.S. v. Harvey Nathan, op. cit.

the look of a beach boy, recalls entering the plant about 7 A.M. that day. Throughout the morning, he had trouble with Nathan. Products were hanging on the wrong racks. Employees were grinding up meat that was improperly labeled. He had to ask Nathan several times to put the proper labels on the meat products Nathan was mixing together. At one point there were two conflicting labels on a meat grinder, and Marzen asked Nathan which one was right. Nathan replied sarcastically, "Do you have to go to Dumb School to be an inspector?" Then, sometime around noon, Marzen walked up to where Nathan was working at a mixing machine. He remembers asking Nathan what was in the mixer. "He said, 'Now, what kind of a fucking question is that?' And I leaned over closer, and he said, 'You get any closer to me and I am going to waffle you.'

"Then he turned around right away, and I had to back up quick, not to be knocked down. He went over to a table on the other side of the room and picked up a container of spices, and came back and he dumped the container of spices in the mixer and stood there watching it mix.

"And I said, 'You still didn't tell me what it is, what is in the mixer.'

"And he says, 'You are baiting me. Do you know what baiting is?'

"And I said, 'No, I don't know what baiting is.'

"At that point he was very angry, he turned around and he threw the spice container on the floor, and it bounced and hit me in the leg, and he said, 'I am tired of playing games. You are baiting me.' And he pushed me with his elbows across the plant."

The small, balding Nathan pushed the young body builder over to the cooler door and said, "How would you like your nose flattened across your face?" Nathan made a fist and gestured as if he were going to flatten Marzen's nose. He stood there with Marzen against the cooler door for a moment, then turned and walked off into the meat cooler. Marzen left the plant immediately to report the incident to his supervisor. "I told him what happened and I told him I was too shaky and nervous to go back into the plant."*

---

*U.S. v. Harvey Nathan, op. cit.

There were conferences that afternoon between Marzen and his supervisor, and between both of them and Nathan. Nathan was questioned about the incident by Marzen's supervisor, Dr. Francis Cavanaugh. Cavanaugh asked him if he had pushed Marzen, and Nathan denied it. He asked him if he had threatened to flatten Marzen's nose over his face, and Nathan denied it. He admitted that, yes, he did ask Marzen if he would like his nose flattened across his face, but he explained that it was just a question, not a threat.

After weighing Nathan's answers, Cavanaugh told Nathan inspection was being withheld again. Nathan said, fine, he didn't want federal inspection anymore. He said that when the inspectors left that day, he didn't want them to come back ever again.

Harvey Nathan wanted nothing more to do with the USDA Meat and Poultry Inspection Service. He remembers telling Cavanaugh, "I just don't have any fun any longer, the business is no longer enjoyable, I cannot physically or emotionally continue as we were going." From his point of view, all he had ever gotten from the federal inspection service was harassment. His attorney, Abraham J. Brem Levy, puts it this way: "Mr. Nathan is an independent American citizen who takes his citizenship very very seriously, and will not stand by and placidly accept conduct on the part of any other citizen, even federal inspectors of the Department of Agriculture, where they engage in small-minded conduct to embarrass a person. . . ." Levy contends that "the word was out in the department to get Harvey Nathan and to embarrass him in any way they can and to aggravate him and to harass him."

Nathan won't go that far himself, but he can think of at least three men who were out to get him, and others who made his life difficult. To hear him talk about his relationship with federal inspectors is to hear a totally different story from the one told by the inspectors.

Nathan's own story goes back to his first days under federal inspection. Stephen Marzen was the first inspector assigned to Nathan's plant, and they had their first run-in after he had been on the job about two months. Marzen complained that a metal tree on which hams were hung was too dirty. There was soot on the tree, but that was hardly abnormal, since the tree was used in the smokehouse. Nathan appealed the ruling to Marzen's supervisor, who said the tree looked fine and allowed work to continue. Nathan says Marzen didn't have any significant reaction at the time to being overruled, but he wonders if maybe his problems don't date to that incident.

All along there were petty problems that seemed to get blown out of proportion. He remembers one morning in April 1976 when two supervisors made a surprise inspection of the plant. He showed them through, and then they walked with him out to a loading dock. One of the supervisors, Dr. Detweiler, pointed to some weeds and paper down the driveway about a hundred yards away. "Dr. Detweiler and I had a running feud sort of relationship where we were continually nitpicking with each other, and I expressed to him that that was fine, I saw it, there were weeds there, but that we didn't process meat there, we processed within the bounds of the plant." Detweiler pressed the point and Nathan said he would get around to it, but he again mentioned that the meat processing was done inside. "He told me he didn't like that answer, that I was being sarcastic, and I told him that I thought he was incompetent and a Yo-Yo."

"Immediately upon the words leaving my mouth, Dr. Detweiler told me that inspection was being withdrawn." Detweiler walked out to a mobile home parked beside the plant that served as the inspectors' office and typed a letter to Nathan: "Because of a general lack of cooperation and harsh yelling statements by you charging our incompetence, all processing operations must cease until acceptable relations between inspection personnel and management are reestablished."

Nathan sat down and wrote a reply. Then the two men met face to face and talked out the problem. Detweiler withdrew his letter and allowed processing to continue. But Nathan doesn't believe the matter was dropped there. A month later, he was operating his plant on a Saturday. To do so, he was required to make special arrangements to have an inspector on hand. Detweiler walked into the plant that day, saw no inspector, and exclaimed, "I caught you!" But Nathan called to the other room, and in walked the inspector. Detweiler quietly left. However, he was back the following Saturday. This time he checked the parking lot for the inspector's car, and when he didn't see it, he again confronted him. "I caught you now!" But again, the inspector was in the other room. Detweiler casually mentioned he had just dropped by to use the phone. A week or so later, a new inspector appeared to make a review of the plant. He pointed out a few minor problems to Nathan, but overall he said he was surprised; Detweiler had led him to believe he'd find a "rat trap."

Nathan said it was all part of a pattern of continual harassment. One new inspector refused to approve some of his products, and after he questioned her, he was sure she was operating on orders from above to give him a hard time.

Then there was the incident where he called in the TV cameras to film while he destroyed twenty thousand dollars' worth of hams. Nathan was upset because the local inspection officials wouldn't help him determine whether the hams were contaminated or not. He had to press the case to high inspection officials in Washington to get a ruling. When he decided to destroy the hams, even though he had finally pushed Washington to OK them, he remembers the inspector on duty told him, "If you are going to do that, you are going to create a lot of enemies."

The real fireworks didn't start until the summer of 1977. For the first half of the year, things had gone smoothly. He got along with the inspector assigned in January of that year, Leo Petkovich, and he didn't have any run-ins with the supervisors either. Petkovich worked at the plant until the beginning of June. On his last day, a supervisor inspected the plant. Nathan says, "He congratulated Leo on a wonderful job of bringing us to compliance and making the facility look as an inspection facility should." The next day, a Saturday, Nathan and an assistant oiled some equipment to make sure it would be in working order for the coming week, because he planned to be out of town. The new inspector arrived on Monday. It was Stephen Marzen.

"On that Monday Mr. Marzen arrived and immediately ceased operations because the plant was filthy dirty," Nathan says. "The same plant that was clean and satisfactory on Friday at the close of business, that had nothing further processed in it

Saturday and Sunday, was now filthy dirty on Monday. On Tuesday, a vat of brine, two hundred seventy-five gallons, was condemned for reason of a housefly. On Wednesday, a similar vat of brine containing two hundred seventy-five gallons was condemned for reason of a feather floating in it."

A few weeks later, a batch of hams was returned by a customer for resmoking because they had been stored in a freezer for about eight weeks and had lost their color. Marzen examined the hams, said they were contaminated and they must be destroyed. He told Nathan he could smell that the hams were spoiled. "I couldn't smell it," Nathan says, "because the hams were frozen solid." Nathan contested the ruling and suggested sending samples to a lab to determine whether or not the hams were contaminated. Marzen's superiors refused the request. The next thing he knew, Marzen had poured Clorox and perchlorine over the hams, destroying them.*

Nathan immediately wrote a letter demanding to know by what authority Marzen could destroy his product. When he got no reply, he sent Marzen and his superiors another letter. This one included bills charging the USDA $3212.60, the value of the hams destroyed, and $462, the value of the brine solutions destroyed a few weeks earlier. "The day after Steve was given these invoices, he entered the plant in the morning, told me my grinder was dirty. I told him I had just cleaned it, he said it wasn't cleaned satisfactorily. Okay. I took it apart and I started to clean it again." When he was done, he told Marzen the grinder was cleaned and asked him to check it. Marzen did not respond. After giving Marzen a few more none too friendly words, Nathan went back into the plant and told his employees to begin production. An hour later, Marzen and a superior informed him that what had been processed that morning was adulterated because Marzen had not given permission to start, and because the processing room was "filthy dirty." There was a confrontation, and when it ended, inspection was formally withheld from the plant.

The attorneys were brought in to work out a settlement, but the peace didn't last long. On August 1, Nathan was making

---

*U.S. v. Harvey Nathan, op. cit.

boiled hams that were then vacuum-packed. "The girls vac-uumed or sealed the hams, affixed the labels, put them into the master cartons, strapped the master cartons, weighed them so they would be ready for shipment the next morning. During this time, Mr. Marzen watched the whole operation." When it was done, Marzen informed him that the hams were improperly labeled and could not be sent out. He said the labels did not contain the phrase "sectioned and formed," so they were incor-rect. Nathan pointed out he had been using the same labels for the past eight months without any problem. Why did he have to change today? "Because this is my decision," Marzen told him. Nathan appealed to Marzen's boss, who said he'd discuss it with his complaint the following day. That didn't help, since Nathan had to meet an early-morning shipment. So Nathan spent three hours unbanding, opening, relabeling, and resealing the hams.

The next morning, August 2, Nathan was still mad. "I was hot off of the confrontation the previous day that was not satisfactorily resolved, and was trying to determine in my own mind at that point how I was going to overcome this situation, because I could no longer tolerate the debating, the harassment that was taking place. I could not either emotionally endure this any longer." When Marzen entered the plant on August 2, he asked him about the hams. Then throughout the morning Marzen kept questioning him and finding fault with production. Finally, around noon, Nathan had had enough. He threw a spice pan on the floor, although he contends he didn't throw it at Marzen. He admits there was an "altercation," but he says he never pushed Marzen or threatened him. After a shouting match, he just walked off into the cooler.

When Marzen returned later with his supervisor, Dr. Cava-naugh, Nathan complained to Cavanaugh that Marzen had been "walking around with a chip on his shoulder." The two men talked about the incident, and then Cavanaugh left. He came back about half an hour later to inform Nathan inspection was being withheld. Nathan said he wanted to make it permanent. He didn't want to see federal inspectors ever again. "While you're here, take anything you want; you may have anything that's within your office," he said. "If you can't take it all at one time, well, you can come back. But thereafter, when you leave, any USDA personnel that comes upon these premises will be considered trespassers, and they will be subject to the ramifications of trespassing, because I can no longer tolerate the nonsense."

Nathan wanted to be left alone. He would just get out of the wholesale business that required federal inspection and go back to retail sales, where he would only have state inspectors to deal with. If he never saw a federal inspector again, it would be too soon.

So on August 10, when he saw three inspection officials approaching his office, he was not pleased. He told his secretary to call the police as the three men entered his office. He said hello to the first man, Dr. Detweiler, and then he said, "Gentlemen, you are trespassing; please leave." He remembers saying it three times, each time more forcefully. Dr. Detweiler turned to leave,but the other two began bantering with Nathan, contending they had a right to be there, they were authorized representatives of the USDA. When they still refused to leave, Nathan got his rifle, put a bullet in the chamber, and said, "Gentlemen, stay right there." But now the three men left—in a hurry—and he followed. He denies saying, "When I get this gun loaded, I am going to start shooting." But these men were trespassers, and Nathan firmly believes he would have been well within his rights if he had shot them. Instead, he waited for the police to come and escort the trespassers off his property.

No one was arrested that day. The police calmed everyone down and they all went home. But as far as the inspectors were concerned, things had gone too far. Something had to be done about Harvey Nathan. On November 9, 1977, a federal grand jury indicted Nathan on two counts of "assaulting, impeding, and interfering with federal officials while engaged in the performance of their official duties." He was charged with assaulting Stephen Marzen on August 2, and with assaulting Marzen and Marzen's two superiors on August 10.

In the trial the following February from which these accounts are drawn, all the petty bickering, all the back-and-forth harassment, came out. It was a bench trial, so when it was over Judge E. Mac Troutman was left to sort out the record of conflicting claims and to weigh the testimony of witnesses whose motives and credibility it was easy to question. Judging the August 2 incident, he ruled the evidence did not support the claim that Nathan had pushed inspector Marzen and hit him with a spice pan. Nathan was found not guilty. But judging the August 10 incident, he ruled the inspection officials were more than justified in returning to Nathan's plant, and they should not have been met by a man wielding a rifle. Harvey Nathan was guilty of the second count and sentenced to four months in jail and twenty months' probation.

Nathan appealed the judgment, and although he lost, the appellate court made it clear the inspection service had little to be proud of. "One can sympathize with Nathan's determination to preserve the sanctity of his private office and dwelling against an unwanted and unsolicited intrusion, as well as with his sense of exasperation at the persistent harassment to which he was being subjected. It is also difficult for a detached observer to condone the conduct of various government officials who allowed the relationship between a citizen and his government to deteriorate over a period of time, and who, though fully aware that they were persona non grata at Nathan's plant, evidently failed to take measures to avoid a confrontation. Unfortunately for Nathan, however, the law as it now stands does not support his position, and ignorance of the law, of course, does not save one from its sanctions."

Two of the assistant U.S. attorneys who handled the case against Nathan, Luther Weaver and Gregory Miller, don't agree with the appellate court's inference that the inspectors had been unnecessarily tough on Nathan. "The inspectors were rather hard on him," Miller admits, "but the moment they weren't there, he would pass some bad meat." Ultimately, however, the court's ruling points to a problem that goes beyond local inspectors who let a personality conflict get out of hand. All too often the USDA management has been guilty of ignoring local problems until it is too late. Perhaps with better oversight, the relationship between Harvey Nathan and the USDA would not have deteriorated the way it did. Maybe the blowup was unavoidable in the Nathan case, even under the best of circumstances. But confrontations are too prevalent for them to be solely the result of bad blood between a few individual inspectors and packers. An ongoing criticism of government inspection and grading services is that the men on the line are too often left to fend for themselves, with insufficient support and supervision from above. For years inspectors and graders have complained of low morale. They say their superiors won't back them up and the USDA bureaucracy in Washington doesn't seem to want to hear their complaints. Most often when inspectors are caught taking bribes, or when the system breaks down as it did in the Nathan case, the real blame lies not with the inspectors on the line, but with the meat inspection management.

A gross example of what can go wrong when inspectors are left to their own devices was uncovered by Florida senator Lawton Chiles in 1976. At that time the Defense Department operated a separate inspection program for the military, and Chiles discovered it was a disaster.

"If Uncle Sam hired family shoppers who live near military bases and gave them a shopping list and fifty dollars each to go to the corner supermarket to buy a basket of groceries to bring back to the military, the result would probably be far better than what the GIs are getting under the present system." These remarks by Chiles opened his hearings in May 1976 on the scandal of military meat procurement. "If a housewife pays for a U.S. choice steak—a rib eye or a tenderloin or a top sirloin—and she gets a tough, low-grade gristly hunk of knuckle, she'll take it back. If a housewife pays a higher price for extra lean ground beef, and a third of that meat cooks away into fat in the fying pan, she won't buy from that butcher or that grocery store again. But Uncle Sam doesn't seem to have the common sense of the average family shopper. Uncle Sam continues to catch many of these meat-packers trying to slip meat past the inspectors, meat that's tough when it should be tender, fatty when it should be lean."

At bases from New England to Texas to Florida to California to Illinois to Virginia to England and to Ireland, when GI's complained about being fed "shit on a shingle," they weren't far off. "What we've found," Chiles said, "is gross waste—not only because some meat companies were engaging in fraud, not only because some military inspectors were on the take—but also because the whole system is like a Rube Goldberg invention. It goes through an awful lot of very complicated motions to get very little accomplished." The Chiles investigation brought major reforms, and the story of the investigation, told through the testimony at his hearings, is still a timely one because many of the underlying problems remain today.

Specialist Fourth Class Nadja Hoyer-Booth* joined the Army for a chance to see Europe. She was a pretty, streetwise eighteen-year-old with long brown hair parted at the side. When she signed up in 1974, she was guaranteed a European tour of duty, and that's all she wanted. Beyond that, the Army could tell her what she would do. In basic training, she was told she would be an ammunition assistant at Fort Knox. But when she reported there, she was told there had been a change: she would be a food inspector instead. She asked what kind of job that was, and she was told, "Well, you just walk into a freezer and go home early."

Hoyer-Booth was shipped to Fort Sheridan in Illinois for basic food instruction. During the eight-week course, she spent a week learning about red meats, a day and a half or two days specifically on beef. "And we learned about potatoes and eggs and hams and it was just another course to me just to study and pass the test and forget about it." Near the end of the course, she got her duty assignment and a rude surprise. She would be stationed at Fort Devens, outside Boston. New England was as close as she'd ever get to Europe.

It was the first of many surprises. When she and two other women recruits reported for duty the first afternoon, all the sergeants and enlisted personnel and officer were sitting around a table playing poker. "And it was working hours and this was a working day and they just sort of ignored us and kept playing

---

*All the information that follows is taken from the transcript of the hearings before the subcommittee on Federal Spending Practices, Efficiency and Open Government of the U.S. Senate Committee on Government Operations, May 10, 1976, entitled "Investigation of Military Meat Procurement."

poker." No provisions had been made for their living quarters. With their meager pay and the expensive housing market in Boston, it was two months before the women found an apartment of their own. In the meantime, they shared a one-room studio with a male soldier who had temporarily taken them in.

To prepare Hoyer-Booth and the two other women soldiers for their new jobs, they were taught a few things, like how to test the fat content of ground beef. And they were given a tour of a large defense contractor in Boston, "to see what a meat-packing plant was like." Hoyer-Booth remembers, "We were in our summer uniforms and the three of us walked in and the whole production stopped and they all turned around and stared and whistled because women just weren't in meat-packing plants. Maybe a secretary. It was very intimidating."

Soon Hoyer-Booth was the military meat inspector for the packinghouse. She was chosen over the other two women, "because I was the largest girl." Now her real education began. Within four or five weeks the other inspectors started to teach her the fine points of military inspection that had been missed at Fort Sheridan.

How to steal a roast was the first lesson. Inspectors were required to test the fat content of ground beef, so they put small bags of samples from various batches of ground beef in a larger bag. "And when you're about halfway through that, you look at an oven roast and stuff it in a bag with the ground beef and cover it up with the ground beef." Hoyer-Booth kept her girl-friends fed that way, and other inspectors did the same. Sometimes the sergeants would ask inspectors to steal for them too. Officers didn't ask for meat, but they, along with the sergeants and the enlisted people, ate the nice stews cooked up in the inspection service office—courtesy of Boston's meat-packers.

Instruction in X-ray vision came naturally after that. Inspectors were supposed to make random samples of the boxes of beef ready to be shipped out, making sure that the right meat was in the right boxes and that the meat wasn't spoiled. But the boxes would be piled high on pallets, and often the proper box to be sampled would end up at the bottom of the stack. At the beginning, Hoyer-Booth would require workers to unstack the boxes, but the workers always grumbled or complained they had bad backs. "And then the other army inspector pulled me aside and said, hey, you know, the bottom is just the same as the top. So that was the end of true sampling." X-ray vision worked just fine. Even if the box was at the top of the stack, the inspectors would not bother to open it. Some days they were still on the job at 6 P.M. after starting at 7 A.M. "That's usually when we had the best X-ray vision." They could check a box even while they were sitting in the lunchroom having a beer.

Late hours could be a problem. Once, Hoyer-Booth rejected some diced beef that didn't meet specifications, and the packer was required to rework the order. "So I stayed there until nine o'clock at night while they were reworking the diced beef, and that was the last time I rejected anything because it wasn't worth staying there until nine at night for a couple of small pieces." But Hoyer-Booth doesn't want to leave the impression that the inspectors were letting unwholesome or spoiled meat get sent to military installations. It didn't meet specifications, but it wasn't unhealthful. In fact, the packing company had a reputation for having the best meat in Boston. She said she would rather steal beef from them than anyone else.

She certainly couldn't complain about the way the packers treated her. "I was given football tickets to a Steelers-Patriots game; and two expense-paid weekends at Cape Cod; four hundred dollars to help me buy my car, which I tried to give back, but they wouldn't take it; my mother got meat." Breakfasts and lunches were cooked at the plant, and sometimes she went out to dinner with the packers. "And for my birthday I was given three suits, two of them tailored." She was on a first-name basis with the assistant general manager and the general manager of the company. "At the time they were my friends more than the vendor. I didn't regard them as a vendor because they were always very friendly to me, always helpful. I have a lot of my own problems, personal problems, and I felt I could talk to them and they would help me with my problems."

But she knew that all that was going on in Boston was wrong. "Yes, I knew it was wrong. It was very surprising at first being taught how to steal a roast and not doing our sampling correctly, but it just was—it didn't seem a big deal. Everyone was doing it and no one really seemed to care about anything." And she wasn't worried about being caught "because no one would care enough to catch me, and if they did, what could they catch me at that they weren't doing themselves?"

The situation was the same throughout New England. The Army inspector assigned to a packer in New Haven, Connecticut, was Kevin Fagan,* a short, square, determined young man of the same age and background as Hoyer-Booth. "When I walked into the unit I had little or no knowledge of the meat-packing industry or how to inspect beef," Fagan says. But he made an effort to learn on his own because he was looking for a career. When he left the military he stayed in the meat industry, working as a quality-control officer for a packer. The problems of military inspection were obvious to Fagan. "They are taking kids that come right out of school, right out of high school like I did, and they bring us to an eight-week course which they give us a week on what I did with meat, and they expect you to run a plant or to even work under a sergeant who in the same case may not know anything either. And they pay you two fifty-seven a day to eat. They gave me sixty-two dollars a month to find an apartment. And I was getting paid something like two hundred and eighty-eight dollars a month."

It was hardly an atmosphere that encouraged the young recruit to do the best job. And once on the job, the desire to do good work was undermined even further. It was standard procedure for the inspectors and even some of the colonels to go out to breakfast with the owner of the plant. Fagan knew it was wrong, and for about four months he resisted, but then he gave in. "Well, when your colonel is eating the same breakfast you are and he is not paying for it, then why can't a private who doesn't make half as much money?" At least Fagan's colonel was creative in taking advantage of the packers. He sent out a directive authorizing inspectors to use the "organoleptic test" to make sure meat was acceptable. That meant inspectors should take a few steaks, cook them, and eat them to make sure they were tender and tasty. "So after we received this in the

---

*Testimony before the Subcommittee on Federal Spending Practices, Efficiency, and Open Government, op. cit.

mail it was normal practice to eat two or three steaks during lunch." Sometimes, in their dedication to protect the stomachs of the military, the inspectors would conduct extensive organoleptic tests for dinner as well.

Still, for a while Fagan tried to do his job right, and when he saw gross abuses he reported them. Once he caught the company switching box tops so that a shipment of beef that had been rejected and sent back was slipped into another order being sent out. The Army inspector in charge of that order admitted to Fagan that, as a personal favor to the plant owner, he was coming into the plant on Saturdays and approving meat that had been rejected and returned to the plant from military installations. Fagan took the information up the chain of command. One superior "didn't want to hear anything about it," Fagan says. Another threatened him. And nothing was ever done about the problem. But the abuses were getting more serious all the time, and eventually the Army brass couldn't ignore them. There was an investigation, but about the only result was that all the inspectors were transferred out of the plant. "When there is an embarrassment, they just move everybody," Fagan says.

Fagan ended up at another beef company in Boston, where he was constantly forced to reject meat. He was doing his job, and he was making the packer provide the military the proper meat. But after about four months, he started getting the message to lay off. First it came from a sergeant, then from a colonel. Fagan and the other inspectors were told they were being "nitpicky." "So that is when I stopped really doing my job right to the letter of the law." From then on Fagan did one thing well for the Army—"played a lot of cards."

Fagan, Hoyer-Booth, and the other inspectors should have been able to look to their superiors for leadership, advice, and support. But that was hardly the case. The inspector in charge was a civilian with a strong knowledge of meat-packing. But not much of it was passed on to his inspectors. Shortly after he started, the inspector was approached by one of the owners of the packing company. "First he came up with that friendly attitude, you know, that we are doing a good job, we are trying to do a good job, and to refrain from hassling. He said, 'Why don't you take a little gift.' And I think it was the first one or two times that I kind of shoved it off. I didn't just jump right at the opportunity at the first onset of the offer." But soon he eased into a routine of taking one hundred dollars a week—later it would be two hundred—"and this was strictly for not hassling the employees." At that time, the packer had a reputation for producing quality meat, so there wasn't much need for hassling the employees anyway. But the owner was setting the stage, and setting it well, for what was to follow.

The inspector began to see more and more low-quality, ungraded beef carcasses in the coolers. The company was obviously slipping inferior meat into the military orders because more high-quality steaks and roasts were being shipped out than could possibly come from the high-quality carcasses on hand. In fact, the amount of bogus meat started to get ridiculous. Finally, he had to complain. "I said, 'The stuff that is coming in here, we should be getting more certified meat. At least you should have a sufficient amount to cover yourself, to cover me. It is getting to the point now that I am just being played as a big dope.' And as I have seen figures in the newspapers, that is exactly what I was, just a big dope."

However, he was not alone. The other inspector in charge was also bought off cheaply and easily by the packers. Sergeant Charles Reidinger* was a twenty-year veteran of the military service when he came to Boston in 1974. He was knowledgeable and well trained, but at this late point in his career, his motives were not exactly pure. For six years he had tried to get himself transferred to Boston so he could retire there. And once he got to Boston, his relationship with the packers was tainted by the fact that he was hoping he could set himself up as a business representative for the packers in some foreign meat deals. Still, the situation he found when he got to Boston would have made it difficult to do a good job, no matter what his motivation. "When I arrived, I couldn't believe what I walked into. What I mean by this, it was total chaos in the unit." His frustration continued to build for three months, and then he went to see his colonel. Reidinger told the colonel, "The

---

*Op. cit.

damned unit was falling apart and somebody better get down there and start looking at it because it's a joke." He gave the colonel a memo stating, "This unit is fast approaching the point of complete mission failure." The memo complained of short staffing and insufficient training. "Conditions are now to the point where new men with no experience in the veterinary service will be assigned and will adopt current procedures or be contaminated by them. Unit morale is at such a low point now that all that is being done is a paper or lip service to inspection requirements."

The scathing memo brought results. The colonel came down for a personal investigation. "He came down for a day and he made the OIC get a haircut," Reidinger recalls. "That was the extent."

At about this time, the Boston packer came to Reidinger with the same request he made to the other inspector in charge—no hassles. For Reidinger, it meant two hundred dollars a month to start, and later four hundred a month. His payoff was only half as large, but he arranged for one bonus the other missed—a one-hundred-dollar hooker at his call about once a month. After so many years, why did a career Army man turn on the military? "I just gave up," Reidinger says. "That's the easiest way. The frustrations just got to the point and I said 'To hell with it.' "

The chain of frustration went one step higher. Captain James Flom* was the officer in charge of the inspection service in Boston. He was an ROTC graduate and a veterinarian, and when he came to Boston in 1974 he was excited about the opportunity. "However, I thought when I was going to Boston that I would be working in fish disease. I expressed a strong interest in marine animal diseases, and I was told that the Boston area worked with a lot of fish and would provide me with the area of my interest." He wasn't prepared for an assignment where his veterinary-medicine background would be practically worthless. "I feel that I am a veterinarian. I do not feel that I am a food inspector, and I made my views very clear very early on this point." Yet there he was, leading the military inspection operation. He was the officer the inspectors ultimately were

---

*Op. cit.

supposed to look to for training and leadership. "But in order to train, you have to understand that area yourself. I myself did not feel when I entered the service that I had the ability to train anyone. I came out of the same school that the privates came out of, so essentially, we were on the same level." Flom was left with no alternative but to rely heavily on his noncommissioned officers like Sergeant Reidinger and his civilian specialist. He says he had no idea they were on the take.

What did the packers get out of this sorry situation? Just about anything they wanted. Edward Kehl,* former quality-control officer for a packer, recalls that he didn't need to concern himself with the quality of his product at all. If there was a problem with the military, "I would lie to them, try to confuse them," which was hardly difficult, since most inspectors didn't know much to begin with. Ironically, Kehl was one of the few people who gave the green inspectors any kind of training. "As a matter of fact, most inspectors, I probably taught them more than the school did so that they wouldn't get in any trouble or cause trouble for us. Of course, I only taught them what we wanted them to know, and just enough so they wouldn't look too stupid if a colonel or someone came to check on us." He had to teach inspectors like Hoyer-Booth something, or their utter ignorance would have ruined the packers' game.

And it was a lucrative game. The packers could take steaks from cheap, low-grade carcasses that were supposed to be used only to produce hamburger, and slip those cuts into the military orders that called for choice steaks. After a while, they didn't care if any of the meat it processed was choice. Kehl estimates that at the peak of the scam, the company was processing eight hundred thousand pounds of this inferior meat a week. Since the company saved roughly ten cents per pound by using the ungraded meat, it was making an easy eighty thousand dollars a week. But there was an even worse abuse. More than half of the meat sent out to the troops as top sirloin steak was actually tough, sinewy beef knuckle. The knuckle was worth roughly $1.45 per pound, but the company had found a way to cut this relatively worthless piece of meat to resemble sirloin steak,

---

*Op. cit.

which it sold to the military for $3.85 per pound—a whopping $2.40 per pound difference. Some days it processed eighty thousand pounds of the stuff—an unbelievable $192,000 bonanza. There were other abuses too, such as price-fixing between packing companies. Two firms would make deals to guarantee each other low bids on various contracts, so each could be sure to get its share of the largesse.

It all made for a total breakdown in the inspection system, and a staggering rip-off on taxpayers. The Chiles revelations sent several packers to jail and ruined the careers of countless officers and enlisted men and women. Unfortunately, the problems in military meat procurement were not limited to Boston. The Boston investigation was the culmination of an inquiry that exposed the military meat-buying practices nationally to be a total disgrace. Chiles had begun the inquiry in 1975 after hearing repeated complaints that the military was not getting what it paid for. In July of 1975, investigators for Chiles' Government Operations Committee stopped two trucks loaded with meat headed for the Norfolk, Virginia, Naval Station. The investigators took samples of the ground beef and diced beef, discovering that the meat was contaminated by a fly, flecks of metal, and cowhide. They also found that the way the meat had been processed violated military specifications. The following week, they made another spot check, this time in Jacksonville, Florida. They found short-weighted meat, off-color meat, and meat with excessive amounts of fat. "The findings indicated a giant rip-off and so we asked for a nationwide audit of the military's beef for our troops," Chiles says. One and one half million pounds of meat at defense supply depots across the country were inspected. Fully two thirds of the meat did not conform to military specifications. Of the $2.4 million spent for that meat, $2 million was spent on products that did not conform to military specifications.

The top military brass were called before Chiles' committee to explain this sorry state of affairs, and their answers were not very good. They presented plans and programs that they said would clean up military inspection, but they convinced no one that they could do the job. Soon the Defense Department was stripped of the responsibility for inspecting meat for the troops. The job was given to the USDA, which had better-trained men and more resources to monitor the system.

But corruption has not disappeared. One persistent problem is that the military bidding procedures can be an incentive to cheat. At the time of the Boston scandal, some packers were submitting bids for contracts at costs below the wholesale value of the meat. The only way they could make any money on the contracts was to substitute inferior-quality meat. William Albanos, the owner of a meat-price-reporting service and a member of the military's advisory committee on meat procurement, says the military must be as concerned about paying too little for its meat as it is about paying too much. "As prices go down," Albanos says, "the cheaters can do it for less, so the other bidders drop out. All you're left with are the cheaters."

Likewise, the USDA has been attacked for not monitoring military meat inspection as closely as it should. Just as with the Boston scandal, there are indications that the USDA men doing military meat inspection have been left to their own devices to a dangerous degree. "You need safeguards that will prevent the present system from deteriorating—and it will deteriorate," says Albanos. "The USDA inspectors are human, just like the military inspectors."

6

Government Responsibility for Meat Scandals

I have good reason to feel this charge is further attempts by the Livestock Division–Meat Grading Branch to DISCRIMINATE, RE-TALIATE, DISCREDIT and HARASS me for uncovering things that has made some officials in the Livestock–Meat Grading Branch look bad and my refusal to SOFT-PEDAL and COVER-UP ROTTEN SITUATIONS.

—John Coplin, memo to Washington

John Coplin is the number one whistleblower in the American meat industry. He's a troublemaker. He's a pain in the ass. He may well be the toughest son of a bitch in the whole industry. For more than thirty years, Coplin has taken on the industry and the USDA bureaucracy. The story of John Coplin is the story of how much one man can do to clean up corruption. Unfortunately, it's also the story of how much one man can be harassed for cleaning up corruption.

Coplin has become a legend in the meat industry. If John Wayne had been a meat grader, he would have been John Coplin. In fact, the tall, beefy, gruff Coplin bears more than a passing resemblance to the Duke. He has the same craggy face and the same now-listen-buster-and-listen-good bluster of Wayne at his best. He's retired now, but there was the same rasp in his voice as he rallied his boys in the grading service to circle the wagons. He commanded the same fierce loyalty and respect. Coplin stood up for his men, and they in turn stood up for him. "He's not above us, we can talk to him. He's like a sergeant in the Army," said one longtime grader, Frank Krzan, who worked with Coplin from the first day he came to scandal-ridden Chicago as the new chief supervisor for the grading service in the Midwest. Coplin cleaned up the meat industry in the Midwest, and then he went after the rest of the country. He demanded just one thing: that packers and graders do things right. As long as you did right by John Coplin, he'd do right by you. "I'm no saint," he was fond of saying, "but I try to do what's right." Too many packers and USDA officials, however, didn't want to play by Coplin's rules. "They're no damned good," he'd say scornfully, and then he'd go after them.There was no use bullshitting Coplin, and scores of packers and bureaucrats found out the hard way that he was unrelenting in his attacks on anyone he considered his enemy.

But there is a dark side as well. In his blind devotion to his crusades, he let nothing stand in his way. Even men who respected him were sometimes wary of him because he made it clear he would turn on his friends if they didn't do what Coplin decided was right. "I'll turn on them when they do something wrong," Coplin would say matter-of-factly. "I don't see anything wrong with that." There are even some who say he could be as unscrupulous as the crooks he was after. He was a volatile, hard-drinking, fearless man, and there was no telling who he'd go after next.

Like many whistleblowers, he saw right and wrong in black and white, so there was no room for compromise. And like most whistleblowers, he found that his efforts were seldom appreciated. There was praise from a small circle of friends, and from muckraking columnists such as Jack Anderson and Clark Mollenhoff, who repeatedly championed his campaigns; there were some glowing newspaper headlines over the years and even a "Ballad of John Coplin." But for the most part, he was a lonely crusader whose reward could come only from knowing that he had blown the whistle. It is a sad fact that people generally don't like informers or tattletales, no matter what great good they are serving. Coplin's bosses in the USDA certainly were not about to applaud his whistleblowing, because they were among his favorite targets.

So Coplin churned out a steady stream of scathing memos to Washington assailing his superiors for failing to clean up their act and clean up the meat industry. "You have permitted the meat graders to be abused by the meat industry for years and the graders are blamed for all corruption even though it is usually faulty USDA Meat Grading Management and USDA Meat Grading Management's reluctance to face up to their responsibility for problems and to clean them up long before the law must step in and fire the *demoralized* graders," goes one vitriolic, if ungrammatical, attack. "In other words, it is always the graders who must assume full responsibility and the USDA Meat Grading Management who permitted the condition to fester and grow—gets off scot-free—making pious excuses. . . . We have no intention of putting up with these retaliations any longer and we expect you to clear the record and correct these most recent abuses without delay."

The memos themselves became legendary, but they seldom brought the desired results. And they surely didn't enhance Coplin's standing in the USDA. When Coplin went to work for the government after World War II, he quickly became the youngest USDA main-station supervisor ever. And when he came to Chicago several years later, he had a bright future. But there he stayed, in a sparsely furnished office on the second floor of a grimy post office building on the South Side of Chicago. On the white office walls were just a couple of meat-grading charts and two crude block-letter signs—"IF YOU SEE SOMEONE WITHOUT A SMILE, GIVE THEM ONE OF YOURS" and, more prophetically, "THERE CAN BE NO PROGRESS WITHOUT CHANGE!!" If Coplin went to the window, he could look across the street to the Chicago International Amphitheatre and, behind it, the Chicago Union Stockyards. At the beginning, the Amphitheatre was attracting the premier national conventions and expositions, and the Stockyards were the center of the American meat-packing industry. Now, the Amphitheatre hosts little more than professional wrestling and roller derby, and the famed Stockyards are nothing more than a partially developed industrial park. Coplin's fortunes have declined as well. In reward for a career dedicated to cleaning up the meat industry, Coplin was forced into retirement in 1980. There was no fanfare, no gold watch, no official recognition of any kind. He had become a bitter man who claimed he was put out to pasture by the USDA—its final means of shutting him up. But packers and USDA bureaucrats alike know they haven't heard the last from John Coplin.

Much of the blame for continuing corruption in the meat industry must be placed on the USDA bureaucracy that regularly turns its back on men like John Coplin. It is a bureaucracy with a life of its own, and all efforts to control it have failed. When the Department of Agriculture was established in 1862, its goals were simple. This nine-employee agency would "procure, propagate, and distribute among the people new and valuable seeds and plants." Who could envision that it would mushroom into today's massive bureaucracy, 128,000 employees strong, that fills five huge buildings in Washington and 16,000 more across the country? The USDA is responsible for a mind-boggling array of tasks, from writing standards for watermelons to building dams to surveying crops to handing out food stamps to paying farmers not to farm to overseeing the many facets of the meat industry. When President Carter took office, he vowed to restrain this runaway bureaucracy and reorganize the USDA. Four years later it was Carter who was cowed, not the bureaucracy. Now it is President Reagan's turn.

The fact is that the USDA is controlled by a core of thirty-five-to-sixty-thousand-dollar-a-year middle-level career bureaucrats and the legion of functionaries beneath them. These men and women serve regardless of whether the President is a Jimmy Carter or a Ronald Reagan or a Pat Paulsen. They are firmly entrenched, and they are most concerned about making it through the day with as few hassles as possible. They certainly don't want to hear about grand schemes of reform from presidents, or grave charges of corruption from complainers like Coplin. In addition, they have long been programmed to identify with the agricultural producers and to promote their businesses. This bias is enhanced by the fact that the USDA draws many of its high-level officials from the industries it regulates. These officials come into the USDA knowing they can go back to their industry, most likely with a jump in pay and prestige, when they get tired of putting in time for the government. When Earl Butz's jokes about loose shoes and warm places to shit were no longer welcome in Washington, he was able to take them back to the boardrooms of Ralston Purina, and countless lower-level officials have done the same. This "revolving door" is continually shuttling men back and forth between the USDA and the packinghouses, from the lowest levels to the highest. A packer can get a friendly laborer a job in the grading or inspection services; the grader can later fall back on a nice job with the packer (sometimes after his favors to the packer have gotten him in trouble with the USDA); supervisory officials throughout the USDA routinely end up as consultants, directors, and lobbyists for trade associations and major companies; and administrators as high as assistant secretary of agriculture find executive posts on the industry payroll after serving the industry well from within the USDA. There are obvious benefits for the USDA in taking advantage of the expertise of people from the meat industry, but there are also obvious conflicts. Unfortunately, the conflicts are usually ignored, and the USDA is overcome by an atmosphere in which everyone is looking out for his friends. It becomes second nature to assume that what is good for the industry is good for the USDA. In this kind of atmosphere, there is little place for men like John Coplin.

John Coplin was a big, burly boy growing up in West Virginia in the 1930's. He was captain of the Buckhannon High School football team, and enough of a scholar-athlete to be offered a football scholarship to West Virginia University. But this was in the midst of the Depression, after all, so Coplin was forced to go to work instead. He followed his two brothers to Chicago, and he got a job with them at Swift and Co. During the next nine years he learned just about everything there was to know about the meat-packing business through his work and through vocational courses offered by Swift. Then World War II came along, and Coplin quit to enlist in the Navy. He served on the aircraft carrier USS *Cabot* in the South Pacific, earning during his tour of duty the Philippine Liberation Bar, the Presidential Citation, and the Purple Heart for injuries sustained during two kamikaze attacks on the carrier. After the war, he returned to Swift in Chicago, but he didn't stay long. He had gotten to know several men in the grading service, and they convinced him to apply for a job. On April 1, 1946, Coplin was hired to be a federal meat grader, assigned to work in Detroit. It would be a few years before he began to realize the April Fool's joke was on him.

Coplin was a bright young ambitious grader, and he was moving up. In 1950 he was named assistant supervisor in St. Paul, Minnesota, and less than a year later he was appointed main-station supervisor—director of all grading operations—in Des Moines. He was the youngest main-station supervisor in the history of the USDA. "Hell, I was moving up the ladder, I was moving ahead," Coplin recalls. "Then I ran into Baltimore." In 1955, Coplin was transferred to the East Coast, where he was main-station supervisor for an area including Philadelphia, Baltimore, and Washington, D.C. Shortly after he arrived, he had reason to remember the stories he had heard back in Iowa. The Iowa packers used to tell him that if Coplin's graders didn't mark their carcasses choice, they could just ship the carcasses to the East Coast, where they would get more favorable treatment. "Well, this is a lot of talk, I always thought, they're trying to tell you things to influence you, but I recalled it," Coplin says. "So when I got to Philadelphia, and I went over to Baltimore, well, I sure found out in a hurry this was true. The cattle that would not grade choice in Iowa, in the Midwest, were being graded choice in Baltimore and Philadelphia. I have records of millions and millions of pounds." Coplin immediately reported the situation to Washington, "And when I reported it, all of a sudden it stopped."

It was only the beginning of Coplin's new insights into the USDA. Shortly after uncovering the misgrading, Coplin made a supervisory inspection of packing plants in Baltimore and Washington with his assistant supervisor. They had finished with the Baltimore plants and were about ready to head for Washington when Coplin's assistant said he had to make a quick stop at one more Baltimore plant; he had to pick up a package. The assistant walked out of the packinghouse with a large bundle of meat. He made a point of showing Coplin the bill, so Coplin would know he paid for the meat. But the bill was hardly reassuring to Coplin. "It had a listing of sausages and hams and assorted meats on there, and a ridiculously low price, like five cents a pound and ten cents a pound. So I didn't say anything. I was amazed, but I kept quiet.

"We get down to Washington, and instead of going to the packinghouses, we go over to the South Agricultural Building. He said he had to drop this off to so and so, an assistant chief. And frankly, I was a little embarrassed, so I made myself a little bit scarce." Coplin walked away from the car as his assistant went inside to make a call up to the meat-grading office. Soon, one of the assistant chiefs of the grading service came down to the parking lot and unlocked his car. Coplin's assistant put the package of meat inside. Coplin was shocked, but he didn't say anything that day. He and his assistant completed their rounds and returned to Philadelphia.

Two weeks later, Coplin and his assistant made a similar inspection trip. The same procedure was repeated. This time, a national technical supervisor came down from the meat-grading office to claim the package. On the trip back to Philadelphia, Coplin had a talk with his assistant. "Now, Charlie, what you're doing is wrong," Coplin remembers saying. "What you do that I don't see is your business, but what you're doing is wrong, and I'm telling you to cut it out. And I will have to report this." The conversation took place on a Friday, so the following Monday Coplin made his call to Washington. He discussed some routine matters, and then he reported the actions of his assistant. "And it's so obvious to me that I'm getting the cold shoulder now. Just like that. And almost immediately after this I get all sorts of offers for transfers to other parts of the country. They offered me the main-station job in Denver. They offered me the main-station job in New York City. And I turned them all down because my daughter had been in several schools and I thought, it's not a promotion."

Coplin had moved around a lot so far in his USDA career, and now he wanted to settle down for a while. But it was not to be. Soon he was informed that one way or another he would have to move anyway: his main-station headquarters was being moved from Philadelphia to Baltimore. "It was obvious to me why," Coplin says. "They wanted me out of there." If Coplin could be forced to take another job, his assistant could resume hauling meat to Washington. Coplin was given another option to transfer, this time to Chicago, and he decided to accept it. He had friends and family there, so it was more attractive to him than the other transfers he had been offered. In addition, the main-station supervisor job in Chicago was then known as the steppingstone for advancement within the meat-grading service—most of the top national grading officials had first served in Chicago. Coplin was told informally that he too could expect to move up if he did a good job.

One footnote: When Coplin moved to Chicago, his old assistant was named to replace him, and the main-station headquarters was moved back to Philadelphia from Baltimore. Coplin's old assistant lived in Baltimore, yet he was never forced to move to Philadelphia.*

Considering that many of the top grading-service officials in Washington had first served in Chicago, Coplin expected to find a first-class operation when he moved his family to Chicago in May 1958. What he found was something else: "It was as rotten as it could be." Coplin could not believe the corruption he found, and he immediately reported the problems to Washington. The response, however, was "Slow down, we'll clean up our own mess," Coplin says. "But I got to thinking, after seeing meat hauled down to Washington, that I'd better not, because I figured down the road about six months from now if I soft-pedaled it, they could say, 'Well, Chicago was in good shape when you came to it, but this is all your doing.' So full speed ahead, I went to work on it." He called in the FBI, the USDA Packers and Stockyards Administration, and the USDA's personnel office in Chicago. "I felt these moves were necessary due to the sheer magnitude of the station's illegal practices, and because I was otherwise dependent on three inherited assistant

---

*Coplin's testimony before the Subcommitte on Federal Spending Practices, Efficienty and Open Government, op. cit.

supervisors [who] I was convinced were involved with illegal practices, whom I reported as such."

His doubts about his assistants were confirmed when one of them refused to cooperate with the FBI. "He returned to the office one day, cleaned out his desk, went on sick leave, and I never saw him again; the other two were soon transferred." What Coplin and his investigators found was staggering. Meat for commercial and military use was routinely misgraded; substandard meat was being certified for use in city, county, state, and federal schools, hospitals and other institutions; and unethical relationships among packers, graders, and supervisors were rampant. One packer was audited and it was discovered he had sold literally millions of pounds of choice and prime meat he never had. Instead, he had taken inferior meat shipped in from the West and bribed graders to come in after hours to mark it choice or prime; this was the "night-grading" scam first reported by lone grader Ted Marugg a few years earlier. "There were unbelievable abuses," Coplin says. "Graders getting payoffs, gratis meat. Most of them just resigned rather than face charges." During Coplin's first three years in Chicago, nearly 70 per cent of the employees of the Chicago main station either resigned or were fired.

"And surprisingly, the packers were coming to me and saying things were so rotten they sympathized with me. Some of them said it's so bad it had to come. And I still have people who tell me that today. It was just a pretty tough row to hoe." Coplin most certainly paid a price for cleaning up Chicago. "I had my auto windshield busted, had my car windows smashed, tires slashed, and on one occasion someone ran broadside into my car while it was parked near one of the packinghouses." And there were threatening phone calls. The message might be "The next time we work over your car, you'll be in it." Or the voice might warn that it would be easy for a rail of carcass beef to accidentally fall on him. Or it might ask what he'd do if the lights went out in a meat cooler. "The dark-cooler situation did happen to me on one occasion," Coplin says. "Let me tell you, it gets dark in the cooler when the lights go out. I had a hell of a time getting out of it." The threats and abuse became so heavy

that Coplin felt compelled to move his family back to Philadelphia for its own safety. He stayed in Chicago to fight on,
however, visiting his wife and daughter on weekends whenever
he could.

The ordeal put a terrific strain on Coplin's personal and
professional life, but through it all the support from his superiors
in Washington was virtually nonexistent. They would send him
new assistants—although not enough of them—but once Coplin
trained the new men, they would be transferred elsewhere;
Coplin had to start training all over again. In addition, his
superiors sent out national technical supervisors and investigators who continually "nitpicked" about Coplin's operations.
He remembers one instance in 1960 when two USDA investigators confronted him with charges he had cheated on his travel
voucher (this was to become a favorite means of attacking him).
Their investigation had consisted of checking the odometer
reading on Coplin's car against what was written on his voucher,
and from that they determined that Coplin had falsified his
voucher. Unfortunately, the investigators had simply misread
the odometer. "The two investigators were so embarrassed that
they apologized and told me that my superiors in Washington
had requested that they check my voucher versus speedometer
reading. Now get this: This incident took place at the end of the
period that I had been working with these same two investigators separating Chicago graders for cause. Incidentally, some
of these graders were friends of some of my superiors in
Washington."

It was now clear that Washington was not on his side, and
it could have been a time for Coplin to back off and give up
fighting his own bureaucracy. But that's not John Coplin's style.
Coplin kept up his fight, and for the next two decades he
continued to strike back at corruption and incompetence. In the
early 1960's he thought back to his first days in Philadelphia,
when he discovered the flagrant misgrading of meat sent in from
the Midwest. As main-station supervisor in Chicago, he was
now in charge of the national record-control office for the
grading service, so he could check up on what kind of meat was
going into and coming out of every packing plant in the country,

including the Baltimore plant where he had found the mis-grading some ten years earlier. "Out of curiosity, I started to look through some of the records. I was amazed to find that from August of 1958 to July of 1963, a period of five years, approximately fifteen and a half million pounds of beef was graded choice at this company that only qualified for good in midwest plants where the meat was slaughtered. It was late June or July of 1963 when I reported this situation to the Office of Inspector General, USDA. Curiously enough, immediately following my reporting this, only fifteen thousand pounds of beef was graded choice at this Baltimore plant in August of 1963, and no beef was graded as such in September of 1963.

"It is my professional opinion that the main-station super-visor in Philadelphia and the national supervisors and my other Washington superiors had to know this was going on, as they regularly visited Baltimore on inspection tours and also visited the originating packinghouses in the Midwest." But when Coplin pressed Washington to investigate further, all he got was a "cover-up." "It was amazing to me no one in the USDA thought it would be beneficial to check these meat-grading certificates after what I reported, but to my knowledge, they did not." At about this same time, Coplin also was hearing alle-gations that his old assistant, now the main-station supervisor in Philadelphia, was soliciting large quantities of meat from packers at nominal prices for meat-grading service weekend parties. But again, nobody else in the grading service wanted to hear about it. Instead, Coplin was the man taking the heat. His superiors kept downgrading his performance ratings and charg-ing him with malfeasance and nonfeasance in office. Coplin would confront his superiors about the charges, and they would withdraw them. Then they'd recharge Coplin and go through the process once again. It got so bad that Coplin finally de-manded an investigation of his performance by the USDA's Livestock Division to clear the air.

All the harassment from his superiors and from the Chi-cago packers continued to escalate until the end of 1963. Then, one day in December, Coplin and an assistant got into an argu-ment with a Chicago packer who was continually giving them problems. After the dispute was settled, Coplin and his assistant went out to dinner before going home for the night. "We got in my car to go back, and I can still see it, this truck that looked like a meat truck sideswiped us, and it was total impact." Coplin's car was forced head-on into a railroad support abutment. "I received cuts requiring forty-two stitches in the right side of my head, above the hairline. A concussion, twelve stitches lower left side—both external and internal. Four broken ribs and one fractured rib—left side. Broken first index finger, left hand. Twisted and bruised right knee and multiple lacertations, and I was unconscious for eight hours—my head had gone through the windshield.

"My assistant supervisor received a broken left leg, lacerations of the left hand and top of hand, and retired never returning to work. My auto was completely demolished. Totaled. The truck was never apprehended. The crash became a hit-and-run accident."

It took six months for Coplin to recuperate from his injuries. During that time the USDA's Chicago personnel office tried to get him transferred for his own safety. "However, my Washington officials' only offer was to reduce me in grade and transfer me back to Philadelphia as the assistant supervisor to my former assistant. With such an offer I decided to remain in Chicago." If it was any consolation, Coplin at least got some recognition for the job he was doing in Chicago. In October of 1964 the Civil Service Commission made a special survey of Coplin's management, and reported that the Chicago meat-grading office was being run efficiently and effectively. Then, the next year, he finally received the results of the USDA investigation he had demanded at the height of the harassment in 1963. The results confirmed that Coplin's superiors had been overly critical of his performance. The investigators concluded that corrective action was necessary to ensure proper recognition of Coplin's performance, and to ensure that he was not denied consideration for promotions in light of his hassles.

But unfortunately, the investigation brought little change. Coplin still had to put up with petty assaults. In 1966 he was called to Washington for what he thought was a routine meeting. Instead, he faced a star-chamber interrogation. For two days his

Washington superiors grilled him and tried to force him to sign a statement that amounted to a confession. Coplin refused, and nothing ever came of the interrogation, but Coplin is sure he knows what the intent was. "In my opinion this was an all-out effort to entrap me into losing my temper and getting me angry."

The small-minded behavior continued that year when Coplin decided it was finally safe to move his family back to Chicago. "I realized long ago my authorization for the movement of my household goods had expired, but I presumed with the unusual circumstances that an exception would or could be made. To my amazement, I was told absolutely nothing could be done." The grading service would provide no money to allow Coplin to bring his family home to Chicago. The only offer from his superiors was once again to allow him to take a demotion and go back to Philadelphia as assistant supervisor to his former assistant. Coplin paid his family's moving bill to Chicago. Later he was vindicated when his congressman, John Erlenborn of Illinois, got a private bill passed reimbursing him.

By this time, something else was clear to Coplin: Chicago was no longer the steppingstone to success in the USDA. He could still remember being assured when he came to Chicago that he could expect a promotion to the national grading staff if he did a good job. "However, after I weeded out the corruption which blighted the Chicago office, no promotion or even recognition was forthcoming. I surmise that part of the reason stems from the fact that many of the national officials of the Livestock Division, including some current officials, served in the Chicago office prior to me. Perhaps they were embarrassed by the fact that I and not one of them brought the problems of the Chicago office to light; or perhaps they were punishing me for bringing attention to the problems and not covering them up."

For whatever reason, Los Angeles was now the place for grading supervisors to be if they wanted to obtain promotions. Los Angeles picked up another old Chicago tradition as well: corruption. While Los Angeles grading supervisors were receiving awards and promotions during the 1960's and early '70's, the grading service there was deteriorating. The scandals didn't break until 1974, but the problems had been common knowledge in the industry for years. And Coplin was complaining about them.

As far back as January 1966, Coplin wrote a memo to the director of the USDA Livestock Division detailing the abuses going on in Los Angeles. He coined the phrase "California choice," which was picked up and used throughout the industry. It was a derisive term referring to the inferior-quality meat that the grading service allowed to be improperly marked choice in California. He also complained about "GRO" grading—Going Right Out. In Los Angeles, graders sometimes did their job right on the loading docks, so the meat could be quickly loaded onto trucks. It was a procedure that left the grader open for abuse from all sides—from the packinghouse workers who had to haul carcasses back and forth from the cooler if the grader judged they were not choice, to the truck driver anxious to get his rig on the road, to the plant foreman in a hurry to get the next truck up to the dock. "It is understandable that some men cannot take this pressure and therefore give in to accepting bribes, permitting the packer to get the grade on the meat that the packer wants, rather than what the USDA specifications call for," Coplin wrote in one memo. Coplin repeatedly brought these problems to the attention of his superiors, and he repeatedly complained about the failure of the Los Angeles supervisors to recognize what was going on right under their noses. In disgust, he once wrote the director of the Livestock Division, "Even a blind pig finds an acorn now and then," yet the Los Angeles supervisors could not find the corruption that was obvious to everyone else in the industry. These officials continued to be rewarded with promotions and awards until 1974. That was when a federal investigation, mounted with the assistance of such people as Coplin and consumer Frank Hogya, finally exposed the grading scandal that had grown to the point where it rivaled even the corruption Coplin found when he first came to Chicago.

It was not only on the West Coast that Coplin was finding corruption. If there was a problem anywhere in the country, Coplin knew about it. He knew the packing industry cold, and he knew all the things that could go wrong in it. Most of all, Coplin knew people. He had a network of friends and informants in the grading service and the packing industry that made his USDA office something of a private corruption-control center. He had an inner circle of close contacts who were on the phone to each other almost constantly. And there was an outer ring of disgruntled graders and supervisors from the East Coast to the West Coast—packers from Denver to Florida to Philadelphia to New York to Boston to Texas and more who all knew they could trust Coplin to get to the bottom of things. "For some reason, a lot of people call me," Coplin says. "But I know a lot of people too. I've been in this business a long time. There's not many places I can't call and say, 'Hey, what the hell is going on over there?' And certain people will come right out and tell me. It's not that hard."

Maybe it wasn't that hard to find problems. But doing something about them was hard—hard on Coplin. In 1975, his network of informants told him about gross abuses in the military meat-procurement system up and down the East Coast. That July, Coplin agreed to cooperate with Senator Lawton Chiles' subcommittee investigation into this military meat rip-off. But the decision hardly pleased Coplin's superiors in the USDA. "Just before I left to testify before the Senate subcommittee, Director Pierce called me at home. He asked me what this subcommittee business was all about. I explained the situation to him briefly, and he questioned whether I should be testifying against a sister agency, I guess he meant the military. I told him I had no intentions of testifying to anything other than the abuses I had seen with my own eyes. I told him I felt there were others in positions such as his and mine that know and that have seen what I have seen, and that I felt they should be coming forth also." John Pierce, director of the Livestock Division, reluctantly allowed Coplin to testify, Coplin says. But he directed Coplin to go to the office of David Hallett, chief of the meat-grading branch, as soon as he arrived in Washington.

David Hallett was a short, pudgy man with a bit of a twang to his thin voice who came up in the grading service through Chicago and was now comfortably entrenched in Washington. He was the man Coplin funneled most of his nasty memos through, and he was the target of many of them. To Coplin and others, he was a prime example of the USDA's producer-oriented tradition that called for simply tuning out charges against the meat industry. On the morning Coplin came to Washington, Coplin and Hallett talked casually about nothing in particular. Then Hallett mentioned he would be accompanying Coplin to the Chiles hearing. "I told him it was wonderful that he was going to testify also," Coplin says. "He replied that, no, Mr. Pierce wanted him to sit in on my testimony. I told him I didn't think it was necessary; not only was it not necessary, it was demeaning." Hurried conferences followed between Coplin, Hallett, Pierce, and three other high-ranking USDA officials. Coplin told them all it appeared they were ordering Hallett to accompany him because they didn't trust him. "I expressed my belief that trust breeds trust, and from my past experiences I did not trust them." But Coplin was finally ordered to take Hallett with him. Once they arrived at the Senate hearing room, however, Chiles' staff was not happy to see Hallett tagging along. There were more hurried conferences, and finally Hallett talked to Senator Chiles on the phone. "After Mr. Hallett hung up, he turned to me and said that I was now testifying on my own as a private citizen, and left," Coplin recalls.

Coplin provided the committee with valuable information for its probe, and committee staff members praised him for his help. However, praise was hardly his reward from the USDA. Instead, shortly after he returned to Chicago, he received a letter by certified mail from USDA headquarters in Washington demanding that he show cause why he should not be suspended for five days for "neglect of duty and failure to follow instructions." The charges stemmed from a rather inconsequential incident some eight months earlier that Coplin assumed had been resolved. At the beginning of 1975, when the nation was still feeling the effects of the first "gas crisis," Coplin sought a clarification from Washington on how much reimbursement for mileage graders could claim on their expense vouchers. There was some question whether graders were allowed nine cents per mile or twelve cents when they used their own cars instead of government cars. Coplin talked to Hallett about the issue, and he thought Hallett gave the okay for Coplin and the graders to claim twelve cents per mile. But once they submitted their expense vouchers, Hallett changed his mind. Coplin contends

Hallett reversed himself for another petty reason: he was upset with testimony Coplin gave in a Milwaukee court case that went against the position Hallett had taken. In any event, when Hallett ruled it was improper for Coplin and his graders to claim twelve cents per mile, they all repaid the excess in March. And they all assumed the matter was closed.

It was a curious coincidence that charges were finally filed some five months after the money had been repaid, but only a matter of weeks after Coplin had testified before Congress. And Coplin doesn't think it was a coincidence at all. "The charge; NEGLECT OF DUTY—FAILURE TO FOLLOW INSTRUCTIONS, is simply unbelievable," reads one Coplin memo to Washington. "I have been aware for a long, long time that my opportunities in the Livestock Division are nil, and this charge is utterly ridiculous and untrue. The Livestock Division and Meat Grading Branch has repeatedly DISCRIMINATED against me and apparently is now using this charge to RETALIATE and DISCREDIT and HARASS me in an attempt to make me look bad for what happened regarding my recent appearance before a United States Senate Subcommittee. . . ."

The memo was but one of many in the record of a long, complicated, and contradictory personnel grievance case that dragged on for months. Finally, Coplin lost. He was suspended without pay, but the case did not end there. Senator Chiles was particularly concerned about the possibility that a government employee was being punished for coming forward to help another branch of government. He had his staff investigate Coplin's charges, and he interrupted his hearings on military meat procurement practices to bring Coplin and his superiors before his subcommittee. After grilling Coplin's bosses, Chiles was unable to find clear evidence of harassment, but he was not at all happy about the way Coplin had been treated. "I just wish that Mr. Coplin had been given the same kind of benefit of the doubt that I guess we have to give the department now," Chiles concluded.

Coplin still didn't give up his fight. He filed suit against Hallett, Pierce, and Larry Thackson,* director of the USDA

---

*John E. Coplin v. David K. Hallett *et al.,* U.S. District Court, Chicago, 1977.

personnel division, charging them with taking part in a conspiracy to deny Coplin promotions and departmental recognition, and with filing false charges against him in the suspension
case. Again, clear evidence admissible in court was hard to
come by, and the case was dismissed.

Vindication came in 1977, when a new administration took
over in Washington. The presidency of Jimmy Carter brought
new faces to government, particularly to the USDA. These were
people not bound by the traditional attitudes of the USDA. In
fact, these were people who had been complaining about the
USDA's biases. Chief among them was Carol Tucker Foreman,
the assistant secretary of agriculture who was responsible for
grading and inspection services. She had been a vocal critic of
the department, and she was willing to listen to those who
wanted to reform it. She reviewed Coplin's case, overturned his
suspension, and reinstated his pay. She told Coplin she was
going to do something about his long-standing charges of
abuses. She even had him come to Washington to discuss what
should be done to improve the USDA. For once, Coplin had
found an official who was interested in reform, and he looked
forward to making the most of the situation.

For starters, Coplin got Foreman's blessing to assist Dan
Rather's *60 Minutes* team in its investigation into meat grading
in San Diego. Accompanied by *60 Minutes* cameras, Coplin and
Rather made a surprise raid on several San Diego supermarkets,
finding a significant amount of misgraded meat at one of them.
The raid outraged both the meat industry and the rest of the
USDA bureaucracy because Foreman had not informed anyone
else in the USDA about the raid beforehand. She feared that
some middle-level bureaucrats could not be trusted to keep the
raid a secret, so now these and other, lower-level officials were
fuming about how Foreman and Coplin had made them look
bad. But Foreman made it clear she was going to continue
making dishonest USDA officials look bad, and that Coplin was
going to be an integral part of her campaign to clean up the meat
industry. Over the next three years Coplin helped uncover
scandals in Texas, New York, Nebraska, Minnesota, and Chicago. Whenever he went to Washington, he didn't bother
talking to his immediate superiors; he went directly to Foreman

and her closest aides. Unfortunately, it was not to last. "I was just tremendously enthused that, by God, we're going to get to the bottom of things," Coplin recalls. "She had me down and I talked to her, and then I appeared on *60 Minutes* and all that, but it just seemed like we could never get things really out in the open, you know?"

The first indication that the time wasn't right even yet for reform came a little more than a year into the new administration. That was when the meat industry made it clear that it would not give in to this new USDA leadership without a fight. One of the new faces Coplin had been counting on was Dr. Robert Angelotti, whom Foreman had brought in to serve as her top assistant. Angelotti, a tall, dapper man with wavy dark hair and a trim mustache, was known as a savvy bureaucrat who had established a solid record of achievement in twenty-three years with the Food and Drug Administration. When the two men first met, Angelotti assured Coplin that he too was committed to cleaning up the meat industry. He told Coplin the meat industry hadn't been regulated in forty years, but he was determined to change that. There was even a special place for Coplin in his plans. Coplin would be what they called informally a "red rover," an investigator whose responsibility was to travel the country, dropping in for unannounced inspections at packinghouses to keep everyone honest.

Coplin was particularly enthusiastic about Angelotti. Here was a man who had no qualms about sticking it to the meat industry. In fact, Angelotti was a more elegant, more sophisticated Coplin. He could be smooth, subtle, and engaging, but he could also be arrogant and abrasive. It was the blunt side of Angelotti that the meat industry most often encountered, and he quickly gained a reputation as the "new bully on the block." Meat-industry groups indignantly denied his many charges of abuses and routinely demanded his resignation. Within the USDA, some employees found him abrasive and "histrionic," and others, loyal to the meat industry, tried to transfer out of his jurisdiction. Then, in August of 1978, Angelotti abruptly resigned. He resigned after being reprimanded for accepting fourteen dollars in industry financed meals, and "inadvertently" filing vouchers for thirty-one dollars in expenses he did not actually incur. These were trivial offenses in a department still reeling from charges that graders were taking four-hundred-dollar bribes, but the meat industry jumped on them and exploited them, creating an atmosphere in which it was impossible for Angelotti to continue.*

Coplin and others charge he was set up for the fall by disgruntled USDA employees working with people in the meat industry. In fact, it was well known that some of his own employees went to the House Agriculture Committee with documents and other information intended to discredit him. Coplin believes Angelotti was doomed because the bureaucrats directly beneath him never wanted to implement his reforms. "They didn't help him," Coplin says, "they weren't on his team." Angelotti's reforms were a threat to their friends in the meat industry and to the way they had done their jobs, so instead they left Angelotti to fend for himself until he was finally forced out. These were bureaucrats who were able to ride out the rough months under Angelotti and then go back to business as usual. For Coplin, the resignation was a severe blow because he lost one of his strongest allies as well as his proposed new investigatory job. He would be forced to continue his barrage of nasty memos charging "retaliation" and "harassment" until the end of his career.

As time went by, Coplin became even more disillusioned. Slowly his relationship with Foreman deteriorated, and he could not as easily get through to her to report the latest scandals he had uncovered. By the end of the Carter administration, he was thoroughly disgusted with her. "I think she got cold feet," he says. "She had good intentions and all, but I think she lost her guts."† Foreman undeniably found that once she was on the inside, reform was not as easy as it had seemed from the outside. Just like any other administrator, she learned that sometimes she had to compromise, and sometimes she had to lower her sights. At her level of responsibility, guts aren't

---

*"A 'Brilliant Bureaucrat' Falls From Grace," by Bailey Morris, *Washington Star*, Aug. 10, 1978, p. 1. See also "Industry Is Silent on Angelotti Resignation," by Jim Ostroff, *Supermarket News*, Aug. 14, 1978, p. 24.

†Author interview with Coplin, Oct. 13, 1980.

always as important as finesse. But her efforts weren't good enough for Coplin. As far as he was concerned, she had a duty to push through every reform and chase every crook, no matter what the consequences. "If she wasn't going to do what her convictions warranted when she took the job, she'd just have to lose her job," he says.*

Foreman was not the only official who fell short of Coplin's expectations. He was even more disappointed by the USDA's inspector general. The Office of Inspector General is the USDA unit responsible for investigating corruption, and the man brought in to head it during the Carter administration was a tough prosecutor who had worked on Watergate, Thomas McBride. He, like Foreman and Angelotti, told Coplin that he was dedicated to cleaning up the USDA, and that he wanted Coplin's help. Coplin gave everything he could, informing McBride of each new scandal, teaching McBride's men all about meat grading so they would know what to look for in their investigations, even snooping around on his own time to gather key information for McBride's men. He talked enthusiastically at the beginning about how much McBride and his men would be able to accomplish. But Coplin soon sensed something was wrong. He had expected McBride to assemble a group of top-notch investigators, but what he got instead, according to Coplin, was "screw-ups." "They hired a lot of people with high IQ's who are stupid, and a lot of schoolteachers, you know, gentle-type people. I'm no saint, and I know to be a good investigator you have to have a little bit of larceny in you." Instead, these men were more in tune with the bureaucratic mind-set that considers anyone who challenges the bureaucracy to be more sinister than the criminals. Their attitude toward Coplin was summed up nicely by one agent who remarked when Coplin's name was mentioned, "Oh, is he still working for *60 Minutes?*"

Coplin soon found that he had to lead these agents around by the hand if there was going to be any chance of their finding corruption, and yet again Coplin was slapped in the face for his efforts. At the same time he was helping some agents mount

---

*Op. cit.

several investigations, other agents were going after him. They grilled Coplin and his graders on small procedural and accounting matters, and they forced him to spend many of his last days in the USDA defending himself against the same office he was trying to help. In May of 1980, Coplin laid out all of his frustrations to McBride. "I hope you have a thick skin, because what I am going to say and what I am enclosing is not a pretty picture for your agency or the USDA," Coplin wrote in a cover letter to McBride. Included was a twenty-nine-page statement and several other documents detailing the incompetence of the Office of Inspector General and the persecution of John Coplin. In his statement, Coplin spelled out numerous instances where, without his help, investigations would have foundered. "I have laid my career and the well-being of my family on the line. I have received threatening phone calls and the destruction of my property. I have also performed unorthodox actions [for the Inspector General's Office] in order to again and again eyewitness abuses in the meat industry such as (1) the excessive over pumping of cured meats, (2) abuses of the Truth and Labeling Act, (3) the flagrant use of the USDA ingredient label, (4) use of spoiled meats in the manufacturing of frankfurters, bologna, etc. (in some cases, this is made possible, simply because a meat inspector cannot be in 2, 3, or 4 places at one time and when he does come upon a violation, his bureaucratic bosses in Washington will not support him, and in time he becomes disgruntled, disgusted and lax), (5) the transporting and slaughter of sick, crippled, and diseased livestock, some so bad that they have to be given 'shots' to even get them up on their feet, or even hold up their head. It would make you sick to your stomach, and you have to see it to believe it and I have seen it!" At the same time, Coplin charged his bosses were using the Office of Inspector General to harass him. In fact, McBride's office had become "a tool to be used by USDA Washington bureaucrats to render ineffective any USDA employee, such as me, who becomes a political liability. . . ." Coplin, who had once praised the concept of the inspector general, now had grave doubts about whether any such unit within the USDA could rise above the bureaucratic infighting to do an impartial and dispassionate investigatory job. It certainly had failed in Coplin's experiences.

If 1977 had been a year of hope for Coplin, that hope was completely gone by 1980. The officials who had vowed to join with Coplin in cleaning up the meat industry were now either departed or, in Coplin's mind, no longer dedicated to the cause. The promised job that would have allowed him to travel the country searching out corruption never materialized; Coplin says it fell through because Foreman and McBride decided after Angelotti was forced out that Coplin would be too controversial for the part. But most disheartening of all was the treatment he was subjected to after one of his most successful investigations.

In 1978, Coplin helped organize a massive raid by graders and inspector-general agents on the second-largest supermarket chain in Chicago. Coplin's informants had told him the chain was mislabeling meat, and the raid confirmed the information: the raiders found meat they contended was upgraded at sixty-two of the sixty-nine stores in the Chicago area. The chain pleaded guilty to intentionally mislabeling meat and was fined two hundred thousand dollars. It had been a stunning investigation, and for his efforts Coplin was awarded a letter of commendation by the U.S. attorney whose office prosecuted the case. "The severity of these charges and the substantial amount of the penalty imposed were directly due to the excellent support and complete cooperation you extended to this office during the many months of the investigation, including your personal assistance in locating and interviewing potential witnesses," reads the letter from Thomas P. Sullivan, U.S. attorney for the Northern District of Illinois. "It is a comfort to this community that federal meat grading standards are being diligently enforced by your agency. The Office of the United States Attorney extends its commendation and sincerest gratitude."

Coplin's reward from the USDA was somewhat different. It seems his superiors considered him a glory-grabber for his role in the raid. And they didn't like the adverse publicity the raid gave the meat industry either. So they honored Coplin by sending inspector-general agents back to Chicago to investigate charges that Coplin was cheating on his expense vouchers, abusing his telephone privileges, and exceeding his authority in his dealings with various packers. Coplin's reward from his superiors was to be a lowered performance rating. Incredibly, they even found a way to discredit Coplin for his role in the raid. During the raid, the function of Coplin and his graders had been to judge which of the retail cuts they saw at the meat counters were misgraded. But USDA regulations prohibit the grading of individual cuts of meat, and now Coplin's superiors were going to punish him for directing his men to break the rule. It's highly ironic that the USDA regularly tells consumers how to use its grade factors to judge individual cuts of meat, while its own graders are prohibited from doing so. And to make an issue of what is at best a technical violation of the rule committed under the unusual circumstances of an investigatory raid borders on the ridiculous.

"I am so weary of defending myself concerning a wide range of manufactured charges made by my agency against me," Coplin wrote in one of his last memos to Washington. This one was to the grievance examiner assigned to hear the attempt to lower his performance rating. Responding to the charge that he had violated USDA regulations in the supermarket probe, Coplin wrote, "This charge is ludicrous and simply not true. All we did was act as experts for the court, and our opinions were a personal evaluation based on years of experience and not the USDA's opinion." He said the graders recognized that grading individual cuts was not the same as grading carcasses, so they didn't make any borderline decisions. But the violations were so gross that there could be no doubt about the mislabeling. "You see, it was like deciding whether the cow was black or white," Coplin wrote. "What would these USDA Washington Officials like us to do, give the $200,000 fine back . . . and take away the Class Action Settlement? Just whose side are they really on, the consumers or the crooks?"

As all this was going on, Coplin had to fight another form of harassment: his own health turned on him. Coplin had developed arthritis in his spine and shoulder as a result of the 1963 accident in which his car was forced into a railroad abutment.

Exposure to cold aggravated the condition, so for a while in 1979 his doctor said he should stay out of meat coolers. Finally he was forced to go on sick leave and then, early in 1980, to give up his position as main-station supervisor in Chicago. His superiors, including Foreman, wanted him to move to Washington to fill a newly created position as a special assistant to the director of the meat-quality division. Foreman said Coplin would be able to help her accomplish many of the reforms he had been suggesting for years. He would be responsible for reviewing meat-grading procedures, instructions, and regulations. But to Coplin, the job was nothing more than a "dead-end post." He complained the transfer to Washington this late in his career was a ploy routinely used by the USDA to inconvenience longtime whistleblowers and force them into retirement.

He would have loved to go to Washington under the right circumstances, such as a promotion to head the meat quality division. He likes to think of what he could accomplish if given the chance. "First, I would go out and make sure people know how to supervise," he says. "The weakest part of grading has been supervision." For years Coplin had contended that if the USDA supervisors in Washington and across the country did their jobs right, most of the corruption in the industry would dry up immediately. But the supervisors were not doing their jobs right. These bureaucrats were either part of the "buddy-buddy system" that was only concerned about covering each other's asses, or they were people whose only ambition in life was to retire. "Anyone who looks that far ahead is no damned good," Coplin says. A snaggletoothed grin crosses Coplin's face as he thinks of what he could do if he were given the power to make all of them justify their jobs. "You know, I'd have so much damned fun," he says with a conspiratorial smile.

But Coplin was never given the chance. The Washington post he was offered was a lateral transfer, not a promotion, and Coplin wasn't buying it. In September of 1980, when his sick leave ran out and an increase in pension benefits went into effect, John Coplin ended thirty-four years with the USDA. He retired to his suburban Chicago home and to his motor home, which had been his one joy outside of his work. He had hoped to be traveling the country these days in that motor home as the USDA's special investigatory red rover. But now he could only contemplate more mundane retirement travel.

The years had taken their toll on Coplin. He had become a hard-drinking man who could be difficult for even his friends to deal with. His doctor told him he drank too much, but considering what he'd been through, the doctor didn't blame him. The frustrations he had experienced would have broken many men, and he had left the USDA with a full share of bitterness. But he hated like hell to be pushed out when there was still so much to be done. It is galling for Coplin to look back at all he had tried to accomplish and to see how little support and recognition he received for his efforts. His last years, which had held such promise, left a particularly bad taste in his mouth. Besides the officials who had given him false hope, and the supermarket raid, which turned out to be just another tool used to harass him, there was a case in Minnesota in which he exposed a packer for slaughtering diseased animals. "Well, I am the guy that took the inspector general's people out there and led them around by the hand, then they came up with the indictment," he says. "Let's face it, if it hadn't been for me, there wouldn't have been anything. But hell, I get nothing out of that, and I don't know if they will either." There was also a case involving a Nebraska packer who sent inferior meat and spoiled meat to state institutions, "And I'm the guy who was right out in front on that. And here again now, shit, I laid everything on the line, all on the line, and when the chips were down at the tail end, well, nobody came to John Coplin's defense."

Coplin vows he will continue his crusades from the outside now, but admits that "as a whistleblower, there's no future."

"You know, it's a sad thing," he says ruefully, "but I have not had any trouble working with the Justice Department, the FBI, with the Senate, the House, you name it, all of them. The only ones I've had trouble working with are the people who should be working with me, and helping."

John Coplin's tales of the bureaucracy are hardly unique. Countless other government employees who made the mistake of trying to do an honest job have found themselves harassed or shunted aside. There are many subtle ways to push trouble-makers at all levels of the bureaucracy off into corners. And there are plenty of officials in high places who can stifle potentially damaging inquiries into the operations of "their" industries.

Ralph Johnson is another man who believes the USDA showed him the door because he dared to say things the meat industry didn't want to hear. Johnson, a paunchy academic bureaucrat in his late fifties with thinning hair and a flat, scratchy voice, was an agricultural economist for the USDA stationed at the University of Nebraska. He is an expert on one of the most serious crises facing the meat industry: the deterioration of the industry's pricing system. The system used to set the price of meat products is primitive, inaccurate, and easily manipulated. As a result, farmers are paid too little for their livestock and consumers pay too much for meat. The only people who prosper are the major packers, who have the leverage to influence prices. The most promising proposal to reform the disgraceful situation is for the industry to develop an electronic, computerized pricing system. However, the major packers, with the help of sympathetic USDA bureaucrats, have been able to short-circuit development of such a system. In the process, they short-circuited the career of Ralph Johnson.

Over the years of research, Johnson developed what may be the most extensive body of knowledge of electronic marketing to be found anywhere, but for the last several years of his USDA career, the USDA didn't want to use that knowledge. Johnson says his experience is a prime example of how the USDA "screws people like me, shuts us up and makes us nonpersons." And he knows why: electronic marketing would be opposed by the major packers who are the friends of his USDA bosses. "What kind of happy crap is that?" Johnson asks.

Johnson's story begins in 1975, when staff members for the Senate Agriculture Committee approached him about doing a study on livestock marketing. They worked out an agreement with Johnson's superiors in the USDA's Economic Research Service, commissioning Johnson to prepare the study for the committee. By the end of 1976, the study was completed. It

was 237 pages filled with the usual dry information of government reports: statistics on areas of cattle concentration and
meat-packing concentration, size and integration of packing
operations, comparisons of livestock marketing methods. But
there was something different about Johnson's report. It wasn't
as dull, boring, and incomprehensible as the reports turned out
by most economists. In fact, it was somewhat readable. And
that's where the trouble began. Anyone reading Johnson's report
would pick up a few derogatory statements about current practices in the packing industry, although Johnson did not blast
any specific companies. Even worse, Johnson violated one of
the cardinal rules of bureaucratic report writing: he made concrete suggestions for change. Specifically, he advocated that an
electronic marketing system was the solution to the pricing
problems of the meat industry.

It is one thing for a bureaucrat to write a report that points
out problems, if it is done in a nonthreatening way. And it's even
all right to make some recommendations for change, as long as
they are hidden beneath innocuous bureaucratic gobbledygook.
But Johnson came right out and said what he meant. He broke
the rules, and he has paid for it ever since.

The first indication that something was wrong came in
February of 1977. That is when Johnson received an ominous
letter from one of his superiors in Washington acknowledging
that Johnson was probably wondering what had happened to his
manuscript. The letter listed the problems Johnson's superior
had with the report. He was particularly concerned that the
report showed "advocacy" of electronic trading, and that it
included some blunt truths about the packing industry. For
example, Johnson castigated packers, saying they would probably attempt to scuttle electronic trading. While Johnson's
superior agreed that was probably true, he said it would have to
be rephrased in more general terms. He also sent Johnson an
outline of general comments on the manuscript, including one
statement that reflects the golden rule for bureaucrats: "Overall, too advocative in an 'inflammatory' sense—be subtle—and
perhaps more effective!!"

Continuing his lesson in proper bureaucratic style, Johnson's superior prepared a revised version of Johnson's report.

He slashed it from 237 pages to 116, and he substituted vague generalities for the specific "advocacy" terms used by Johnson. Most important, he toned down support of electronic market trading; only the most careful reader would pick up the impression that Johnson thought electronic marketing was a good idea. In all, it was a masterful bureaucratic rewrite.

Johnson was not pleased. He claimed the revision was inaccurate and misleading. "It eliminates statements the producers, packers, or consumers might not like," he wrote at the time. Johnson battled with his superiors over the report throughout 1977, and finally in December he took his case to Secretary of Agriculture Bob Bergland. "There is little doubt that the Department's tremendous loss in credibility and prestige is due to our uncanny knack of selecting too many middle level administrators who are more concerned with not saying or doing anything that someone might not like, than they are in furthering public interest," Johnson wrote. Specifically, he claimed that many employees had been rendered ineffective by this "middle level administrative syndrome" that calls for avoiding topics someone, "especially someone in the 'trade,' might not like."

Johnson's letter was referred to Kenneth Farrell, acting administrator of Johnson's division in Washington. Little did Farrell know that he would spend the next several years rehashing Ralph Johnson's complaint. At first he tried to be sympathetic to Johnson and generally supportive of his position on his report. But this one 237-page report became an obsession with Johnson, and he ignited a bureaucratic paper war that was to rage for years. He may not have known how to write a good bureaucratic report, but he sure knew how to play bureaucratic bingo.

The stack of official memos on the case was already about three inches thick by October of 1978, when Farrell received one more memo on the persecution of Ralph Johnson: "It is quite obvious to anyone familiar with the facts that [one of Johnson's bosses] tried to gut my report and prevent me from reporting my findings to Senator Huddleston and to the Senate Agriculture Committee," Johnson wrote. "It is also quite apparent that [his] actions were not due to an honest difference of professional opinion. It was a deliberate attempt on [his] part to alter my report." Johnson contended that because he would not go along with the attempt to "bias my report and mislead the Senate Agriculture Committee," the administrator, with the help of other Washington bureaucrats, retaliated against Johnson by a series of actions. Johnson claimed they lowered his performance rating, denied him a raise, made threatening phone calls and sent threatening letters, prohibited him from discussing the report with the Senate committee staff, and tried to get him transferred to Washington, among other things. "I am sure that we both recognize the above pattern of retaliation as a classic example of how administrators punish their subordinates for nonpunishable offenses," Johnson wrote.

During these two years, Johnson did two more rewrites of his report. Finally, his superiors authorized release of the report to the Senate Agriculture Committee, although they warned that the report did not necessarily represent the views of the USDA. Ironically, this version was almost identical to Johnson's original manuscript—a manuscript that two years earlier was unacceptable and "inflammatory." Now, Johnson received a favorable performance rating and a raise for his work on the report. But Johnson's relationship with his superiors had been ruined, and he still felt they were out to punish him. He was denied the opportunity to do further work on electronic marketing, his area of greatest expertise. Instead, he was given what he considered make-work projects that would be no use to anyone. And his superiors kept trying to transfer him to Washington. Just like John Coplin, Johnson believes the transfer was an attempt to force him to retire. So Johnson kept up his bureaucratic paper war; the stack of official memos was now just about a foot tall.

Johnson was not alone in questioning whether his superiors were giving him a hard time mainly because his work might be controversial. Congressman Berkley Bedell of Iowa came to his defense in a letter to agriculture secretary Bergland. Bedell charged that it was clear to him that Johnson was being punished because his high standards of research had clashed with his superior's perception of "political expediency." Bedell also noted that he had uncovered additional cases in which the conclusions in USDA reports may have been tampered with because individual administrators have feared the potential political ramifications.

The whole Johnson affair was complicated by the fact that the frustration and aggravation were affecting his health. He developed a heart condition that was apparently "anxiety-induced," and his doctors warned that the transfer to Washington that his superiors kept trying to push on him would complicate the condition. His superiors persisted in demanding the transfer, however, and Johnson stood by his doctors' orders that his heart condition would not permit the transfer. As the bureaucratic paper kept flying back and forth on this issue, Johnson went on extended sick leave instead. He put up his fight until April 1981, when his sick leave ran out and he was forced to retire.

The USDA has been deprived of his expertise on what may be the most important issue facing the meat industry. And other government investigators concerned about meat prices are wary of approaching him because his personality conflicts in the USDA became so virulent. Johnson, who sees himself as the leading authority on electronic marketing, can find no one who will listen to him. "My study is still the best thing that's out, that's available, that's ever been done," he contends. But he says his bosses in the USDA only wanted him silenced. "They've screwed up electronic marketing," he says disgustedly, "and they know I know it."

There are plenty of other Ralph Johnsons who would like to make an honest contribution to improving the meat industry, but who know that doing so will only cause them grief. And there are plenty of other high-level officials who are more concerned about what the industry might think than about what is best for the public.

One of them is another official who was worried about Johnson's electronic marketing report. Charles Jennings was administrator of the USDA's Packers and Stockyards Administration during part of the Johnson flap. This is the agency that is most directly responsible for keeping packers honest, and the one that should be most concerned about the industry's deteriorating pricing system. Unfortunately, this has been traditionally the most complacent, do-nothing, and industry-fearing branch of the USDA. In a review of Johnson's final report in 1978, Jennings warned that "there should be great concern in this agency about a report that recommends the establishment of a U.S. Government-operated ELAM Market [electronic marketing system], or even a government-supervised market operated by the industry. The industry would not accept it." That kind of knee-jerk reaction can have grave consequences. Imagine Las Vegas officials writing a memo after the tragic MGM Grand fire to the effect that "there should be great concern in this city about a report that recommends requiring fire sprinkler systems. The casinos would not accept it." Jennings had another concern with Johnson's report as well: "There should be concern about our image in being party to a report that makes such sweeping suggestions. . . ."

It could be argued that sweeping suggestions are precisely what his agency should have been making, considering the serious problems with meat pricing. In all, these were the kinds of comments that would have been more appropriate coming from an industry lobbyist than from a USDA administrator. Ultimately, even Jennings figured that out: after only two years with the USDA, he went back on the industry payroll. His brief government tenure is a textbook example of the problems inherent in the revolving door that connects the meat industry and the USDA.

Jennings is a smooth, amiable, grandfatherly man who has spent his life in the meat industry. He was president of the Kansas City Stock Yards when an old friend, assistant secretary of agriculture P. R. "Bobby" Smith, convinced him to come to Washington to take what has been called the most powerful job in the meat industry. As head of the Packers and Stockyards Administration, he would have at his disposal vast regulatory and enforcement powers over the industry. In fact, he was called by some the "dictator of the meat industry." But critics argue that Jennings lost his perspective, and often times his sympathies lay with the industry. During his two years in the USDA, Jennings ignored the incredible tools that could have been used to reform the meat industry. Instead, critics claim that too often he overlooked problems.

Particularly disturbing was his treatment of the most powerful packer in the nation. During the past decade the rise of a company called Iowa Beef Processors, Inc., has concerned officials both in government and in the meat industry. This company pioneered a new packing concept known as "boxed beef" that is one of the few real innovations to be introduced in the packing industry in this century. Iowa Beef discovered that it is cheaper and more efficient to chop carcasses into wholesale or even retail cuts at the packing plant than to ship out carcasses that must be cut up eventually anyway. Boxed beef is the new standard for meat-packing, and Iowa Beef has established itself as the General Motors of the meat industry. It would seem obvious that boxed beef and Iowa Beef would be major concerns in the Packers and Stockyards Administration. Yet during the tenure of Jennings, and those who preceded him, the agency developed no hard data on what boxed beef was all about; it couldn't even tell for sure how many packers were involved in boxed beef. And under Jennings' direction, two investigations into Iowa Beef were closed despite evidence of apparent questionable activities.

Before Jennings came to Washington, the Packers and Stockyards Administration was worried about Iowa Beef. This was a company as shrewd as it was dominant, and there was a strong possibility that Iowa Beef was moving into a position to monopolize various segments of the packing and slaughtering industries. In 1975, the agency mounted an investigation into practices by Iowa Beef that were potentially anticompetitive and illegal. The investigation uncovered five practices that the USDA believes violated the Packers and Stockyards Act. Among the violations were charges that Iowa Beef gave "volume discounts in the sale of boxed beef during 1972–73," which could potentially have been a means to favor certain customers; and it paid brokerage commissions to one meat broker "when no brokerage services were performed, or under circumstances where it was not always clear that brokerage services were performed," which could potentially have been a means of bribery. But no action was ever taken against Iowa Beef for these alleged abuses. Less than a year after Jennings came to the USDA, he closed the investigation. Virtually all of the evidence gathered during the investigation was then destroyed. "Since the situations described above apparently have been corrected or discontinued by IBP, and it appears that recent policy and management changes have brought about improvements in your method of operation, I believe these matters can be handled informally," Jennings wrote to Iowa Beef in April 1978, in one of the few documents that remain from the investigation. All Iowa Beef had to do was tell the USDA that the practices "have been discontinued and that you have taken affirmative action to prevent their recurrence," and the USDA would forgive and forget. Iowa Beef responded that it didn't believe it had done anything wrong, but it wouldn't do it again anyway. So the USDA returned all the business records and documents it had subpoenaed during the probe and destroyed most of its own files.

None of this was publicly disclosed until a year later, when a reporter for *Supermarket News,* a trade journal for the supermarket industry, discovered the agreement. Mark Hosenball, an aggressive investigative reporter who has played an important role in bringing attention to questionable activities by Iowa Beef, came across the agency's closing letter in the case when he made a Freedom of Information request on the USDA. When he confronted USDA officials, they confirmed that their investigation had been quietly dropped, and they also acknowledged that this supposedly comprehensive investigation had overlooked more serious allegations that Iowa Beef had given one supermarket chain a preferential price break on its meat. All these revelations outraged other government investigators concerned about the power and conduct of Iowa Beef. Congressman Benjamin Rosenthal of New York, who was investigating charges that Iowa Beef might have been part of a scheme to manipulate meat prices, demanded an explanation from agriculture secretary Bergland for the USDA's conduct. Considering that valuable information from the probe had been destroyed, he wanted to know "when and how investigations like this one are opened or closed, when documents are returned or maintained by USDA, and when summaries, notes, and other memoranda are stored," so the USDA would not quietly sweep charges under the rug again.

Unfortunately, this was not the only time Rosenthal and others would have reason to question the USDA's hands-off approach to Iowa Beef. After this first inquiry was dropped, the USDA had a second chance to scrutinize Iowa Beef. This time, the USDA looked into charges that Iowa Beef was trying to monopolize slaughtering and cattle-feeding operations in the Pacific Northwest. The company had entered into exclusive contracts with the cattle feedlots in the region that could give Iowa Beef control over virtually all of the cattle raised in the Northwest. The potentially anticompetitive implications of this move were serious enough for the USDA to file suit to halt the Iowa Beef takeover. But after an initial rebuff in court, the USDA dropped its investigation. Packers and Stockyards officials decided the "anticipated adverse effects of the joint venture have not occurred." Two years later, however, a confidential memo surfaced questioning whether the agency really had been interested in finding anything wrong with Iowa Beef.

The memo, prepared in late 1977 by Richard Davis, Jr., the lawyer in the USDA's Office of General Counsel who directed legal activities involving the Packers and Stockyards Administration, indicates that USDA lawyers felt the Packers and Stockyards Administration was doing a less than thorough job of investigating Iowa Beef. The memo states that the agency had not dug deeply enough into the charges about Iowa Beef's activities in the Northwest to determine whether or not the practices were monopolistic. In addition, by concentrating the probe on the situation in the Northwest, the USDA was ignoring the real issue: potential monopolization of the meat industry nationwide. "This complaint does nothing to attack the real cause of concern over IBP—its size and market power," reads the memo, which goes on to warn that unless the scope of the investigation was broadened, it was doomed to failure.

The lawyers were not at all happy with the information Packers and Stockyards' personnel were giving them either. They "have either failed to recognize evidence in their possession supporting a monopolization case or haven't felt it of sufficient importance to forward to OGC [Office of General Counsel] for review," the memo states. Specifically, Packers and Stockyards officials didn't look into charges that Iowa Beef was withholding certain grade carcasses from the market to push chain stores into buying IBP's boxed beef instead; and that an IBP-commissioned study suggested a scenario by which IBP could drive up labor costs in such a way that it would "saddle competition with high-cost plants while increasing [IBP's] own strength in both slaughter and market positions." Additionally the lawyers were upset that Packers and Stockyards' investigators did not discover, or didn't turn over to them, an Iowa Beef document "indicating a potentially predatory policy aimed at driving competitors out of business." The lawyers learned about the existence of this document by reading *The Wall Street Journal.*

The memo was a blunt attack on the Packers and Stockyards Administration. In fact, officials in the general counsel's office decided it was "too blunt," so it was never forwarded to Jennings. But the lawyers contend the contents were fully discussed orally in meetings attended by Jennings. They are certain he knew how strongly they felt about the soft treatment Iowa Beef was getting.

When the memo finally surfaced in May of 1980, it was particularly embarrassing to Jennings. He had been telling people that he was the one who wanted a more aggressive investigation of Iowa Beef; it was the lawyers who held him back, he said. But others find that hard to believe. Congressman Neal Smith of Iowa, whose House Small Business Committee has conducted the most vigorous inquiry into Iowa Beef and meat-industry practices, says the Packers and Stockyards Administration "deliberately" pursued only a "limited" action against Iowa Beef that conveniently turned up evidence so weak that there was no alternative but to drop the probe.

There's a more compelling reason to doubt Jennings: he is now vice-president for public relations for Iowa Beef Processors, Inc. Six months after leaving the meat industry's most powerful regulatory job, he was hired by the most powerful packer. The move was branded as cynical at best by outraged consumers, government reformers, and even meat-industry groups. Now he played an active role as spokesman for this very company.

The outcry over Jennings' new job prompted the USDA to call for an investigation from its Office of Inspector General. The inspector general agents merely interviewed a few of Jennings' associates in the USDA and a few officials of his new employer, and left it at that. Jennings was cleared of any impropriety or conflict of interest, but critics contend the investigation can only be called superficial.

Jennings doesn't understand what all the fuss is about. He gripes that nobody complained of any conflict of interest when he left the Kansas City Stockyards to serve the government, so why should anybody complain now? And he readily admits he left the USDA when he did because new ethics legislation was about to go into effect that would have limited his options in seeking employment in the meat industry. He had merely taken a stroll through the revolving door, as countless men had done before him, and as countless more will do in the future. Few officials in the USDA seem to be worried about all this shuffling back and forth, and the ones who are worried are mainly the troublemakers like John Coplin or Ralph Johnson, whom no one wants to listen to anyway. It's no wonder that USDA bureaucrats find it more appealing, and certainly more rewarding, to give the meat industry what it wants. It's no wonder that whistleblowers like John Coplin and Ralph Johnson don't have a chance.

7

The Healthfulness of Meat

For one thing, I've yet to see a woman who could pack a front quarter of bull... or side of beef... or bump legs. It has just never been a woman's place around a packing house.

—*"The Old Timer,"*
Meat Industry *magazine, p. 49, July 1980.*
Oman Publishing Inc. © 1980

When the heavyweights of the meat industry came to Washington during the Carter administration, they invariably spent some time in the USDA headquarters building just a few blocks from the Washington Monument doing battle with an assistant secretary of agriculture. They would climb to the second floor and walk down the hall to the first door past the secretary of agriculture's office. Here they were ushered into a richly paneled office furnished in greens—bright-green carpet, lime-green and green-plaid furniture, leafy green plants all around. They were met by a delicate five-foot-two-inch woman with curly red hair, a pleasant smile, and a disarming Arkansas drawl. To these macho meatmen, she must have looked like a pushover. But they soon enough learned otherwise. The first indication was her viselike handshake. Then her straightforward greeting that made it clear she had no time for unnecessary pleasantries. This woman meant business. Carol Tucker Foreman, assistant secretary of agriculture for food and consumer services, was every bit as tough as any of the meatmen.

128

And the meatmen didn't like it. They didn't like it that this woman could boss them around. Some of them didn't like it that she was a woman, period. And they all didn't like it that she was asking pointed questions and making difficult demands from USDA headquarters.

The meatmen were used to thinking of the USDA's top bureaucrats as their friends. An assistant secretary of agriculture was usually one of the boys, a man sympathetic to the needs of meat producers, slaughterers, and processors. Certainly the assistant secretary was not a woman. Few industries are still as male-dominated as the meat industry, so taking orders from a woman is not something meatmen accept easily. Their attitude is neatly summarized by one packer, "The Old Timer," who writes a column for *Meat Industry* magazine: "For one thing, I've yet to see a woman who could pack a front quarter of bull ... or side of beef ... or bump legs. It has just never been a woman's place around a packing house. Of course, some of the sidelines we've developed are well suited to their size, strength and aptitudes. Portion control comes rapidly to mind along with most weighing, packaging and, of course, clerical work. There have been some pretty fair truck drivers as well. But, by and large, it's been a man's world in the meat business as long as I can remember." It was bad enough that the meatmen had to deal with a woman, but Foreman was something even worse as well: a consumer advocate. The meatmen who in the past could count on the USDA to take their side in the fights with those pesky consumers were now faced with an administrator who had been quoted saying things like "Consumers have not been just ignored by this department, they've been abused."

Carol Foreman was clearly not the kind of administrator the meat industry and its supporters were used to. And they made sure she knew it. Former secretary of agriculture Earl Butz called her appointment the "ultimate insult to farmers." A Kentucky congressman said, "If Carol Foreman and her cronies have their way, the nation will exist on wheat germ and organic bean sprouts." A Nebraska congresswoman charged, "Carol Foreman, one of agriculture's biggest enemies, is at work right now discrediting the meat industry and causing the public to lose confidence in American farm products." The *National Provisioner,* trade organ for the meat industry, snidely referred to her as "Chatty Carol" and other derogatory names while attacking her every move. To meatmen she was a "dictator," and analogies linking her to leading tyrants became favorites throughout the industry: her press releases came from the "Idi Amin School of Diplomacy"; she was, simply, the "Ayatollah of the USDA."

What did Foreman do to deserve this vilification? Basically, she took the branch of the USDA whose actions most directly affect consumers, and she tried to make it stand behind consumers. That is what she was supposed to do, but it shocked the hell out of the meat industry. Foreman was a voice for consumers and a tough administrator who tried to make the USDA more responsive to the needs of consumers. She cleaned up some of the corruption in meat grading and inspection, and she tried to make grading and inspection more useful tools for consumers. Meatmen groused that all she was really doing was giving the industry a bad name and piling on unnecessary regulations. But there was something that riled them even more about Foreman: she had the audacity to ask basic questions about the healthfulness of meat products. She wanted to know the effects of all the chemical additives poured into livestock and into meat. She wanted to know if processing and labeling regulations really helped consumers figure out what they were buying. And worst of all, she wanted to know if it was really healthy for Americans to eat all the meat we do.

The meat industry doesn't want anyone talking about these things. Increasingly, talk about chemicals leads to links with cancer and other disorders. Talk about labeling leads to evidence that a lot of what we buy as meat is actually fillers and by-products. And talk about health and nutrition leads to evidence that meat may not deserve its spot at the absolute center of the American diet. The meat industry despises the consumer advocates who harp on these points, and it certainly doesn't want a top government regulator bringing them up. In Carol Foreman, however, it had both.

When Jimmy Carter took office in 1977, Foreman was one of the many "outsiders" brought in to run his administration. At the time she was known as one of the most aggressive consumer-interest lobbyists in Washington, heading the Consumer Federation of America, a coalition of 240 consumer groups nationwide. She was quite familiar with the USDA because it had been one of the Consumer Federation's favorite targets. Foreman and the Consumer Federation sued the USDA twice, first for giving in to the meat industry by relaxing meat-grading standards, and then for allowing the sale of processed meats that contained bits of ground bone resulting from a mechanical deboning process. Foreman also attacked the USDA for listening only to food processors and big farmers while ignoring consumers. Once, while Earl Butz was secretary of agriculture, she and a group of consumer advocates marched into a meeting of a USDA advisory panel wearing gags to draw attention to the fact that they were silenced by the USDA decision makers. In that same room about a year later, Foreman was sworn in as assistant secretary of agriculture.

Foreman was chosen for the post because she was known for more than just symbolic acts. "People expect a consumer advocate to be some hysterical lady out of a supermarket," Foreman told one interviewer shortly after her appointment. "But one thing all Carter's 'consumer types' have in common: We know an awful lot about how government operates and how to work within it. When it's screwing you all the time, you learn." Foreman was a savvy, pragmatic strategist who understood politics and the inner workings of government. She had been born into a political family: her father had been Arkansas state treasurer and her younger brother became Arkansas attorney general and, later, a U.S. representative. She was married to an international vice-president of the Retail Clerks Union (which briefly snagged her appointment as assistant secretary while the Senate considered charges that she was, literally, "in bed" with organized labor). On her own she developed a wide range of governmental experience; she worked as a congressman's executive assistant, as a congressional liaison aide for the Department of Housing and Urban Development, and as chief of information and congressional liaison for Planned Parenthood. If there was any question about how tough and gutsy Foreman was, she dispelled it when she lobbied aggressively on Capitol Hill for Planned Parenthood while in a visibly advanced stage of pregnancy.

As assistant secretary of agriculture for food and consumer services, Foreman was in charge of a staff of thirteen thousand and a yearly budget of $9 billion. She was responsible for programs ranging from meat grading and inspection to food stamps, school lunches, and nutrition research and education. She charged that the USDA catered solely to the interests of food producers, and no matter how much it upset them, she was going to make the USDA the "people's department" Abraham Lincoln had envisioned when he set it up.

"I want to kick some ass, I just don't know where to kick it," she told one visitor shortly after taking the job. It wasn't long, however, before she started booting, and the backside of the meat industry smarted for the next four years. Foreman was not afraid to take stands she knew would infuriate the meat industry. And she was not afraid to tell the industry about her stands in languge it understood. Foreman may be physically small and delicate, but she could come on like a Marine drill instructor when necessary. She was known for one of the foulest mouths in government, an attribute that endeared her to some of her male audiences and at least got her the attention of others. In addition, she surrounded herself with a band of young, idealistic assistants who shared her zeal. These were not the usual bureaucrats who easily accepted whatever the meat industry told them. And they were not the kind of bureaucrats that the meat industry felt comfortable dealing with. Meatmen could not use their old-buddy routines on such assistants as Tom Grumbly, an earnest young man still in his twenties who was not afraid to stand up before meat industry groups and say the industry was corrupt; Sydney Butler, who came to the office in blue jeans and shoulder-length hair until a promotion forced him to clean up his act; and Jody Levin Epstein and other women assistants whose insistence on using three names was an implication of women's liberation that some meatmen found offensive.

For the next four years this small band of idealists took on the meat industry and the USDA bureaucracy. They talked continually about restoring the "integrity" of USDA officials, such as graders and inspectors, whose reputations had been tainted by scandal. They proposed reforms and new programs that for once showed concern for the needs of consumers, not just the meat industry. In the process, they made a lot of enemies.

To the meat industry, the sins of Carol Foreman were many, and they were succinctly inventoried early in 1980 at a gathering of West Coast meat-packers. The setting was the annual Western States Meat Packers convention at the Disneyland Hotel. Here was a spectacle that was in its own way as bizarre as anything to be seen at the famed amusement park just a short monorail ride away. There was a convention hall filled with the latest in meat industry fashions, from space-age sausage makers and burger grillers to the Anyl-Ray Fat Analyzer and the Inject-Jet Bone-In Pickle Injector. There were intriguing signs: "Are you EXTRACTING SHROUDS so they can take up brine?" There were short, bull-necked, leisure-suited packers, tall, weatherbeaten, heavy-on-the-rawhide-look packers, and dapper, citified packers. There were speeches on such important topics as electrical stimulation of meat and world meat research. And Richard Lyng was on hand to accept the Floyd Forbes Award, a bronze steer trophy that is the packers' highest award for service to the meat industry.

Lyng had once been an assistant secretary of agriculture, just like Foreman. He had recently retired as president of the American Meat Institute, the dominant national trade organization, for whom he had feuded with Foreman continually. Now this husky, aging man stood before the assembled packers to accept an award given, among other reasons, for keeping the pressure on Foreman. In his deep, sure voice he highlighted for his Disneyland audience the issues that drove the meat industry crazy about Carol Foreman, and, as it turned out, the attitudes that no longer would be welcome in the USDA under Ronald Reagan.

He warmed up with some general statements about the problems facing the industry, such as inflation, energy, and government regulation. He complained about Washington officials who were making matters worse for the meat industry instead of better: "The fuzzy-wuzzies, in too many instances, are in charge," he griped as his audience nodded agreement. He attacked the Consumer Federation of America as an organization that is "antibusiness" and "antimeat." Then he turned to his favorite target.

"You know that the Consumer Federation was the training ground of the assistant secretary of agriculture, who has given this industry, in my opinion, a dreadful time during the past three years. Most of the industry's regulatory problems during that time were the brainchild of what I would call the Ayatollah of the USDA, Carol Tucker Foreman." Lyng gave a rundown of her many "Ayatollah-like" actions. First of all, he said Foreman "went into the USDA with an antimeat attitude." As evidence, he pointed to the fact that in 1977 she helped sponsor a meatless dinner at the White House. "We objected to that," Lyng said, "but even the secretary of agriculture went to the dinner." Nothing is more sickening to meatmen than the idea of vegetarianism.

Foreman's next sin was to bring in Dr. Robert Angelotti as her top assistant. Angelotti was the abrasive bureaucrat who took seriously the USDA's regulatory powers and who vowed that he would apply them to the meat industry for the first time in decades. Meatmen quickly came to despise him as much as they despised Foreman—if not more. Then, when this reformer was charged with filing false expense vouchers, the meat industry pounced on the issue and forced him to resign. Lyng sarcastically told his Disneyland audience that Angelotti's term had been a "great experience for us." About the only thing great about his leaving was that the meatmen could now focus all their wrath on Foreman.

Lyng moved on to the two controversies that had turned meatmen absolutely livid about Foreman: her stands on the use of the chemical additive nitrite and on a mechanical meat-deboning process.

Sodium nitrite and sodium nitrate are time-honored chemicals in the meat industry, important to the production of processed meats such as bacon, hot dogs, lunch meats, and pet foods. They add color, making hot dogs a pleasant pink rather than an unappetizing gray; they add flavor; and they inhibit spoilage and prevent deadly forms of food poisoning like botulism. But they also may cause cancer. For twenty years, the link between nitrites and cancer has been studied, and enough evidence has been discovered to prompt some countries to limit or ban nitrites. But the definitive evidence of the link has not yet been found, and the American meat industry has resisted all efforts to tamper with its use of nitrites. It's an understandable position, since nitrites are used in an estimated $12.5 billion worth of food—7 per cent of the food supply.

The charge against nitrites is that they can combine with other substances to form nitrosamines, which are known to be potent carcinogens. Nitrosamines have been found in a variety of products—in 1979 there was a major scare when large concentrations were found in some brands of beer—but bacon is the product that has raised the greatest fears. There are indications that nitrosamines can be formed during the process of frying nitrite-cured bacon, and also that they can be formed simply by the interaction between nitrites and other substances in the human stomach. Then, in 1978, a government-commissioned study by an MIT professor found supposedly more compelling evidence. The study concluded that there was an increased rate of cancer of the lymph system in laboratory rats fed nitrites. Based on the results, the USDA and the Food and Drug Administration quickly called for a total ban on nitrites. The meat industry mobilized to fight the initiative against one of its most precious additives, and the battle raged until 1980. That was when an independent review of the MIT study revealed serious flaws, indicating that the rate of cancer in the laboratory rats was actually much lower than originally reported. The USDA and the FDA reluctantly dropped their attempts to ban nitrites, although Foreman warned a House committee reviewing the controversy that "it would be a grave mistake for us to be lulled into a false sense of security." She reminded everyone that there was still serious concern in the scientific community about nitrites, and she promised that the USDA would continue to study nitrites and vigorously push for development of alternative chemicals to replace them.

But Lyng didn't buy Foreman's concern. To him, the assault on nitrites was nothing more than "scientific McCarthyism." "Nitrite has been charged with a lot of things that have not been proven; and more and more, it looks like they will never be proven—nitrite is innocent of these charges. I cannot quantify the tremendous harm that this has done, not only to the meat industry, but also to the consumers of the world."

Even the meat industry's wrath over nitrites, however, paled in comparison to one more issue: the controversy over mechanically deboned meat. It may sound like a rather technical kind of dispute, but it was one that pointed out most graphically how strongly the meat industry will fight being forced to tell consumers what they are buying. For Lyng, it was Foreman's "most irresponsible and most Ayatollah-like action."

The meat industry has developed machines that mechanically separate meat from bone, so ideally packinghouse workers should be spared the time-consuming and inefficient task of scraping out by hand as much meat as possible from inaccessible bones and joints. With mechanical deboning machinery, an estimated five to fifteen pounds of additional meat can be extracted from a single carcass—quite a significant amount. But the machinery also extracts bits of bone and bone marrow. The bits are ground into a fine powder by the process, so there is little danger of unsuspecting consumers biting into large chunks of bone in their wienies. But the bits are certainly not meat, even though they were included in the makings for hot dogs, sausages, luncheon meats, and other processed meats as if they were. Even without the powdered bone, some meatmen know enough about what goes into processed meats to avoid eating them. And the recipes themselves are hardly enticing. Take, for example, the ingredients in one recipe for liver sausage: 160 pounds of pork livers, 100 pounds defatted pork stomachs, 160 pounds pork snout trimmings, 30 pounds pork cheek meat, 5 pounds ring liver seasoning, 8 pounds salt, 40 pounds water. Consumer groups were not about to accept the addition of powdered bone to the list without a fight, so in 1976 they sued the USDA. They wanted to halt the use of mechanical deboning machinery until the USDA made sure manufacturers spelled out on the product labels just what was going into processed meats. The consumers also wanted the USDA to determine for sure whether it was healthful for consumers to eat this powdered bone. Carol Foreman, then heading the

Consumer Federation, led the fight, and she won. Mechanically deboned meat was banned, although the following year the industry pushed the USDA to reconsider its decision. This time, the official the meatmen had to deal with was all too familiar to them: Carol Foreman was now assistant secretary of agriculture. Foreman did reconsider the USDA's decision and she approved the use of the machinery. But there was a catch: all meat products containing meat processed by the machinery had to include a statement on their label warning that they included "tissue from ground bone." The meat industry argued that the statement sounded awful, and consumers would never buy products that carried that warning. So the haggling continued. In 1978, the USDA issued a revised regulation. This one decreed that mechanically deboned meat had to be labeled, in lettering at least one half the size of the product name, "Mechanically Processed Beef Product [or Pork, etc.]." And in lettering at least one quarter the size of the product name, "Contains up to $x\%$ powdered bone." The industry once again complained the statements were repugnant, and consumers would still conjure up images of chomping down on bone bits. Now, few packers use the process while an estimated $20 million worth of mechanical deboning equipment stands idle.

"This is a ridiculous situation in which this product—because of the unreasonable labeling requirements for mechanically deboned meat—is being denied the public, while at the same time, the identical product coming from poultry is not being discriminated against," Lyng charged. And since Foreman originally led the fight against the machinery when she was with the Consumer Federation, he contended she was biased and should have removed herself from deliberations on the issue.

Foreman was equally firm in her stand that the regulations were fair and informative: consumers should be told what they are buying, and consumers shouldn't be paying meat prices for bone and marrow. In addition, since it was admittedly inconsistent that poultry products using the machinery were not labeled, she said she would look into requiring the warning for poultry products as well. Her adamant position only served to further infuriate meatmen. "It's about as easy to negotiate with her on this issue as it is for the United States to negotiate with the people of Iran," Lyng charged at Disneyland, to the delight of the assembled packers.

Now he had gotten all the bitter charges out, and he decided to back off just a bit. He conceded "it may not be fair, and it certainly is an overstatement, to compare Carol Foreman with the Ayatollah, but it brings home the concept of unreasonable and probably inexperienced leadership." Lyng had made his point, however, and the Ayatollah nickname stuck. It quickly spread through the industry, becoming an epithet used with glee against Foreman.

And it hurt. Foreman and her staff were used to abuse, but they considered the comparisons to the Ayatollah a low blow. They didn't expect the meatmen to agree with everything they were doing, but they did expect some respect for going about their jobs in a responsible manner. Instead, meatmen such as Lyng made them out to be irrational zealots simply because they were concerned about considering more than just the parochial interests of the meat industry. Foreman was ostracized for hiring assistants such as Angelotti who did not blindly accept whatever the meat industry said. She was attacked on the nitrite issue because not enough rats had died in one test to convince meatmen of a health hazard well established in other tests. And on mechanical deboning of meat, it wasn't even a question of how many rats died; it was merely a matter of asking meatmen to label products so consumers know what's inside.

All of these attitudes are incomprehensible to Lyng and the Disneyland packers. They still want the good old days when the USDA was "their" department, and nobody was questioning what was going into their products. They hang on to attitudes and practices out of Frontierland, and by not recognizing the changing conditions in their industry and the changing desires of consumers, they are living in a fantasyland. This time, Lyng and the Disneyland packers won out. Less than a year after Lyng gave his speech, Carol Foreman was out of a job. And Richard Lyng was deputy secretary of agriculture, second in command, in Reagan's new Department of Agriculture.

When the Carter administration came to an end, she had

yet to come to terms with the virulent criticism from the meat industry, the impatience of her former colleagues in the consumer movement, and the indifference of the bureaucracy. During her four years, Foreman was able to earn a grudging respect from some quarters of the meat industry as a woman who stood up for what she believed in. Producer groups in particular came to respect her as a person, if they didn't always agree with her policies. They were impressed with her gutsiness and her down-to-earth personality, and some even considered her "one of the guys." But many other meatmen never came to an understanding with Foreman; they attacked her viciously and relentlessly until the end. Equally frustrating to Foreman was the fact that while she was fending off charges from the meat industry that she was going too far, she had to contend with charges from the consumer movement that she wasn't going far enough. Even Ralph Nader, who had enthusiastically praised Foreman at the start, later complained that she "sold out" to the food producers. Regardless of what Foreman had set out to accomplish, the fact remained that she and her staff were isolated against the rest of what is one of the slowest, dullest, most corrupt, and most entrenched bureaucracies in all of government. The career bureaucrats who were there before Foreman came and who stayed after she left were not very interested in implementing her reforms, so many of them were stalled.

Possibly she was in a no-win situation, considering all the conflicting desires and interests of producers, consumers, and bureaucrats she had to please. In any event, she ran out of time. Carol Foreman's reign turned out to be just a brief aberration in the history of the industry-oriented USDA. When Ronald Reagan was elected, it was clear the USDA would turn back to its old ways. Reagan's supporters and advisers were the people who despised Foreman, and now they would have the opportunity to undo her attempts at reform.

If Carol Foreman's tenure with the USDA was important for one reason, it was for focusing attention on the new jungle facing the American meat industry. The concerns today about the American food supply and the American diet are potentially as serious as anything revealed in Upton Sinclair's 1905 classic. Back then, the public was outraged by the gruesome tales of what went into our meat. After all, who could not be revolted by descriptions like this: "There would be meat that had tumbled out on the floor, in the dirt and sawdust, where the workers had tramped and spit uncounted billions of consumption germs. There would be meat stored in great piles in rooms; and the water from leaky roofs would drip over it, and thousands of rats would race about on it. It was too dark in these storage places to see well, but a man could run his hand over these piles of meat and sweep off handfuls of the dried dung of rats. These rats were nuisances, and the packers would put poisoned bread out for them, they would die, and then rats, bread, and meat would go into the hoppers together. This is no fairy story and no joke. . . ." No joke indeed, and the government inspectors were not doing anything about these and other problems. Sinclair writes in another section of *The Jungle,* "If you were a sociable person, he [the inspector] was quite willing to enter into conversation with you, and to explain to you the deadly nature of the ptomaines which are found in tubercular pork; and while he was talking with you, you could hardly be so ungrateful as to notice that a dozen carcasses were passing him untouched." *The Jungle* caused such an outcry that immediate steps were taken to overhaul the U.S. inspection system. The reforms that resulted and the improvements made over the years since then have established the American food inspection system as possibly the best in the world at what it does. But there are serious new problems.

One afternoon during the summer before Carol Foreman left the USDA, she was leaning back in the lime-green armchair in the corner of her USDA office. Her sandaled feet were propped up on the coffee table, and her fingers were on her temples as she tried to explain about the new jungle—a jungle that does not lend itself as easily to graphic horror stories like the ones told by Sinclair. "Keeping dirt and hair and bones out of meat is something the inspection system was set up to do many years ago, and we've conquered those problems and we do them very well," Foreman said. Today's problems are more subtle than rats in the sausage meat, tubercular steers, or workers falling into the vats of Durham's Pure Leaf Lard. "The massive use of chemicals in agricultural production is a phenomenon that has begun since World War II, over the last thirty-five years. And it's only in the last few years that we've begun to discover that the chemicals which have made it possible to increase the food supply very substantially also have some unintended and sometimes very unfortunate consequences. That is, for example, pesticides used on corn crops contaminate the corn and then the contaminated corn is eaten by hogs and the contamination ends up in the hog meat at a health risk to consumers."

This chain reaction gives the USDA hundreds of potential contaminants to worry about. There are growth promoters like DES, there are sulfa drugs fed to swine to prevent disease, there are nitrites and pesticides, and there are PCBs and other toxic chemicals that can contaminate the ground on which animals graze without anyone knowing about it until it's too late. A 1979 study by the U.S. General Accounting Office indicates that 14 per cent of dressed meat and poultry sold in supermarkets may contain illegal residues of drugs, pesticides, and other contaminants. Of 143 drugs and pesticides likely to leave residues in raw meat and poultry, the report says 42 are suspected of causing cancer, 20 of causing birth defects, and 6 of causing mutations. The federal Environmental Protection Agency has limited or abolished the use of some of these chemicals and now the inspection service tests for residues so contaminated meat is not passed on to consumers. "However, that turns out to be a problem that requires a great deal more sophistication than we have," Foreman said. "We were late in recognizing it, not by malfeasance but just because we weren't wise enough as a country to question what the side effects might be to the use of those chemicals when we first decided to use them."

The problem of detecting chemical contamination starts with one very frustrating fact: "You can't see it. Unless an animal has so much of it that he's staggering, you can't see it. It's not like a disease or a broken bone or gross physical contamination. Furthermore, the tests we have to do to find those residues are extremely expensive, technologically very sophisticated, and require a long time to perform. You can't do them on every single animal. We inspect every single chicken for disease, but we can't inspect every single chicken for every single chemical that might contaminate it. By the time we took every sample, there wouldn't be any chicken meat left to sell. Plus the fact that the cost of doing all those tests on the chicken would far outweigh the cost of the chicken itself." That means the USDA must rely on statistical sampling, choosing a small group of chickens or hogs or cattle at random on which to conduct the tests. Then it must hope it sampled a sufficient number of animals to catch any harmful residues. Even so, the process is time-consuming and inefficient, and there is no way the USDA can test for every single chemical that could contaminate meat. "The meat inspection laws never contemplated that there would be a problem that you couldn't recognize immediately," Foreman said. "They say that we shall not stamp as wholesome any product that may be contaminated, but we stamp all of these products that we later call contaminated because we have no proof at the time that they're contaminated. We get it two weeks later. Then we have to go back and try to recall the product. It's very expensive, it's damaging to the reputation of the company, and it's inefficient."

Even more disturbing is the fact that the link between residues and health hazards is seldom direct, so the actual danger presented by residues is open to debate. Particularly frustrating are the potentially carcinogenic chemicals. Cancer may wait ten years or more to strike, and when it does, it leaves no clue to its identity, so who is to say some meat eaten a decade ago was the culprit? In addition, the research on chemical residues is highly contradictory: for each study claiming a chemical is hazardous, there is another showing that it is not. And as the list of chemicals suspected of causing cancer and other maladies grows, so does public cynicism about cancer claims. After all, is it always necessary to change time-honored procedures and eliminate chemicals that have been accepted for years just because a few mice died?

There are enough issues in the controversy over chemicals in meat for an entire book, but the dilemma can be stated briefly. The meat industry says the risks of chemicals must be weighed against the benefits. Chemicals combat disease in livestock and contamination of meat products. They help producers raise healthy animals quickly, lowering the cost of meat to consumers. Therefore, to the cattleman struggling to keep his livestock healthy and his operation economical, or to the meat processor striving to combat botulism and other potent poisons, the benefits of chemicals could not be more clear. But the fear of health hazards from this ever-increasing list of chemicals is very real, and to the consumer, the risk could not be more serious.

The concern about chemicals in meat is part of a larger concern in the new jungle: is it safe for Americans to eat as much meat as we do? In recent years researchers have discovered unsettling evidence that Americans should not only be concerned about the additives that go into meat; they should also be concerned about the meat itself.

The United States has become a country where eating too much, not too little, is a major problem. In the twentieth century, the American diet has become rich in meat, dairy products, alcohol, and processed foods, all laden with fats, cholesterol, sugar, salt, and calories. In the past few decades, public health researchers have linked this diet to many of the major killing and crippling diseases, including heart and blood-vessel disease, stroke, high blood pressure, diabetes, cirrhosis of the liver, and cancer of the colon and breast. Meat, with its abundance of fat, has become a major source of concern. There is research indicating that diets high in saturated fats such as those found in most meats lead to increased risk of colon cancer in men and breast cancer in women. There is concern that even the ways meat is cooked can cause cancer: when fat is combined with the chemicals in charcoal, a reaction takes place that is potentially harmful; when meat is heated at high temperature on a metal surface, a feared carcinogen called benzopyrene can be formed.

In light of these concerns, Foreman pushed a campaign to study the American diet and even to recommend changes in it. One result was that in 1980 the USDA and the Department of

Health, Education, and Welfare issued the report "Dietary Guidelines for Americans," a first step toward a national nutrition policy that could reshape the American diet. The guidelines were hardly revolutionary, recommending in summary that Americans should "eat a variety of foods; maintain ideal weight; avoid too much fat, saturated fat, and cholesterol; eat foods with adequate starch and fiber; avoid too much sugar; avoid too much sodium; if you drink alcohol, do so in moderation." There were no direct statements that any one product was bad for you, but there were implications. Particularly, there were implications that we should eat less meat—especially the succulent prime and choice meats most abundant in fat.

These subtle implications were enough to set off the meat industry. "By repeating statements about saturated fats and cholesterol, the Government is perpetuating a theory that is unproven," the National Cattlemen's Association complained when the report was released. The Cattlemen and other industry groups said it was premature for anyone to recommend dietary changes, and they pointed to research (much of it funded by the meat industry) claiming that present dietary habits pose no confirmable health hazards. Most of all, they complained that when the government starts telling people what to eat, it is getting into an area where it has no business. But Foreman had planned to push further into this area. She had expected to expand on the "Dietary Guidelines" and to continue pursuing all the serious questions of the new jungle. Now that she is gone, the meat industry can expect an easier time. There will be less talk about chemicals and the American diet from within the USDA. But Foreman was hardly alone in raising questions about the healthfulness of meat, and the pressures from outside the USDA will only increase.

This new jungle has the meat industry extremely touchy these days. Health fears, combined with high prices, have resulted in a decline in meat consumption that is expected to continue. Beef producers are particularly concerned, because through the first half of the nineteen-seventies they had happily watched consumption rise to the highest levels ever: in 1976 every American ate an average of nearly 130 pounds of beef. Now that figure has dropped to just over 100 pounds, back to the level of the mid-sixties. Meatmen are understandably wary of the economic implications of this trend. But they are equally upset that now they also must contend with attacks on the healthfulness of meat. Until recently, meat went unquestioned as one of the most important sources of protein and other nutrients. It was one of the pillars of the Basic Four Food Groups that every American was taught to worship. Now a growing number of critics are chipping away at meat's reputation, and they keep finding more cause for concern. The meat industry knows it must aggressively defend its products.

The first strong indication to meatmen that they were in for some trouble came in 1970 when Frances Moore Lappé's book *Diet for a Small Planet* was released. This book complained about the "incredible level of protein waste built into the American meat-centered diet" and raised questions about the tie between America's rich diet and hunger elsewhere in the world. The meat industry quickly dismissed the book as the ravings of a food faddist. Nevertheless, it sold more than a million copies, marking the beginning of a new awareness of diet and nutrition that was to grow during the 1970's.

The next major blow came in 1976, when Senator George McGovern sensed enough concern about the American diet to call for a study by his Senate Select Committee on Human Needs. The committee held hearings and in January 1977 issued a report, "Dietary Goals for the United States." The report was intended to be simply a guide of nutritional information, so neither McGovern nor the staff director in charge of the project expected it to be particularly controversial. But they had overlooked the implications of one brief recommendation. It read: "Decrease consumption of meat."

The meat industry was irate when it found out the government was telling the public not to eat its products. This time, the industry counterattacked. Such groups as the National Cattlemen's Association and the National Livestock and Meat Board pressured McGovern to withdraw the report. McGovern, as the senator from a heavily agricultural state, was vulnerable to the wrath of meat producers, so in the spring of 1977 he called additional hearings. The meat producers presented their attacks, and McGovern's staff members and consumer groups defended the report. "We wrote the report with simple guidelines for meals, and one of the things we wanted to say was eat less meat," recalls Nick Mottern, who was on the McGovern committee staff at the time. "We got away with a lot because nobody knew we were doing it; so the first edition was not touched by politics." Mottern, now an earnest, aging activist with a slight paunch and a scraggly beard, doesn't believe any of the testimony presented at the spring hearings refuting the report's recommendations. But when a revised report was issued that fall, the simple four-word recommendation on meat had been changed. It now read: "Decrease consumption of animal fat and choose meats, poultry and fish which will reduce saturated fat intake." That may not seem like a major difference, but Mottern points out that the idea behind the report was to present information that would be easy for consumers to understand and use. By changing the recommendation, he charges that the staff deliberately obscured the importance of reducing meat consumption and misled the public. He argued vociferously against the change, and when he lost he resigned from the committee staff. "Every time you attempt anything in terms of public information that hurts an interest in the food industry, there's concerted action to cut it off," Mottern says now. "Most people don't realize how information is being manipulated."

"Manipulation" is a strong word, maybe too strong. But the nutritional value of meat is a sensitive topic, and the McGovern incident taught the meat industry to gear up to fight for its products. The industry is now well prepared to marshal its strong lobbying forces both in Washington and in the home districts; legislators from agricultural regions know they will pay a heavy price if they go against the industry position. In addition, the industry has always operated strong educational and public-relations programs to keep Americans thinking positive thoughts about meat. Trade groups are a major provider of educational materials on nutrition (obviously stressing the importance of meat) and they are always looking for new ways to hype their products. In 1980 the California Beef Council asked its members for $4.6 million to fund an advertising and marketing campaign to sell "sensual" beef. "Sex sells everything else," said a spokesman for the council, "so why not beef?"

The industry is also heavily involved in research aimed at reassuring the public that meat is a healthful food. Its experts can point to studies that rebut all the charges of potential health hazards associated with meat. Unfortunately, it is here that the charge of manipulation may not be too strong. Ideally, scientific research should be the objective middle ground where health concerns could be calmly and rationally investigated. But science has fallen prey to politics, and the motives, as well as the results, of research conducted by groups that have chosen up sides on the debate over the healthfulness of meat have become suspect.

There are many subtle ways to bias research or to structure studies so they will support preconceived positions. An industry like the meat industry is in a particularly good position to support research that will tell it what it wants to hear. Scientific research of all types relies on grants from the industries that will be affected, so it should be no surprise that sometimes research can be bent to serve the needs of industry. There can be a tendency for researchers to concentrate on how new technology and new chemicals can serve industry rather than to question whether these new applications of science and technology might have detrimental consequences. In addition, industry can woo researchers and professors with consulting fees and appointments to boards of directors, so it can become difficult for researchers to bite the hand that feeds them. More than a few researchers and professors have found grants and research opportunities hard to come by after their research has gone against industry's position.

One of the most distressing controversies over research surfaced in 1980 when a report, "Toward Healthy Diets," was released by the Food and Nutrition Board, an advisory group of the National Academy of Science. The academy is a respected governmental advisory body originally established by Abraham Lincoln to give the government unbiased advice, but this report badly damaged its reputation. The report concluded that the dangers of cholesterol had been exaggerated: for healthy Americans there is no reason to limit cholesterol and fat intake in an attempt to avoid heart disease. It also questioned the link between diet and health that was at the base of McGovern's "Dietary Goals" and Foreman's "Dietary Guidelines." This was the first high-level study to reject the theory that cholesterol is closely linked to heart disease, and a shocking rejection of the conclusions of most recent research.

Cholesterol is a fatty substance produced by the liver that is essential to the structure of cell membranes and to the production of certain hormones. But it is also carried in the bloodstream, and it has been found to be an ingredient of the waxy atherosclerotic deposits that clog the coronary arteries and cause heart attacks. Foods that are high in cholesterol, such as eggs, beef, pork, cheese, and butter, have therefore become the targets of researchers and nutritionists concerned with limiting the intake of cholesterol. And the meat, dairy, and egg industries, of course, have been anxious to find evidence refuting the cholesterol-heart disease link. When the Food and Nutrition Board report was released, the industry groups were ecstatic. "We are pleased that finally sound science has come back into the arena, rather than politics we've felt we've been in for some time," said Peyton Davis of the National Livestock and Meat Board.

But to others, politics is precisely what the Food and Nutrition Board report reflected. It turns out that several members of the research team that prepared the report were paid consultants to food producers affected by the controversy over cholesterol. The scientist who presented the report to the media was a paid consultant to the egg industry; two more scientists had conducted studies funded by the egg, meat, and dairy industries; and the chairman of the board was a consultant for food companies including Pillsbury and Kraft. The report was immediately attacked by groups ranging from the Consumer Federation to the American Heart Association. The Food and Nutrition Board's own Consumer Liaison Panel disassociated itself from the report. The consumer panel, comprising representatives of consumer and nutrition research groups and government, complained of the conflicts of interest among the researchers and charged that the researchers ignored evidence against cholesterol. "We can only conclude that the board is dominated by a group of change-resistant nutrition scientists who share a rather isolated view about diet and disease," reads a statement from the consumer panel.

Other scientific research organizations have also been attacked for their slavish defenses of industry positions. The most notorious is the Council for Agricultural Science and Technology (CAST), an organization for farmers, agricultural scientists, and industrialists that is based at Iowa State University. It supposedly gathers the best minds from universities across the country to study agricultural issues. But it has been called by detractors the "agro-industry truth squad." Virtually all of its reports back the industry line, and some have sparked divisive internal controversies. For example, in 1978 several academic scientists resigned from a CAST task force studying the use of antibiotics in animal feeds. Six of the scientists signed a sharp letter of protest accusing CAST of omitting from a draft of the final report evidence on the risks associated with drug use. Instead, the report stressed favorable evidence on the benefits of drugs. In a review of the controversy, *Science* magazine noted dryly, "CAST devotes much of its time to showing the federal government why chemicals used on the farm are less dangerous than someone has claimed them to be."

That attitude continues. In 1980, CAST issued "Foods from Animals: Quantity, Quality, and Safety," a report that runs down the laundry list of charges against meat. The report purports to be an objective discussion of the pros and cons, but it is hardly an even-handed look at the serious controversies facing the meat industry. Instead, the report is obviously structured to refute criticisms of meat. To read the report is to learn that all the fears about meat are groundless; it blithely dismisses concerns on such topics as the banned growth stimulant DES ("the cancer risk factor from DES residues in edible beef tissues is essentially zero") and cholesterol ("the research of a quarter century has not clearly confirmed the hypothesis" of a link between cholesterol and heart disease), while hardly acknowledging the substantial body of unfavorable research on these topics.

But none of this should be particularly startling. Meat is undergoing an unprecedented amount of scrutiny, so meatmen must find means to defend their products and their way of life.

At stake are the livelihoods of the men and women responsible for the largest portion of the food dollar—from the farmers growing the grain used to feed the livestock, to the ranchers raising the livestock, to the packers, processors, and supermarkets preparing and selling meat products.

So of course they find research to support their positions and of course they attack those people who question their products. They will fight the Carol Foremans, who are indeed a threat to the way they have traditionally done business. Even Foreman realized her rules and regulations would not be accepted easily by the meat industry. "Most of them force the food producers to change some of their long-cherished practices," Foreman said. "They resist them in every way they can, and some are sure that either they or the consumer will be devastated by them."

Early in 1980, Foreman looked back on the uproar she had caused in the meat industry. "Three years ago some of the farm and food industry was in a total panic about a consumer advocate coming into the department," she said. "I can't see that the food industry isn't better off now than before. And I'm sure the public is." Less than a year later, Foreman was gone, but the concerns she raised about the integrity of the USDA and the healthfulness of meat are very serious, and they won't go away.

8

The Meat-Pricing Rip-Off

Anything, in theory, is open to manipulation, up to the President of the United States being bought off by the Arabs. But that doesn't mean it's going to happen.

—Lester Norton, 1980

Lester I. Norton, a crusty old man in his seventies, is unceremoniously perched atop a chair in his booth in the exposition hall at the 1979 Western States Meat Packers convention. His shirttail is out and his ample belly is protruding as he stretches to tack up one of his signs for the *National Provisioner,* trade organ of the meat industry—"Serving Meat Processors, Purveyors, and Renderers. World's Greatest Readership." Norton seldom misses the conventions of any of the myriad meat industry trade organizations. These get-togethers are the bread and butter of his weekly magazine. He emblazons "WSMPA Show Issue!" or "AMI Pre-Show Issue!" or "AAMP Convention Report Issue!" above the full-page, full-color front-page ads for such products as Brechteen Natural Curvature Casings, the Bettcher Slice-N-Tact, or the Townsend Model 900 Bacon Skinner ("Increase yield skinning up to 1,500 bellies per hour"), and he carries a full report of the proceedings inside.

Norton is the industry's cheerleader. He is the self-appointed spokesman for the meat industry. And he is a powerful force in his own right. In addition to his *National Provisioner,*

151

he also publishes the *National Provisioner Daily Market and News Service,* or, as it is more commonly known, the Yellow Sheet. Because of this daily one-sheet newsletter of meat prices printed on distinctive yellow paper, Lester Norton is a respected and feared man. Some consider him the man with the power to set the price of meat.

After he got his booth in order at this particular convention, Norton donned his rumpled sport coat and headed for the main auditorium to address the conventioneers. His was a familiar face to just about everyone in the audience. They had heard him attack the enemies of the meat industry in speeches and editorials peppered with old bromides and dripping with irony. But this speech would be a little different. As the words dragged out of the right corner of his mouth in his resonant voice, Norton was not lashing out at the enemies of the meat industry; he was lashing out at the enemies of Lester Norton.

Norton has spent much of his time recently defending himself against charges that his Yellow Sheet is inaccurate and outdated. The most serious allegation is that the Yellow Sheet is the tool used by major packers and supermarkets to manipulate meat prices. Norton vehemently denies this and other allegations, and he has been striking back at his critics. But time may be running out on Lester Norton and his Yellow Sheet.

The entranceway walls in the office of William Albanos, Jr., are covered with black-and-white photos of pigs with funny sayings printed underneath. Inside Albanos' personal office there is a big pig cookie jar on top of a file cabinet, several more pigs of various shapes, sizes, and materials on the shelves, and a poster bearing the message "Those who indulge ... Bulge" illustrated with the picture of one exceedingly round pink pig on the wall. Bill Albanos sits behind his desk in a garish, ill-fitting suit with a silver pig pin on the lapel. He is a short, squatty man in his forties with a round boyish face, double chin, and a world-class beer belly. "Hello, da Meat Sheet," he says in his fast, reedy voice with a heavy Chicago accent when he answers the phone. The conversation usually centers on whether steers are steady today, if hogs and picnics are soft, if choice heifers should really be going for 68, and the like.

Albanos is managing director of the *Meat Sheet,* also

known as the Pink Sheet, as opposed to the Yellow Sheet. In this confusing little color-coded world, he is Lester Norton's main competitor. But Norton's power is such that Albanos is a distinctly minor competitor, and he is continually facing financial difficulties. His office is an unimposing collection of rooms at the back end of a light industrial building on the outskirts of the Chicago suburb of Elmhurst. But it's just a couple of miles from Oak Brook, the office-research center where the General Electric Co. has an imposing research and development office. Albanos spends much of his time these days rubbing elbows with these more stylish R/D men, particularly the computer men. Albanos doesn't know too much about computers, although he and his daughter are taking some computer courses at the local junior college. But he's learning fast. Albanos and the GE computer men have come up with an idea that could put Lester Norton and his Yellow Sheet out of business. The question is whether Albanos can stay in business long enough to make it happen.

These two men, Lester Norton and Bill Albanos, may be the most important individuals in the country to everyone who is upset about the price of meat. They are on opposite ends of a struggle over the mechanism used to set the prices of meat products. Norton is trying to hold on to his system, and Albanos is trying to replace it. Their fight has been going on for years, and it will probably be several more before it is resolved. For now, the reality facing everyone who eats meat is that the prices we pay for the meat products we buy every day are made up by a handful of men in a "ramshackle"* brownstone on Chicago's Near North Side—Lester Norton's Yellow Sheet reporters. These men have no space-age computer technology at their disposal to assist their calculations, no panel of economic advisers, not even hard facts. The price consumers pay for meat products is what these men say it will be, and there's little use in asking them why.

Consumers, already groaning under prices that have made

---

*"Yellow Sheet Guides Prices of Meat, but How Reliable Is It?," *Wall Street Journal*, Dec. 6, 1974, and in testimony by William Sellhorst before the subcommittee of Livestock and Grains, House Agriculture Committee, Aug. 6, 1977.

meat the most costly food product, may be paying as much as $1 billion a year extra on their meat bills because of this system. Ralph Nader, who has begun to investigate the situation, says meat prices today result from a "hidden form of price fixing using a third party to bilk millions of dollars a year from consumers at the meat counter. Yet it has received less attention in the press than a corner grocery store burglary." During the past few years, the evidence against the meat pricing system has been mounting. An investigation by the House Committee on Small Business* found that the vast majority of meat prices are "fabricated" † by the Yellow Sheet. The suppressed version of a USDA study of meat pricing states that a few large packers nationwide dominate the pricing system and conceivably have the power to manipulate the market. The study also raises the possibility that these packers may have the power to influence livestock futures trading as well. Another recent USDA report‡ states that information on who is buying and selling meat has become "so scattered, so fragmented, and so limited that it is difficult to say what happened in the market on a given day." A report by the General Accounting Office puts it more simply: meat prices are set in an "information vacuum."

The stakes are high. An increase of just a penny a pound on carcass beef prices means about nine hundred thousand dollars a day to packers nationally. Some critics contend that wholesale prices are routinely pushed up two to five cents per pound. By the time the meat is sold at the supermarket, the overcharge jumps to five to ten cents per pound, costing consumers hundreds of millions of dollars a year. Exactly how much consumers are being ripped off is hard to pinpoint because this curious price-setting mechanism baffles even those in the meat industry who depend upon it every day. The heads of some packing companies will sheepishly admit they don't understand how the Yellow Sheet works. All they know is their meat clears the market each day, and that's good enough for

---

*Information derived from the hearing transcripts of the U.S. House Committee on Small Business, 1977–1980.
†Ibid., May 22, 1978.
‡Report of the USDA Meat Pricing Consultation and Evaluation Group.

them. Meatmen fear change, so they aren't anxious to fiddle with their pricing system. Stll, they know the system has not advanced much beyond the days when the New York Stock Exchange was conducted beneath a tree.

Imagine that the prices quoted on the Stock Exchange were gathered by a few aging men who merely called a few buyers and sellers on the telephone to figure out prices. And imagine that the daily stock tables listed only the closing prices—no highs, no lows, no volume traded. And imagine that everyone buying or selling stock had to agree to accept whatever price would be listed in next week's stock table—with no opportunity to negotiate. Dow Jones would crumble immediately. Yet that is essentially the system that for years has determined the prices ranchers are paid for their livestock, the prices packers charge for carcass meat, and the prices supermarkets charge consumers for everything from roasts to hot dogs.

Lester Norton went to work for the *National Provisioner*, a publication established in 1891 as "A journal of record and information in the interest of packers, provision dealers and auxiliary industries," when he was just seventeen. This was in the early twenties, when the meat industry was in some disarray as the result of a recent court order intended to lessen the domination of the packing industry by the "big four" packers of that era. By 1923, conditions had gotten particularly bad, as Norton recalls in one of his standard speeches. "This was a year of chaotic marketing conditions in the meat industry, when product prices were going through wild gyrations. Identical product was simultaneously selling at ridiculously high and disastrously low prices. Markets were affected by rumor and conjecture, in the absence of trading facts." Major packers such as Thomas Wilson and Oscar Mayer warned that these wild gyrations in prices were threatening the entire industry.

"Conditions demanded that someone with courage and foresight accept the risk and the challenge of helping to bring order out of marketing chaos, so that sensible production, marketing and selling decisions could be made," Norton continues.

"That was when Paul I. Aldrich, who was then president of the *National Provisioner,* decided to accept the challenge. With the help, advice, and encouragement of many, he assembled an operating staff, developed basic reporting and production techniques and launched the service late that year." This was the start of the Yellow Sheet. At first it only listed pork prices, and it could count on only token support from a handful of subscribers. But slowly it grew. The Yellow Sheet was performing a service that was essential to meat traders in need of accurate price information, and over the years it became a dominant force in the industry. It is regarded now as the bible of the meat industry.

Norton was there at the very start, and by 1948 he had worked his way up to become the president of the National Provisioner, Inc., responsible for both the magazine and the Yellow Sheet. He made a name for himself as a spokesman for the industry, and he tirelessly promoted the Yellow Sheet as an objective arbiter of meat prices. "Fact *without bias* is what we consider an apt description of the Daily Yellow Sheet," he would proclaim in speeches at trade association meetings and other meat industry forums in one convention hall after another. "The Yellow Sheet is really simple to define," he told the Cooperative Food Distributors of America in his booming voice.* "It is a price report. A report of the actual prices being paid in the open market for the meat items it quotes. The Yellow Sheet quotes the actual going market at the close of the trading day. Five days a week. The prices we quote are not judgments of what people should ask for meats they want to sell. They are not our opinion of what you should bid for the meats you want to buy. They are not opinions of value. They are not suggestions as to what prices ought to be. The prices we quote are the actual closing prices being paid in the open market—by willing buyers to willing sellers—where neither party is under undue pressure and is negotiating freely in competition with others who are also in the market."

---

*Submitted as testimony before the Joint Economic Committee of Congress, Dec. 12, 1974, p. 59.

If only it were that simple. Despite Norton's oft-repeated disclaimer that his Yellow Sheet is merely a guide to help traders arrive at a fair price for meat products, everyone in the meat industry knows it has become much more than that. The Yellow Sheet, alone, sets the prices for as much as 90 per cent of the meat traded each day; the Yellow Sheet is not a guide, it *is* the price.

When the Yellow Sheet was developing its reputation for "fact *without bias,*" the meat industry was based around the Chicago stockyards, and the trading was fast and furious. It was easy for Norton's reporters to discover all the trades they wanted. But now the stockyards are gone, the meat industry has become decentralized, and finding open-market trades is a difficult task. Most meat buyers don't negotiate directly anymore. Instead, they trade on what is called the "formula basis." They discuss how much meat and what kind of meat they want to trade, but when it comes to deciding the price, they agree to buy "at the sheet": they will pay whatever price is listed in the Yellow Sheet on the day of delivery, plus or minus a penny or so for a few specified variables. It's like agreeing to buy a thousand shares of IBM at whatever is listed as the closing price in the newspaper two weeks from today. Twenty years ago, only a smattering of trades were made on the formula basis. Now, industry sources generally agree that 70 to 90 per cent of all wholesale meat transactions are formula-basis trades. It's a lazy man's device that is hard for a trader to screw up because everyone pays the same basic price. For the industry, it is a simple way to trade large quantities of meat daily. But for the consumer, it can be a rip-off. Critics say the system kills the incentive for buyers to push for the lowest price. "What do you care what you're paying as long as your competitor pays at least the same price?" asks one investigator. And the system places a terrible burden on the Yellow Sheet.

Five days a week, Norton and his men are on the job. In the *National Provisioner*'s offices, past the entranceway wall painted with stylized steers, pigs, and lambs prancing on a yellow background, a group of men wearing headsets sit at desks separated by plywood partitions. Norton says he has a staff of twelve reporters on the phone constantly to meat-packers, meat processors, and meat brokers, gathering the latest pricing information for the Yellow Sheet.* There are four men gathering beef prices, and two more gathering pork prices, and the additional six gather information that is incidental to the Yellow Sheet. For all these men, Norton doesn't have a WATS line, yet he says they are on the phone all day, talking to buyers and sellers across the country, compiling prices in 337 separate categories, from "U.S. Grade Carcasses" to "Beef Variety Meats" to "Skinned Hams," "Bellies," "Picnics," and "Tallows and Greases."

An estimated fifteen thousand meat industry subscribers pay $190 a year to receive the Yellow Sheet. It is an indispensable part of their businesses. But more and more its users complain that the Yellow Sheet is open to manipulation. For large packers, a price swing of only a penny or two a pound can mean millions of dollars in profit, so there's an obvious incentive to try to influence the Yellow Sheet. In fact, critics contend that reporting prices to the Yellow Sheet gets to be a contest, with sellers trying to feed the Yellow Sheet reporters high prices, and buyers low prices, in an attempt to swing the market to their advantage. And since traders are not required to report all their trades, there is an obvious incentive to report only those trades that will do them good.

The process is helped along by the form of the Yellow Sheet. It prints just one price for each item, supposedly the going rate at the end of the trading day, so there is no way to judge how widely prices varied during the day. And the Yellow Sheet doesn't bother to list the volume of trading for each item, so there's no way of knowing whether the price has been set on the basis of the sale of one carload of meat or one hundred. Few meatmen deny that from time to time the market makes some highly suspicious swings, but with the sketchy information provided by the Yellow Sheet, it's virtually impossible to prove the swings are manipulated.

However, meatmen agree that there are several standard

---

*Telephone interview with Norton, July 31, 1978.

schemes that can be used to try to influence the market. One of them is known as the "packer-to-packer highball." Essentially, the way it works is that if a packer knows he will be selling a large quantity of meat on the basis of the Yellow Sheet price for a specific day, he will try to push up the Yellow Sheet price for that day by buying a couple of small loads of meat from another packer at an inflated price and reporting the sale to the Yellow Sheet. Just a two-cent rise in the Yellow Sheet price could mean an eighty-thousand-dollar bonanza on a one-hundred-carload sale. There are numerous variations on this scheme, as well as other schemes, and then there is the option of ignoring the Yellow Sheet completely: if a packer fears a particular trade will adversely affect his position in the market, he can simply stipulate that the trade not be reported to the Yellow Sheet. Lester Norton cannot require packers to report all their trades, so no matter how hard his reporters try, they are helpless if packers won't cooperate. Meatmen know these things happen, and they grumble about the Yellow Sheet from time to time, but when anyone suggests they do something about the situation, they just shrug. This is an old-time, change-resistant industry, and few want to mess with the traditional ways of doing business.

Lester Norton gets irate when he hears these charges of manipulation. "You have a perishable product, and the law of supply and demand is certainly operating full tilt in this industry," he says. "The market is very sensitive, it seems to fluctuate properly in accordance with supply and demand, and nobody has any problem trading in it."

However, during the past decade the Yellow Sheet has been the target of a barrage of complaints from within the industry as well as from government. At least one packer has been forced to sign a consent order to stop manipulative practices, and many more have been fingered by fellow packers. Norton has been called before the House-Senate Joint Economic Committee, the House Agriculture Committee, the House Committee on Small Business, and a USDA task force, among others, to defend his pricing apparatus. At these hearings he would repeat his convictions about "fact *without bias.*"

He would be questioned about how many trades his reporters were actually finding and, therefore, how many trades were actually setting meat prices. There have long been fears that the Yellow Sheet was setting prices for the bulk of meat trades based on very little information. Norton was able to turn aside all these fears.

Then, on May 22, 1978, Nick Wultich stood before his charts set up in the conference room of the House Committee on Small Business. He is a tall, scraggy man, and his balding head was bent slightly forward as he peered over his glasses to make his points to the congressmen. Dressed in his standard austere black suit set off against his white shirt and black-and-white-striped tie accented by a white handkerchief peaking out of his coat pocket, he slowly picked away at his prey. In a voice reminiscent of Eliot Ness, Wultich, chief investigator for the committee and a former FBI white-collar-crime specialist, was presenting the findings of his year-long investigation into the operations of the meat industry's pricing system and the Yellow Sheet. "I would describe it," he told the congressmen, "as a mess. During the period of the last several months, I would say I have talked to close to a hundred people, and that covers everyone from the cowboy out there to the big packers," he said in his deep, clipped voice. "Basically, the story is the same. They are cornered." They are cornered, Wultich told the congressmen, by a system based on the work of Norton's handful of men in that "ramshackle old brownstone."* Wultich found that these men who were supposed to be monitoring meat prices were actually fabricating meat prices.

Studying the actual work sheets used by the Yellow Sheet reporters to record the trades they were calling all over the country to uncover, Wultich checked the Yellow Sheet's accuracy. He found it to be woeful. An average of 75 per cent of the time, prices were quoted in the Yellow Sheet even though the reporters had been unable to uncover any trades; the reporters set prices on absolutely no information. And these prices without trades to back them up changed from day to day: 569 prices changed over a twenty-five-day period despite the

*Op. cit., p. 153.

fact that no trades had been reported. An additional 5 per cent of the quoted prices did not jibe with what the reporters had recorded on their work sheets. So on the average, Wultich said, 80 per cent of the prices quoted each day were in effect fabricated by the Yellow Sheet reporters. He concluded that there was only one time when the Yellow Sheet reporters were providing useful information. "They were of most guidance to the public," Wultich said, "when they reported they didn't know the price."

Along with his findings of inaccuracy, Wultich found that the prices reported in the Yellow Sheet—even when they were backed up by trades—were based on minuscule volumes of trading. An average of only 4 per cent of the total trades daily were surveyed by the Yellow Sheet reporters, which Wultich warned was an inadequate sample. In fact, subsequent studies by the USDA, the General Accounting Office, and others have confirmed the fact that there is an extremely "thin" market of negotiated trades. The Yellow Sheet is trying to do an impossible task, because even if it were to uncover every openly negotiated trade, there may not be enough of these trades anymore to provide reliable pricing information for the rest of the industry. When Wultich had finished, Congressman Neal Smith of Iowa, chairman of the committee and a major crusader for meat industry reform, summed up the situation: "All concerned in the multibillion-dollar meat industry are now faced with the fact that prices are being determined noncompetitively, virtually in the upstairs room of a Chicago trade publication building, rather than in an open, competitive process."

This was the first solid evidence against the Yellow Sheet, and since then Smith and others have pushed hard to reform the meat industry's pricing system. Even the reluctant USDA has been dragged into the fight. The USDA, particularly its Packers and Stockyards Administration, should have been the agency keeping tabs on the Yellow Sheet all along. Instead, it has been an apologist for the meat industry's pricing system, and it has turned its back on the mounting complaints. It has extensive powers to police meat trading, yet it seldom uses them. It has heard charges of manipulation for years, yet it has never charged a packer with attempting to manipulate the Yellow Sheet. In addition, the USDA operates its own price-reporting service with a staff and budget many times larger than Lester Norton's, but its reporters are considered incompetent and the price report is considered to be little more than a joke in the meat industry.

It wasn't until Smith's committee findings made head-lines that the USDA was forced to recognize the serious defi-ciencies of the meat industry's pricing system. Finally, the Packers and Stockyards Administration commissioned a study of beef pricing, but when it was completed in late 1978,* it was suppressed and three thousand copies were ordered destroyed. The official reason given was that some of the data were incorrect. But, one of the few copies of that original report that escaped the shredder tells a different story. The original report, obtained by the authors, has virtually all of the same data as the revised version that was finally released a few months later. † Missing from the revised report are critical comments pointing out the grave pricing problems. The original report supports Wultich's findings that the Yellow Sheet set prices even when no trades had been reported. It also points out that the number of trades used to set prices in each category was either "none or small"; at no time were more than seven trades found to determine the market in any one category.

In addition, the report states that eight major packers nationwide provided more than half the information used by the Yellow Sheet, indicating that they could have a disproportion-ate influence over prices. Those eight packers were also heavily involved in cattle futures trading, and the report suggests a possible link between control of the Yellow Sheet prices and control of livestock futures prices. Unfortunately, by the time a revised version of the report was finally released, all that was left were a few innocuous statements, such as "From price analy-sis it could not be concluded that, on the average, prices quoted

---

*"Beef Pricing Investigation," USDA Agricultural Marketing Service, Oct. & Dec., 1978.
†Ibid.

by the Yellow Sheet inaccurately reflect the sample of negotiated prices," and "There was no strong evidence that the
Yellow Sheet quotes, on the average, fail to reflect prices logged
in by reporters." These conclusions only serve to cover up the
problems. As an editorial in the Yellow Sheet's competitor, the
Meat Sheet, cleverly pointed out, the statements "seem to
indicate that there was evidence, although not strong, on the
average. Does this mean that it was strong, occasionally, or that
it was weak, or what?" Since the report was issued, the USDA
has been forced to be a bit more forthcoming in its recognition
of the sad state of meat pricing, but it is still reluctant to do
anything to improve the situation.

Meanwhile, the Yellow Sheet is being attacked on another
front. It's common knowledge that cattle buyers use the Yellow
Sheet to help determine what they will offer cattlemen for their
livestock. While many cattlemen go along with the system, a
vocal minority charges that the major packers and supermarket
chains use the Yellow Sheet to rig prices, shortchanging them in
the process. Sixteen suits filed by more than a thousand cattle
raisers throughout the Midwest and West have been consolidated in federal court in Dallas, naming as defendants or co-
conspirators eighteen of the largest supermarket chains, four of
the largest packers, and the Yellow Sheet. The suits charge that
they are partners in a conspiracy to depress the price cattlemen
are paid for their livestock and to raise the price consumers pay
for meat. The way the scheme allegedly works is that the major
packers and supermarkets report artificially low prices to the
Yellow Sheet early in the week when they are buying live
animals for slaughter. Then, at the end of the week when the
packers are selling the slaughtered products and the supermarkets are establishing prices to the consumer, they report
high prices to the Yellow Sheet, pushing up the cost to
consumers.

There is a precedent for the suits, because in 1975 the
Great Atlantic & Pacific Tea Co. was found liable for $32.7
million in damages by a federal jury in San Francisco for
conspiring to fix high retail prices and low wholesale prices for
meat (the judgment was later reduced to $9 million in an

out-of-court settlement). Although the Yellow Sheet was not
a defendant in that case, the evidence proved that, at the very
least, the Yellow Sheet was an example of an "otherwise legitimate endeavor that may be manipulated to exploit an illegal
design."*

The Dallas suits may push the link further. The campaign
for these suits is led by Glenn Freie, the short, barrel-chested
Iowa farmer who heads the Meat Price Investigators Association, the group of five hundred midwestern cattlemen taking on
the giants of the meat industry. In testimony before a variety of
congressional and other governmental bodies, Freie has pressed
the case. He says his group has developed evidence showing
that, at the very least, livestock producers are being paid six
cents per pound less for their animals than they should. As for
consumers, Freie says there have been periods when supermarkets "could have shaved 20 per cent off of the price they
were charging you, the consumer, and still had a very, very fine
return."

Not all cattlemen agree with Freie; in fact, many vigorously *oppose* his activities. But Freie is continually bending the
ears of elected officials, farmers, packers, and anyone else who
will listen. "It takes two things to control the beef market—
superior power and superior information," he says in his
standard presentation. "The supermarkets and the packers
control the marketing system of beef in the United States today.
They have the market power. They also control the information
on beef prices." Freie maintains that the Yellow Sheet was
established at the request of the leading packers, and it has
always been "the packers' sheet."

Lester Norton has not taken all this criticism well. During
the past few years, he has increased his attacks on his detractors and his defenses of the Yellow Sheet. The editorials
that lead off many issues of his magazine are often filled with
name-calling and attacks on his enemies. At the trade association meetings and government hearing he attends these days,

---

*From the order of Judge Oliver J. Carter in Bray v. Safeway *et al.*, U.S.
District Court, San Francisco, 1975.

he takes the offensive against all his critics. One of his strongest speeches came in 1979 at the annual Western States Meat Packers convention. In one speech, he was able to neatly tie together all of his detractors.

Norton, still a spry old man, mounted the podium and spoke of his enemies in a deep resonant voice with a sarcastic tinge. Topping the list was Congressman Smith, his most persistent critic, whose hearings have done the most to damage the credibility of the Yellow Sheet. He characterized Smith's hearings as "carefully planned and programmed." He accused Smith and his aides of "hiding behind a cloak of Congressional immunity that enables them to slander and distort without concern for the consequences." Even witnesses "are encouraged to make outrageous statements for reporters to seize upon," he said. Nick Wultich, Smith's investigator, didn't fare any better in Norton's estimation. As far as Wultich's investigation disclosing the incompetence of the Yellow Sheet was concerned, Norton responded that Wultich knew nothing about meat marketing or reporting and didn't understand the papers he was working with. "He put on a vivid demonstration of incompetence while posing as an expert," Norton pointed out. None of which, he charged, deterred him from putting "deceptive and slanderous testimony on the record." In all, Norton charged that for Smith's investigations into the Yellow Sheet and the meat industry, he deserved "the Christopher Columbus Government Planning Award ... in honor of old Chris, the greatest forward planner of all time. When he started, he didn't know where he was going. When he arrived, he didn't know where he was. When he got back, he didn't know where he had been. And he did it all with someone else's money."

When the laughing quieted down, Norton moved on, taking apart the Bray case, the 1975 San Francisco decision in which A&P was found guilty of conspiring to fix meat prices. He harped about a U.S. Justice Department review of the case that questioned the decision, and then lamented that the case set the stage for all the attacks to follow. He called the Bray decision a monstrous miscarriage of justice that nevertheless mobilized the Yellow Sheet's detractors. "People with names like Smith and Hawkins . . . teamed up in the hopes of harassing people into lawsuit settlements," Norton said, linking them to the Meat Sheets and Market News Services who saw a chance to attract attention as did politicians seeking publicity and reporters looking for something to sensationalize. "Bray brought them all crawling out from behind the woodwork," he concluded.

Now he had tied everyone together. There was Glenn Freie and his Meat Price Investigators Association, "whose theories on agricultural economics are right out of *Alice in Wonderland*," and their attorney, Lex Hawkins. "Having proved they couldn't make money raising cattle, they wanted to see if they could make money in court," he said. There was Bill Albanos and his *Meat Sheet.* "The *Meat Sheet* found that selling subscriptions on merit was a slow process, so they decided to see if they could speed up the process by creating distrust of the Yellow Sheet." Norton charged that the *Meat Sheet* even hoodwinked respected *Wall Street Journal* reporter Jonathan Kwitny into printing an exposé of the techniques used to manipulate the Yellow Sheet. "It was Bray and the *Meat Sheet*'s slandering of the Yellow Sheet that led Hawkins and his rag-tail band of agricultural ignoramuses into trying to get bailed out of the bad business decisions they had made because they didn't know the live-stock business," he said. There was one final tie-in. He pointed out that Smith and Hawkins were law school classmates from Des Moines, and that Hawkins was a former State Finance chairman of the Democratic Party in Iowa. "He has helped Smith get elected. He has raised money for Smith's election campaigns. He holds plenty of political I.O.U.'s. Some are surely Smith's," he said.

It was a virtuoso performance of attacking the congress-men, attorneys, reporters, farmers, and others who had dared to question the Yellow Sheet. When it was done, Norton opened the floor to questions so that he could candidly clear up any other misconceptions and misrepresentations about his Yellow Sheet. The first questioner asked Norton to reconcile conflicting statements he had made regarding the critical question of the Yellow Sheet's accuracy. He had stated repeatedly, even under oath, that the Yellow Sheet was accurate because his reporters wrote down absolutely every trade they uncovered; but once doubt was cast on how many trades his reporters were actually finding, he started responding that his reporters kept some of the trades in their heads. Which statement was right? He tried to sidestep the question, and when that didn't work he concluded, "I don't think this is the proper forum to go into it." The moderator stepped in and abruptly ended the question-and-answer session after only one question and no answers. Some of the packers in the audience could be heard grumbling.

However, the questions about the Yellow Sheet will not go unanswered, so Norton must continue his defenses. In the process, he and his Yellow Sheet are becoming an embarrassment to some of the powers of the meat industry. While these powers still publicly support him, privately they wish he would just shut up and go away. Norton is as much a victim of the decline of the meat industry's pricing system as anyone else. Few doubt that he is sincerely dedicated to his quest for "fact *without bias*." But many doubt that there can be any such thing today. The pricing system based on the Yellow Sheet is collapsing, while Lester Norton tries to hold on a few more years.

It is amazing that the second largest manufacturing and processing industry in the country still depends on Lester Norton's group to set meat prices. Equally amazing is another pricing mechanism that may have a bearing on the prices we pay for meat. This one is even less understood and less rational: commodities trading, also known as futures trading.

While Norton's men are at their phones on Chicago's Near North Side, hundreds of younger men are in two trading pits downtown screaming at one another. These are the futures traders at the Chicago Mercantile Exchange and the Chicago Board of Trade. They are buying and selling cattle and hogs that haven't even been born yet, and that none of them wants to own anyway. They are moving prices up and down from day to day for even less reason than Norton's men, and for the most part they couldn't care less what the effect might be on farmers, packers, or consumers. They are only out for a quick buck, and they don't really care if the commodity is frozen pork bellies, feeder cattle, heating oil, or silver.

Futures trading is the arcane sport of betting on what the

price of some commodity will be several months, or even years, in the future. Speculators have found that the commodity markets can be extremely volatile, and thus a perfect place to gamble under the guise of serious investing. The commodities markets were brought into the headlines in 1980 when it was said two Texan brothers, Nelson Bunker Hunt and W. Herbert Hunt, almost cornered the silver market, sending silver prices skyrocketing. Then they almost went bankrupt when the market turned on them. The Hunt episode raised serious questions about the worth of futures trading and the potential for a few people, or even one person, to take control of a particular market and dictate the price of that commodity to everyone else.

All of this is not what commodity trading was supposed to be about. Years ago, the commodity markets were places where contracts for grain and soybeans and other perishables were bought and sold with the idea that some months down the line the products would actually be delivered to the contract holder. It was a tool for farmers to "hedge" their investment in their crop or livestock. The farmer fearful of being wiped out by bad weather or a wrong turn in prices could use futures contracts to "lock in" a price for his product, guaranteeing himself a profit or minimizing his loss. And the people buying produce and livestock could do the same. But speculators found that the commodity markets could move up and down quite quickly, so it could be great fun to play these wide swings for quick killings. Now, speculators greatly outnumber true "hedgers": by some estimates only 5 to 20 per cent of the traders are using the markets for this originally intended purpose. In recent years the commodities markets have expanded considerably into some rather bizarre areas. There are traders speculating on wine vintages, there is serious consideration about setting up futures trading in Dow-Jones stock quotes, and there is even talk about trading futures contracts on the weather. Can a futures contract on jelly beans be far behind?

What effect these futures prices have on the actual cash prices of the product is a matter of much debate. There are disturbing implications that manipulators can play cash and futures prices off against each other to make a bundle. Trading in cattle futures has been particularly suspect. Some critics charge that large packers control futures prices, using their extensive market information and buying power to run them up and down at will. The suppressed version of the 1978 USDA* report investigating the Yellow Sheet pricing system raised precisely that possibility. The report suggested there could be a link between control of Yellow Sheet prices and control of livestock futures trading. In one instance, the report found that eight major national packers, who provided more than half of the information used by the Yellow Sheet to set prices, were also heavily involved in cattle futures trading. After one of the few days all eight of the packers did not report any trades to the Yellow Sheet, the cash market declined. That same day the futures market followed suit, and the packers liquidated their futures contracts for a combined profit of $822,780. The report doesn't allege that there was anything illegal about these activities, but it points out they were at least a disturbing coincidence that should be studied further. The findings were particularly alarming to some critics, who have even suggested that cattle futures trading should be eliminated. Congressman Neal Smith said at the time the findings indicate that there could be strong incentives for major packers to manipulate the futures prices. "The fact of the matter is that they can make twice as much in the futures market as they could in a slaughter operation," Smith said. Then, in 1981, Smith uncovered a more shocking flaw. He revealed a scheme that could be used to predict "with 100 per cent accuracy" when the futures market would turn. "This is operating with such clockwork that someone trading with this system could have made at least $4.7 million over the last three years," Smith said.† "Some people did make profits of that amount." He said 32 large futures traders were able to reap profits totalling $110 million by selling their futures contracts at just the right time.

Smith is not alone in fearing potentially manipulative schemes. In 1979 the House Government Operations Subcommittee on Commerce, Consumer, and Monetary Affairs, headed

---

*Op. cit., p. 162.
†Press conference by Smith on Feb. 27, 1981, Washington, D.C.

by New York congressman Benjamin Rosenthal, charged that major packers were interfering with both the Yellow Sheet and the futures market. The scenario Rosenthal found goes like this: A few packers depressed the wholesale market by reporting artificially low prices to the Yellow Sheet; farmers then sold cattle cheaply and quickly because they were afraid the market would go even lower, causing the futures market to decline also. The packers who had started the downward trend bought futures contracts at the lowered prices and then bought large quantities of cattle, driving up the futures prices; the packers then sold their futures contracts for a quick profit; and then they manipulated the Yellow Sheet upward again. It is a tortuous process, and it is one that is extremely difficult to prove. Commodity-exchange officials adamantly maintain that critics like Smith and Rosenthal simply don't know what they're talking about. "If even a large combination of interests got together to try to manipulate prices, the effect of their efforts in our large, active cattle market would be erased within minutes," says Clayton Yeutter, president of the Chicago Mercantile Exchange. "There is just no feasible way to manipulate a market of that magnitude."

But from time to time the wholesale and futures markets both make some inexplicable swings, and the charges of manipulation are brought out once again. Several packers have been accused of possibly manipulative practices, although none have been caught red-handed. Several meat brokers have been disciplined for possibly manipulative actions in both futures and wholesale trading. and at least one high-level official has been forced to resign by the nation's largest packer, Iowa Beef Processors, Inc., after it was disclosed that he was trading on the futures market while also handling wholesale marketing for Iowa Beef.

The impact on consumers of all this screaming in the trading pits is still uncertain. Futures trading may be no more than a bizarre game that moves prices up one day and down the next with no long-term impact. But there is little hope of determining when futures prices are out of line until they can be judged against rational, dependable cash price information. And there is little hope of building confidence in cash prices until there is something better than the Yellow Sheet to do the job.

Although the Yellow Sheet is unquestionably the bible of the meat industry, it has always faced competition. Even before the Yellow Sheet was born, the USDA was putting out its Market News Service, but its influence has always been minimal. For a while there was a Red Sheet, which, some claim, was copied and then forced out of business by the Yellow Sheet. And now there is the Pink Sheet. Officially, it's the *Meat Sheet*, but it is just as commonly known by the color of the paper it has been printed on since shortly after it was begun. The *Meat Sheet* is Bill Albanos' challenge to the Yellow Sheet, and Albanos may be the man responsible for putting Lester Norton's Yellow Sheet under.

Bill Albanos, the short, squatty man with the pig pin on his lapel, is somewhat new to the price-reporting business, but not to the meat industry. His introduction to the industry came in the Army, where he started out as a venereal-disease inspector and moved on to become a meat inspector. For five years he served in the Army Veterinary Corps, and when he left the military he set up his own consulting firm to teach packers how to work with the military. Later he went to work for Dubuque Packing Co., overseeing its pork-processing and distribution operations in Chicago. Soon he opened his own pork plant, and before long he was doing $20 million in business. He was so successful that Dubuque eventually bought him out to eliminate the competition, and Albanos went back to work for his old company. But in 1974 there was a disagreement, and Albanos decided to go out on his own once again.

Like most meatmen, he had complained about the Yellow Sheet over the years. "I parallel this with the old cliché that when two Greeks meet on the street they talk about opening up a restaurant," Albanos says from his pig-infested office. "Well, when two meat people meet on the corner, they talk about the Yellow Sheet and how bad it is, how there should be an alternative, and how we're forced to use it." Albanos decided to take on the Yellow Sheet. He doesn't have much of a formal education, and he is undeniably rough around the edges. But in his own way he is an articulate, intelligent man with deep insights into the pricing problems of the American meat industry. He knew the inadequacies of the Yellow Sheet, and he knew there was money to be made if he could come up with something better. He mounted a slow but steady campaign to expose the failings of the Yellow Sheet and establish his *Meat Sheet* as a viable alternative.

The first issue of the *Meat Sheet* was distributed on August 2, 1974, and it wasn't long after that before Albanos found out that his challenge would not be appreciated by Norton. "It has just come to our attention that you have recently begun publication of a competing meat price reporting service which is unfairly and confusingly similar to our service in appearance, format, size, yellow color, masthead location and alignment, and name," read a letter to Albanos from Norton. "The obvious effect of the design of your service, if not the calculated intent, is to deceive a reasonable user in the trade into believing that your service is or may be ours, and to appropriate to your service, unfairly and illegally, to our damage, the reputation, good-will and business that has been built up and identified uniquely with our service over a long period of time and at great expense." If changes were not made, Norton warned, the Yellow Sheet would take "more formal action" to protect itself against the "unfair competition" of the *Meat Sheet.*

There was no denying that the *Meat Sheet* was patterned after the Yellow Sheet in form and content. And the color of those first issues was suspiciously similar too, although Albanos indignantly insists his color was "ivory," not yellow. He agreed to change the color once the original stock of paper ran out, and soon it became known as the Pink Sheet. The pink paper gave it a separate identity, and Albanos made sure the meat industry recognized the other significant differences between his sheet and the Yellow Sheet. The *Meat Sheet* listed several meat products not included in the Yellow Sheet; it included the volume of trading and the high and low prices for the day in addition to the closing prices; and it separated from the rest of the trades the "packer-to-packer" transactions—the ones most prone to manipulation. Albanos told everyone who would listen that these changes made his *Meat Sheet* a more reliable price sheet. He said his prices were not necessarily higher or lower than the ones Norton reported, but they were presented in a more useful fashion and his reporters were more accurate. Albanos' *Meat Sheet* won the respect of many in the meat industry, but that did not translate into great acceptance as a pricing tool. While many meatmen told Albanos they liked his sheet, they also told him they were locked into using the Yellow Sheet and they weren't about to rock the boat. "I've had thousands say they would like to use the *Meat Sheet*," Albanos says, "but they say the other traders won't, so they can't." Albanos' contention was confirmed in a survey by the California Public Interest Research Group (CalPIRG). As one meat buyer told CalPIRG, he thought the *Meat Sheet* was more accurate, but he used the Yellow Sheet because "meat packers won't have anything to do with the other sheets."

From the start, Norton and Albanos went head to head. Or maybe belly to belly. They both engaged in petty bad-mouthing to discredit each other. In one memorable case of overkill, Norton lashed out at two New England trade associations who passed a harmless resolution suggesting that packers use both the Yellow Sheet and the *Meat Sheet* when determining prices. "It is your privilege to take the risks that might go with such activity," read an ominous letter from Norton to the New England Wholesale Meat Dealers Association. "Whatever your motives and however innocent your resolution may be in fact, there will be inevitable suspicions of impropriety and price fixing read into your resolution." The wholesalers had passed the resolution after a meeting with Albanos, so Norton concluded that they only made their decision "at the urging of an opportunist more concerned with his survival than your welfare."

For his part, Albanos kept a list of everything Norton had done to "harass" him. Albanos and a partner told a congressional committee that even before the *Meat Sheet* started publishing, Norton tried to pressure meat brokers to stay away from it: Norton's employees warned the brokers that they wouldn't be as friendly and they would take away the brokers' free subscriptions to the Yellow Sheet if they went to a cocktail party for the *Meat Sheet*. Albanos also complained about the time

Norton's *National Provisioner* magazine refused to accept an ad for the *Meat Sheet*. But Albanos had some more substantial avenues of attack as well. He hammered away at the inadequacies of the Yellow Sheet and of the meat industry's pricing system in general. In fact, he shares much of the responsibility for bringing attention to the sad state of meat pricing. But that has put him in an awkward position. At the same time he has been tearing down the Yellow Sheet, he has been trying to establish his own publication based on the same archaic system. It's a ludicrous situation, and Albanos knows it. "The *Meat Sheet* and the Yellow Sheet work by this system which is antiquated, lousy, and indefensible," he admits. "It's the only thing that operates today, but you cannot defend it."

Ultimately, Albanos has no desire to defend the system, or even his *Meat Sheet*. He wants to replace them both. While he has been struggling to keep his *Meat Sheet* afloat, he has also been promoting the American Meat Exchange, Inc. This is a proposed computerized marketing system for the meat industry that could make both the Yellow Sheet and the *Meat Sheet* obsolete.

For the past decade, as the evidence against the Yellow Sheet has been building, support for electronic, computerized marketing of meat has been building as well. To its proponents, electronic trading may be the only way to guarantee farmers, packers, and consumers fair meat prices. A 1979 USDA report concludes that electronic marketing "could provide a most efficient device for negotiating transactions. It could provide the most competitive market that is conceivable for the wholesale products that provide the cash receipts for a most important segment of American agriculture—that of livestock production." Secretary of Agriculture John Block and former secretary Bob Bergland are both on record as supporting at least a test of electronic marketing. But several serious obstacles must be overcome before it can be accepted. The first problem is the meat industry's traditional resistance to change. Secondly, meatmen fear that electronic marketing will bring with it government supervision. At one USDA hearing on electronic marketing a representative for a livestock association spoke for many throughout the meat industry when he said "cattlemen distrust Government even more than they distrust Lester

Norton." Thirdly, and most important, the largest packer, Iowa Beef Processors, Inc., opposes electronic marketing. The other large packers are not exactly thrilled about the concept either, but they have at least agreed to give it a try, if only for public relations. The major packers are in a position to dominate the present system, guaranteeing themselves the most favorable prices, so there is no incentive for them to back something that gives the other guys a better chance. The major packers have postponed development of electronic marketing by questioning the operational aspects and painting proponents such as Albanos as mere opportunists only out to make a buck at the expense of the rest of the industry.

For the past several years, Albanos has been trying to overcome these obstacles. Working with economists at the University of Illinois and computer experts at the General Electric Co., he has developed a system that may be the one best suited to the meat industry's needs. He has been cajoling packers, supermarkets, and government officials to test it. He has slowly built a group of staunch backers, as well as a group of skeptics who are at least willing to give it a try. Under his system meat traders, linked by computer terminals with video display screens, would be able to negotiate complicated trades and consult up-to-the-minute information on meat prices. One rap detractors have given electronic marketing is that it isn't flexible enough for meat, a perishable commodity that traders must either "sell or smell." But the Albanos system, if anything, expands the flexibility because it could give traders a broader range of potential buyers and allow them to consummate numerous transactions in the time it would take to complete just one trade under the present system. It would be, in effect, an electronic stockyard, bringing together traders scattered over a wide area. Proponents argue that this electronic trading system would reverse the trend toward formula trading and once again make meat a commodity that is traded through open negotiation. The benefits would be more competitive prices and, since the computer system would record every single trade, more accurate trading information available to all. The system wouldn't guarantee lower meat prices, but it would guarantee that there would be some reason behind prices.

Each year, Albanos moves closer to making electronic

trading for the meat industry a reality. Each year he is able to dispel more of the fears about electronic trading and convince a few more meatmen of its benefits. But at the same time, Albanos can still be heard repeating one of his favorite sayings: "Help me, I'm dying." Albanos' fight has kept him continually on the brink of financial disaster. The Yellow Sheet's dominance is still strong enough that the number of subscriptions to Albanos' *Meat Sheet* hardly pays the bills. And he is in a constant fight to hunt up grants and backers for his American Meat Exchange. The day when his new system will be a success seems to be approaching, but there are still too many days when he fears the money will finally run out. "I could have stopped fifty times already," he says. "It's a miracle I'm still around." He pauses to reflect on the struggle, and then adds, "It's more than a miracle." But he intends to keep pushing. "Every day I'm here is one more nail in the coffin of this old system," he says. "The only question is whether I have enough nails and enough time."

If he succeeds, he will supplant a man he has been fighting for nearly a decade, although the two men have never actually met. Albanos and Norton go to the same trade shows and testify before the same government hearings, but they have never spoken. "I've tried to say hi," Albanos says, "but he just looks the other way." Still, Albanos has a grudging respect for this cantankerous old-timer who has been a fixture in the meat industry for so many years. There are times when he seems to be in awe of Norton, just as some young ballplayer might be in awe of the aging superstar who has lost a step and needs to come out of the lineup. "I hope I can be as strong-willed on this thing as Lester Norton has been," Albanos says. "I just don't want to be as blind."

9
The General Motors of the Meat Industry

Well, kid, I have other expenses too. There are three kinds. I pay meat buyers off at 15 per cent. I pay union people off at 7 per cent. And it costs me 10 per cent to convert the corporate money to cash, and I have to deal in cash.

—Moe Steinman, explaining his services to Iowa Beef

As far back as the Depression, Currier Holman was complaining about how terribly inefficient the meat-packing industry was. This tall, rangy Sioux City, Iowa, boy was working his first real job at the town's Swift & Co. plant in the early 1930's. It wasn't much of a job—he was stripping the guts and offal from freshly slaughtered carcasses in the "gut shanty"—but in the Depression you took what you could get. In an interview with *Meat Processing* magazine in 1975, he recalled his first night on the job: "About one o'clock in the morning I was hauling a barrel of sheep guts—or what was left of them—over to the rendering works. In the process of moving them from one department to the other on the barrel truck over a slippery floor, I lost my footing and down we went—barrel, guts, and me. I came up on the bottom and the contents of the barrel came up on top. I pulled myself out of that awful mess, leaned against a column and cried real tears. I was tired, all alone on my first night doing clean-up in that big plant."

It was hardly a pleasant welcome to the meat industry, but it would have taken much more to discourage Currier Holman. This was a man of intense confidence, drive, and vision. From the start he saw the gross inefficiencies in the traditional methods of meat-packing, and he talked about them to anyone who would listen. He knew he could do a better job if he ever got the chance. It would be nearly thirty years before that chance came, but when it did, he made the most of it: Currier Holman took over the American meat-packing industry. Unfortunately, his drive to power was marred by Mafia influence, labor unrest, and charges of conspiracy, predatory practices, and monopolization.

There has always been something ominous about giant meat-packers. Back at the turn of the century, Upton Sinclair's hardworking Jurgis Rudkus was awed by the sinister power of the packers in *The Jungle*: "He had learned by this time that Packingtown was really not a number of firms at all, but one great firm, the Beef Trust. And every week the managers of it got together and compared notes, and there was one scale for all the workers in the yards and one standard of efficiency. Jurgis was told that they also fixed the price they would pay for beef on the hoof and the price of all dressed meat in the country; but that was something he did not understand or care about."

By 1920, the real-life Beef Trust, the "big four" packers of that day—Swift, Armour, Wilson, and Cudahy—had become so powerful that the federal government was forced to step in and break up their monopoly. As the result of a consent decree signed by the packers and a new Packers and Stockyards Act, the meat industry became a model of fair competition during the next several decades. But it also became a complacent industry. The meat industry today is in many ways an old-fashioned industry that has not advanced much since the Depression. The dominant justification for business practices has been, "What was good enough for my daddy and my granddaddy is good enough for me." That goes for the small farmer raising fifty head of cattle and for the big-name packers. Now they are all finding that the old ways won't do anymore. A few farsighted packers who were willing to innovate and modernize the packing business have taken over, and it may be too late for the others to catch up. Startling evidence of the changing order of the meat industry came in 1980 when Swift—for years the nation's largest packer—was dumped by its conglomerate owners because of a declining bottom line. The other packers with the old familiar names slide farther down the list of major packers each year. They are being replaced by a few faceless companies with names like IBP and MBPXL who can produce meat more quickly, cheaply, and efficiently than the old-line packers. They may be the new Beef Trust.

Chief among them is Iowa Beef Processors, Inc. This is the firm founded just over twenty years ago by Currier Holman and a few backers who shared his vision of revolutionizing the packing industry. It is now the world's largest packer. It is the unquestioned king of the beef-slaughtering business, controlling about one out of every seven head of cattle slaughtered. And during the 1980's it is expected to come to dominate the pork business as well. Iowa Beef broke into the *Fortune* 500 within two and a half years of the day it slaughtered its first steer, and by 1979 it was seventy-seventh on *Fortune*'s list of industrial corporations—ahead of such firms as General Dynamics, General Mills, Johnson & Johnson, and Uniroyal. It sells some $10 to $15 million worth of beef a day. Its annual sales are in the $4.6 billion range, and its profits after taxes are nearing $50 million.

The rise to power of Currier Holman's Iowa Beef has come at a furious pace, but every step has been marked by controversy. Although it has won high praise for its innovations and the quality of its products, it has not won praise for its methods. Iowa Beef is known as a ruthless, humorless organization that is bent on growing ever larger and more dominant. The attitude was shaped by Currier Holman, a man of ambitious dreams. But as a New York judge was to remark, he was also a man who sold his soul to the devil to make his dreams come true.

After those first nights in the gut shanty, Currier Holman stayed with Swift for several years, and then he moved on to another major packer, Armour, where he became a cattle buyer. Soon enough he went off on his own, working through the forties and early fifties as a cattle buyer based at the Sioux City Stockyards. He was building his contacts and his capital, and in 1955 he was finally in a position to take action on his dream. He and a few backers formed Sioux City Dressed Beef, a new packinghouse that would implement some of the innovations Holman had been talking about all these years. Instead of sending out entire carcasses to its customers, Holman's company sent out trimmed quarters of meat, which made transportation easier and eliminated the waste of fat and bones that the buyer would have to discard anyway. And instead of the standard practices of preparing each carcass individually, Holman's company developed an assembly line—or actually a disassembly line. Carcasses were hung from a conveyor chain so each man along the line could do one specific job.

Sioux City Dressed Beef was not exactly a rousing success, however, and after a few years Holman was bought out. But he kept talking up his ideas, and he kept looking for backers who wanted to modernize the packing industry. In 1960, he was ready to try again. Holman and his new backers formed Iowa Beef Processors, Inc., the firm that would put together a slaughtering-and-processing system that would put many packers out of business and put giants such as his first employers, Swift and Armour, on the run. Iowa Beef was not the first company to try many of the innovations it would perfect. In fact, few of the ideas were actually originated by Holman. But Holman pieced them together, and then he added aggressive management to make the total operation succeed.

Holman expanded on his disassembly-line process, which speeded up production and also allowed his company to replace some skilled butchers with lesser-skilled—and lower-paid—laborers on the lines. Then he made a point of locating his plants in rural areas near the supply of cattle. This allowed him to buy cattle directly rather than using the cumbersome stockyard system that added time and transportation costs. It also allowed him to save more money by paying his employees rural wage rates rather than city wages. But the most important advance was the fact that Holman decided to perfect a concept known as boxed beef. That is the rather unglamorous term for a process of cutting carcasses not just into quarters, but into what are known as the "primal cuts," the wholesome loins, ribs, chucks, and rounds that supermarkets buy. These chunks of meat are vacuum-packed, placed in boxes and shipped off to the supermarkets. The supermarkets have to do little more than open the boxes, slice up the chunks almost like loaves of bread, and place the retail cuts on the meat counter. Supermarkets can buy more selectively, since they don't have to make use of everything that comes with a carcass, and they can save on butchering costs. In addition, the vacuum-packed pieces have a longer shelf life than carcasses, and shipping costs are reduced, since the 25 per cent portion of the beef carcass that is fat and bone remains on the packing-plant floor.

There are concerns about boxed beef, however. There are charges that the extended shelf life can be a tool used by boxed beef firms to influence prices: if prices are too low, they can hold back large quantities in storage until the market improves. A second concern is that the process leaves more room for grading abuses, since once the meat is cut up it is harder to keep track of what pieces go into each box. In fact, until the USDA prohibited the practice, some suppliers stamped a small p or c on boxes that could have been confused with markings for prime and choice grade meat. A third concern is that the vacuum-packed meat may be more susceptible to microbiological contamination, including salmonella. No serious health hazards have been confirmed, but tests are continuing. Despite these complaints boxed beef has become the standard of the industry, and Iowa Beef is the company that made it happen.

In putting it all together, Holman would talk about bringing General Motors technology to the meat industry. And no one can dispute the fact that Iowa Beef is now the General Motors of the meat industry. In fact, its hold on its industry may be stronger than GM's. Some midsized packers are in effect captives who sell carcasses to Iowa Beef in order to survive; it's as if Ford were supplying engines for GM cars. And some of the old-line firms seem headed for a fate similar to that of Chrysler. Iowa Beef has far outstripped the old powers, Swift, Armour, Wilson, Cudahy, and Morrell; in fact it does about as much slaughtering as all of them combined. Its closest competitor is now another company that has embraced the new technology:

MBPXL Corp. This is a firm about half the size of Iowa Beef, but it has the backing of a conglomerate that one day may give it the strength to challenge Iowa Beef.

With its new technology and its aggressive management, Iowa Beef grew to become the nation's largest packer within ten years. At this point, however, the budding empire nearly collapsed. When Holman was mapping out his plan for taking over the meat industry, he didn't fully realize the power of two forces he would have to reckon with: the unions and the Mafia.

It's an unfortunate fact that unions often oppose innovation because it will mean the elimination of jobs. And boxed beef was certainly no boon to the butchering unions. Iowa Beef's disassembly-line process meant that skilled butchers could be replaced by semiskilled laborers. And when the pre-butchered boxed beef was delivered to supermarkets, there was less work for the butchers at that end. In fact, there are some people who claim that Iowa Beef and boxed beef are successful not because of the technological innovations but because of the savings in labor costs.

As Iowa Beef was establishing its plants throughout the Plains, it had to fight the unions, and by 1969 the fight had turned into a full-scale labor war reminiscent of the vicious labor battles of the turn of the century. In August of 1969 the Amalgamated Meat Cutters and Butchers Workmen of North America struck Iowa Beef's main plant in Dakota City, Nebraska. This was Iowa Beef's corporate headquarters, and the modern plant there was its pride and joy. For the next eight months it would be the site of shootings, fire-bombings, and dynamitings. At least one death was attributed to the labor battle, shots were fired into Holman's office while he was seated at his desk, and the house next door to Holman's, owned by Iowa Beef's general counsel, was destroyed by a radio-controlled bomb (Holman contended the bomber was really after his own house but made a mistake). Labor problems have plagued the company ever since. One strike lasted ten months, another fourteen months, and Iowa Beef has remained a hard-nosed, stingy employer when it comes to dealing with unions. Even now, only about half of its plants are unionized.

By the time the Dakota City strike was settled, Iowa Beef

was in a desperate situation. The strike had cut deeply into the company's finances, and the banks were talking about calling in Iowa Beef's line of credit. The last thing Iowa Beef needed was more labor trouble. But now it had to deal with disgruntled butchers and supermarket officials in the one market that was crucial to its success: New York.

If Holman had miscalculated about the power of the unions in general, he had really miscalculated about the power of the unions and another sinister force deeply involved in the sale of meat in New York. A few years later, Holman would complain, "Anyone that's in the meat business in New York is a crook," and he may not have been far wrong. Throughout the sixties and early seventies, New York was wracked by meat scandals that entangled the unions, the meat wholesalers, and the supermarkets. Behind many of them was the Mafia. Next to gambling, no industry has a higher cash turnover than the meat industry, so it has long been a prime target for organized crime. Mafia ties have been suspected in scandals throughout the country, but its involvement has been mostly clearly documented in New York. Even today law-enforcement officials believe a few of New York's Mafia families retain influence in the meat business, although nowhere as much influence as in the past. In the early sixties the Mafia was behind a scheme that resulted in twenty tons of horsemeat and meat from diseased cows unsuitable for human consumption to be sold as "boneless beef" to supermarkets, hospitals, restaurants, and the military in New York and elsewhere along the East Coast. In another scandal, the Mafia caused processed meats made with diseased and rancid meat to be sold throughout the New York area. And at the time Currier Holman was trying to break into the New York market, it was common knowledge that very little meat could be moved without paying a tribute to the Mafia.

As all the labor problems were threatening the future of Iowa Beef, Holman began hearing about a man who might be able to get his boxed beef into New York without further hassles. His name was Moe Steinman, and Holman would soon enough learn that he could be Iowa Beef's salvation. All Holman had to do was sell out to Steinman and the Mafia.

The story of how the largest meat-packer in the country

bowed down before the Mafia would come out three years later. By then, boxed beef was a success in New York, and Iowa Beef was back on its path toward dominance of the meat industry. But there was a price to be paid. On March 12, 1973, Currier Holman, Moe Steinman, and Iowa Beef were indicted on a variety of charges, including conspiracy to commit commercial and union bribery. The case made headlines: here was the nation's largest packer not only in bed with the Mafia, but apparently at the mercy of the Mafia. Holman maintained his innocence, arguing that the money his company had paid Steinman was for legitimate brokerage commissions, but when his trial ended in September of 1974, Holman had been found guilty.

One of the reporters who covered the trial was Jonathan Kwitny of *The Wall Street Journal.* The case had come to his attention when a reader sent his editor a small clipping from deep within the New York *Times* about the impending trial. Kwitny is a highly respected investigative reporter who for years had been fascinated by the Mafia and, thanks to this trial, he would develop a deep fascination with Iowa Beef. Over the next several years he exposed countless shortcomings of this growing company in the pages of *The Wall Street Journal.* And in a book that grew out of his reporting, *Vicious Circles,* he chronicled in painstaking detail the influence of the Mafia over Iowa Beef.

Kwitny explains* that Moe Steinman was a longtime New York racketeer who had the distinction of uniting three powerful Mafia families, the Genovese, Gambino, and Lucchese families. He was their front in the meat industry, and little meat could be moved in the New York area without his approval. Steinman was the man who could guarantee "labor peace" in the meat business, and supermarkets, unions, and meat wholesalers knew he was the man in charge of the kickbacks and bribes that would keep meat moving.

When Holman found out he would need some labor peace in 1970, a meeting was set up in a downtown New York hotel,

---

Vicious Circles: The Mafia in the Marketplace by Jonathan Kwitny, W. W. Norton & Co., N.Y., 1979, p. 251.

the Stanhope, that would set in motion an uneasy partnership between Iowa Beef and the Mafia. One of the lawyers present at the meeting was quoted as describing the participants in *The Wall Street Journal*. He said Steinman "was a furtive-looking character out of *Guys and Dolls*. . . . I thought he was there to get coffee for the Iowa Beef people. I had no notion until later that I was in the presence of a famous character. . . . This fellow, he looks like a worm." As for the Iowa Beef contingent, they "looked like a bunch of Texas Rangers."

It was unclear at the meeting just what Steinman would do to help Iowa Beef. He was asking for a commission on all boxed-beef sales in New York that ran twice the normal rate, but it wasn't clear that he would be performing an actual service. When Iowa Beef officials were forced to recall in court what Steinman's services really were, they quoted Steinman as telling them later, "I've got to buy a union steward down there, I've got to buy a guy a broad. I may have to buy a chain store buyer and, er, I've got to pay in cash." Another time he told one of them, "Well, kid, I have other expenses too. There are three kinds. I pay meat buyers off at fifteen per cent. I pay union people off at seven per cent. And it costs me ten per cent to convert the corporate money to cash, and I have to deal in cash."

When it became clear to the Iowa Beef officials just what Steinman was all about, there was a significant amount of disagreement about whether they should have anything to do with him. A few officials ultimately left the company, partly because of those disputes. But Holman knew he had to sell his meat in New York if he was going to survive, so the partnership was struck. It was a decision that may well have saved the company, and although Holman ultimately had to answer in court for his decision, he and Iowa Beef may have come out ahead anyway.

The 1974 trial of Currier Holman was a bench trial, so the verdict was solely up to Judge Burton B. Roberts. Roberts took pity on Holman, considering him a "victim of the extortionate practices" common in New York, rather than a willing partner in a conspiracy scheme. "If IBP was to survive it had to sell to New York," Roberts said. "In order to sell to New York it had to join the corrupt system there. It was as simple as that and of course, Holman knew it. Somewhat to his credit, it was not until the company was on the brink of financial disaster that he agreed to pay the price and when he did so it was with reluctance. But the distaste he had for participating in such methods proves that he made a conscious choice. Sadly, like a modern-day Dr. Faustus, Currier J. Holman sold his soul to Moe Steinman."*

Roberts had to find Holman guilty, but he didn't have to punish him. "I like you. I like you as a man," the judge told Holman. Then he freed him without fine or penalty of any sort. Iowa Beef was fined seven thousand dollars, a pittance compared to the millions of dollars it was able to make because of its scheme to get into the New York market.

Reporter Kwitny had difficulty accepting the picture of Holman as a victim. After the trial he continued to dig into the Iowa Beef story, finding more and more questionable practices to expose in *The Wall Street Journal*. He discovered that Mafia influence lingered long after Holman's day in court, and it had a profound impact on the future direction of the company. He writes in *Vicious Circles*: "As a result of the meeting in the darkened suite at the Stanhope that day in 1970, Iowa Beef would send millions of dollars to Steinman and his family under an arrangement that continued at least until 1978. After the meeting, millions more would go to a lifelong pal of Steinman and his Mafia friends, a man who had gone to prison for using slimy, diseased meat in filling millions of dollars in orders (he bribed meat inspectors) and who wound up on Iowa Beef's board of directors. Consequent to the meeting in the Stanhope Hotel, Iowa Beef would reorganize its entire marketing apparatus to allow Steinman's organization complete control over the company's largest market, and influence over its operation coast-to-coast. In 1975, Iowa Beef would bring Moe Steinman's son-in-law and protégé to its headquarters near Sioux City to run the company's largest division and throw his voice into vital corporate decisions. But, most important, a mood would be struck in the Stanhope that day—a mood of callous disregard for decency and the law. Iowa Beef would proceed to sell its butcher employees out to the Teamsters union, to turn its

---

*Kwitny, op. cit., p. 356.

trucking operations over to Mafia-connected manipulators, and to play fast and loose with anti-trust laws."*

All the way until his death in 1977, Holman refused to acknowledge that he had done anything wrong in New York. In the *Meat Processing* interview in which he talked about his start in the gut shanty, he also confirmed that if he were confronted with the New York situation again, he'd do the very same things. Now that he is gone, the present Iowa Beef officials are weary of hearing the Mafia story brought up again and again. President Robert L. Peterson has been known to kick his desk when reading news stories that dredge up the old charges. He and other officials say that the Mafia scandal has nothing to do with what the company is like today. However, critics continue to chip away at Iowa Beef's reputation. Investigative reporters such as Kwitny and Mark Hosenball, a reporter for the trade newspaper *Supermarket News* who in recent years has been even more aggressive than Kwitny, plus congressional investigators, and others have developed evidence that indicates the Mafia may not be the only problem with Iowa Beef.

At the same time Iowa Beef was selling its soul to the Mafia, it had other headaches to deal with as well. Even outside of New York, the boxed-beef concept was not meeting with the acceptance Iowa Beef had hoped for. The company needed to shore up its sales and spur the acceptance of boxed beef nationally, so it turned to a man with a national reputation for his sales savvy and management ability. Hughes Bagley, a short, slight man with a fast, high-pitched, Mickey Rooney voice and a quick dry wit, was brought in as a consultant in 1971 to shape up boxed beef. A few months later he was officially hired as vice-president for retail sales development, and during the next four years he helped establish boxed beef as a solid success for the company. During that time he also collected several piles of papers that became known as the Bagley Documents. These internal memos and other papers have been the objects of numerous court battles in recent years. Some men who have seen them claim they contain potent evidence against Iowa Beef.

Hughes Bagley is known as a man who understands just

---

*Kwitny, op. cit., p. 252.

about every aspect of the meat industry. His father was in the meat business, so he got an early introduction to it. Then he worked his way through college in the St. Louis packinghouses, and his first job after graduating from Washington University in 1947 was with a packer, tagging cattle in the coolers and selling beef to chain stores. In the next twenty years he worked for a succession of supermarket chains managing their beef operations. He developed a reputation as a man who could take a foundering operation and turn it into a smashing success. But he also developed a reputation as the kind of guy who always thought he was smarter than his boss. Most of the time he probably was, but that didn't get him very far. What particularly insulted Bagley was the fact that supermarkets and packers turned to unfair and dishonest marketing practices to make a profit. His position was that if you only had a brain in your head, you could make more money doing an honest job than a crooked job. That, unfortunately, was not a widely held position, so he bounced around the industry a good bit.

When he came to work for Iowa Beef in 1971, he said the situation there was "chaotic." The company was losing money on boxed beef, and it needed help fast. Bagley used his supermarket expertise to alter Iowa Beef's boxed-beef program, making it more attractive to supermarkets. He was successful in turning the situation around, but he was disturbed about some of the things he saw along the way. "During the time I worked at IBP, there were several areas of marketing which caused me great concern," he testified later before the House Committee on Small Business. "While I was not knowledgeable as to legal matters and definitely had no understanding of anti-trust laws, I did have experience in the retail segment of the meat industry. Because of my experience, I found reason to question some of the practices at IBP in the marketing of its product." He brought the problems to the attention of Iowa Beef's attorneys because "I sincerely felt IBP could get into serious legal problems over some of its activities. Legal counsel, at that time, confirmed my concern."

Bagley claimed that Iowa Beef offered discounts to some big customers, which an Iowa Beef attorney confirmed to him could be a violation of the Robinson-Patman antitrust act forbidding preferential pricing. He also claimed that his company had the motivation and the opportunity to manipulate the Yellow Sheet, and that the company devised a variety of tactics aimed at making supermarkets and other packers dependent upon Iowa Beef. Bagley even questioned whether union opposition and the Mafia were the real problems with getting boxed beef established in New York. Instead, he charged that Iowa Beef had been misrepresenting how much beef supermarkets would be getting for their money, so the supermarkets just weren't interested in the product.

The more he saw of these and other practices, the more he related them to what seemed to be the goals of Currier Holman and Iowa Beef. "You have to understand that during this period, Currier Holman totally and completely dominated that company. IBP was Currier Holman and Currier Holman was IBP. Currier Holman was totally dedicated to continually increasing both IBP's slaughter and thus their share of the market. . . . Mr. Holman had complete and total disdain for the old line packing companies such as Swift, Armour and Morrell. I am convinced that Mr. Holman's ambition was to totally dominate the meat industry."

Bagley retains a deep respect for Holman as a tenacious, hardworking, extremely thorough executive. But he was also a man to whom the end justified the means. "When he wanted to, he could be one of the most personable men in the world," Bagley says now. "But when he wanted to be mean, nobody could be meaner. Nobody."

Bagley's experience with Iowa Beef was like his experience with some of his other jobs: he helped turn a drain on the company into its biggest money-maker, and then he was fired. "In July 1975, after a business trip back East, I was advised by the executive vice president of IBP that my services were no longer required even though I had another year to go on my contract. I was then told to clean out my desk and files, and to leave." Cleaning out his desk was not as easy as that may sound. Bagley was what one investigator later called a "squirrel": he saved just about every piece of paper he received. It took several Iowa Beef beef boxes to hold all the files he took.

Bagley next went to work for Spencer Foods, one of Iowa

Beef's competitors, and while he was there another ex-Iowa Beef employee gave him some more Iowa Beef documents to add to his collection. "These documents outlined and summarized the marketing concept of IBP, and after reading them, I became concerned generally for the future of the meat industry and directly concerned for the small packers and retailers and even the ultimate consumers of meat products. I could see that somebody somehow had to stand up and be counted, or IBP was going to swallow up all of its smaller competition, including my new employer."

Bagley decided he would be the man to stand up and be counted. He had heard about a lawyer who was investigating alleged antitrust violations by Iowa Beef. "I did not know this lawyer, and I did not know what his relationship to IBP or the meat industry was, but I felt that he might be a starting point of my becoming involved in at least trying to prevent a massive takeover by IBP of the packing industry." Bagley made an appointment with the attorney, who turned out to be one of the men working with Glenn Freie, the Iowa farmer who had formed the Meat Price Investigators Association. What followed was a collaboration that helped Freie and his band of disgruntled cattlemen mount what has become the most serious threat to Iowa Beef. The so-called Bagley Documents are at the base of the suits charging Iowa Beef, along with a few other dominant packers and the dominant supermarket chains, with conspiracy to control the marketing of meat. Most of the documents are being held under protective order by the court, so the full extent of Bagley's allegations may not be known until the suits brought by Glenn Freie and his cattlemen come to trial—if then. But the few documents that have been made public* lend credence to charges that Iowa Beef may have become the world's largest meat company through predatory practices, misrepresentation of its products, and a campaign to drive its competitors out of business. The House Committee on Small Business fought a long battle to obtain the documents, and it

---

*The House Committee on Small Business, July 23–24, 1979, and in "IBP Complaint and related matters," memo from the USDA Office of the General Counsel.

released some of them at the 1979 hearing at which Bagley
testified. When the committee was still fighting for the right to
release the documents, it filed a court brief arguing that the
documents show "significant, deliberate and repeated violations of this nation's civil and criminal laws by Iowa Beef Processors, Inc." Furthermore, "the Bagley documents could also
expose past and present high corporate officials of IBP to felony
criminal charges for violations of antitrust laws." The brief goes
on to state that "these violations have resulted in the loss of
millions of dollars to the customers and competitors of IBP."

In the meantime, Hughes Bagley, who felt strongly about
the need to bring his fears about Iowa Beef out into the open,
has paid dearly for it. He has been sued by Iowa Beef for $4
million for taking the documents and for sharing them with
others. He has bounced on to a few more jobs, and he lost his
latest one amid charges that his employer was pressured by
Iowa Beef to let him go. Now he feels as if he has been
blackballed within the meat industry. "No one in the industry
will talk to me, they don't even understand the issues," he says
now. "All I can hope is that my day in court will come."

Iowa Beef officials scoff at the continuing barrage of
charges, and at the people who are making them. In testimony
before the House Agriculture Committe, IBP president Peterson said, "It is our view that certain individuals have developed
an unhealthy appetite for the spoils of antitrust litigation, and
perhaps ultimately a desire to serve the goals of unions which
oppose innovation and efficiency in the beef industry." That
wouldn't be so bad, he said, "if these accusations were con-
fined to the courtroom where they belong and can ultimately be
tried on their merits. What is of concern is that these allegations have been moved into the public arena through congressional auspices and the media, which seem to find scurrilous
comments about the beef industry more newsworthy than an in-
depth look at the real problems it faces."

As for the specific charges of Bagley, company officials say
he is a disgruntled employee who has a "vendetta" against his
former firm. They point out that the USDA's Packers and
Stockyards Administration, the agency with extensive powers
to police the meat industry, reviewed the Bagley Documents,

yet chose to take no action against Iowa Beef. However, it should be noted that the USDA found several practices it judged to be potentially anticompetitive and illegal, although it decided to handle the matters "informally." It also should be noted that the Packers and Stockyards administrator who decided to drop the inquiry into Iowa Beef was later to become vice-president for public relations of Iowa Beef. Iowa Beef officials point out that the documents have been scrutinized by other governmental bodies as well. When the House Committee on Small Business released some of the documents, Graham Purcell, an attorney for Iowa Beef, said, "Every syllable of this has been heard before and has been considered by the Justice Department, the Internal Revenue Service, and no violation of law has been found." Purcell, it should be noted, is a former Texas congressman who once chaired an influential subcommittee of the House Agriculture Committee. Some critics charge that inquiries into Iowa Beef by that subcomittee have been blocked because of his lingering influence on Capitol Hill.

Regardless of whether or not the Bagley Documents prove some specific wrongdoing in the company's past, what may be more chilling about them are their implications about Iowa Beef's future—a future the documents indicate may be aimed at monopolizing the meat industry.

Iowa Beef is a no-nonsense operation. Executives and production employees work six-day weeks, and the plants operate on two-a-day shifts. Company president Robert L. Peterson told the *Des Moines Register* in 1980 that he devotes 99 per cent of his time to Iowa Beef, 1 per cent to his family, and nothing to anything else. Any other packer who is willing to do the same will have no trouble staying in business. But as he told one livestock organization, "the little packer who won't do that— who wants to spend a lot of time away from the shop and have the fun things in life—won't be around, because our business won't allow that kind of life." Business is what Peterson and Iowa Beef are all about. "We do not spend a great deal of our time in civic functions," he told the *Register*. "We spend it on business. Our primary role in every community we're in is to deposit the payroll. Companies that liken themselves to civic ambassadors end up not serving the business purposes they're supposed to." Iowa Beef's purpose is to produce meat, and it does it with a vengeance.

The blueprint for that effort was developed by Currier Holman, and the present executives such as Peterson are building on Holman's plan. Their efforts have been bolstered by consultants like the Boston Consulting Group, a high-powered conservative economic think tank that has helped Iowa Beef develop its hard-nosed marketing strategies. All of these people are very clear about the goal of Iowa Beef: to grow even bigger. The company recently completed building the world's largest slaughterhouse in western Kansas, and it operates nine more plants in seven states. Its next announced intention is to move into the pork-producing business, and few doubt that by the end of the decade Iowa Beef will come to dominate pork as it already dominates beef production. Every time Iowa Beef expands, it sends shivers through the existing packers in the neighborhood, who fear they will be gobbled up by this giant. It's an understandable fear, because the ranks of small and medium-sized packers are dwindling each year while Iowa Beef continues to grow.

An example of the power the small and medium-sized packers fear occurred in 1977 in the Pacific Northwest. Iowa Beef bought and remodeled two dormant packing plants in the region and then signed exclusive contracts with six of the largest feedlots. Almost overnight, it had become the largest packer in the region. And its exclusive contracts with the feedlots made it conceivable that Iowa Beef could control virtually every head of cattle raised in the region. Packers and cattlemen alike worried that Iowa Beef would dominate the market and dictate prices. Even the USDA challenged the potentially anticompetitive implications of the move, although it later dropped the inquiry, deciding that the "anticipated adverse effects of the joint venture have not occurred." Many packers and cattle feeders in the Northwest aren't sure they agree with that ruling, although others are happy that Iowa Beef has come in to stimulate the industry.

Farther down the West Coast, the California meatpackers dread that the day is approaching when Iowa Beef will come in and put them all out of business. There is no doubt that, for all the criticisms, Iowa Beef is an efficient, innovative packer, and the California packers are mainly the opposite. When more than a dozen of the largest Southern California packers stood in court in 1978 to be sentenced for price-fixing, one of their justifications for their scheme was that it was the only way they could hope to survive in their struggle against packers like Iowa Beef. "The public has the idea these packers [the Southern California packers] are a bunch of big, vicious dogs depriving the puppies of their food," said the attorney for one of them. "In this case, however, it was the puppies combining to hold their own against the bigger dogs out of a will to survive." Everywhere Iowa Beef goes, existing packers fear they are doomed, and cattlemen don't know what to think. On the one hand, an Iowa Beef plant guarantees a steady demand for their animals. But on the other, cattlemen are worried that Iowa Beef will control prices if it forces out competition.

Iowa Beef officials contend that those who criticize its expansion plans are trying to penalize the firm for being successful and efficient. Iowa Beef has built a better mousetrap, and its detractors don't want to let the company make the most of its invention. But that begs the real question: Is Iowa Beef's size, whether achieved legitimately or not, nearing the point where the company will monopolize the meat industry? Company officials deny that there is any chance. "There is no monopoly in the beef industry," Peterson says flatly. "Some have charged IBP is out to create a monopoly. That isn't so. The fact is, we are only out to be the lowest-cost producer in this least concentrated of industries, and we are out to achieve that goal so we may pass part of the benefits back to the cattle feeder and part of the savings on to the consumer." Indeed, many economic studies have been prepared in recent years by the USDA, Congress, and the meat industry on potential monopolization, and most of them confirm that the meat industry is presently a competitive industry. But most of them also point out that the industry is in transition, and many of them point out what seems to be a trend toward concentration of power in the hands of a few packers—with Iowa Beef heading the list.

In addition, USDA attorneys have indicated there is cause

for concern over potential monopoly power by Iowa Beef. When Charles Jennings, now an Iowa Beef vice-president, headed the Packers and Stockyards Administration, USDA attorneys chided his agency for not attacking "the real cause of concern over IBP—its size and market power." A memo prepared by the USDA lawyer who directed legal activities involving the agency stated that the agency "has not yet investigated IBP nor analyzed its various activities in terms of monopolization or attempt to monopolize. Moreover, agency personnel have either failed to recognize evidence in their possession supporting a monopolization case or have not felt it of sufficient importance to forward to OGC [Office of General Counsel] for our review." As an example, the memo cited a study prepared for Iowa Beef by the Boston Consulting Group that outlines a "possible competitive scenario" under which "IBP would saddle competition with high cost plants while increasing its own strength in both slaughter and market positions." Another part of this study hints that IBP may have been withholding carcasses from the market "in order to hasten the conversion of chain stores from carcass beef to boxed beef." All of this suggests to some critics that if monopoly in the meat industry is to be headed off, now is the time for action.

The most vocal critic has been Congressman Neal Smith of Iowa. For three years, as chairman of the House Committee on Small Business, he studied Iowa Beef, and he came to the conclusion that immediate steps are necessary to stop a takeover of the meat industry by Iowa Beef and just a few additional packers. Critics say Iowa Beef came off as a villain in his hearings, and it is a main target of legislation Smith has proposed to protect against monopolization. Iowa Beef has taken Smith's attacks very personally. In an angry thirty-two-page letter to Smith after he had given Hughes Bagley a forum to air his charges against the company, Peterson accused Smith of trying to make "political capital" out of "an anti-IBP crusade." He also charged that Smith had staged his hearings mainly to aid an old law school chum, Lex Hawkins, who is the attorney for the cattlemen suing Iowa Beef. Another Iowa Beef official went to a member of Smith's committee and warned that Iowa Beef would not consider building a proposed plant to that congressman's region until such time as Smith and another congressman "cease and desist from their attacks upon a company that has done more to contain the 'farm-to-market' spread, to the benefit of both producers and consumers, than any other food processing company in modern history."

Back in Smith's home state, Iowa Beef made it a point to give financial support to his opponent when Smith was up for reelection in 1980. And Iowa Beef officials have warned that even though Iowa is the largest hog-producing state and one of the most important cattle-producing states in the nation, they may not expand their operations there, largely because of Smith's continued attacks. "We don't want to build plants in a state where the Congressman is nickin' at us all the time," Peterson told the Des Moines *Register.* "When you're from North Carolina, you don't knock tobacco." As Iowa Beef sees it, Smith is knocking meat in cattle and hog country, and for that he may be the company's biggest enemy.

Neal Smith does not seem like the kind of guy anybody would make much of a fuss about. This small, unimposing man has been the U.S. representative for the Fourth District of Iowa for twenty-two years. You don't normally build up that kind of seniority by making waves, and Smith has always been on the quiet side. His speeches, which drone on in his slow farm-country drawl, could put you to sleep, and his statements and reports, while long on facts, are short on excitement. He doesn't smoke, drink, or swear, and he is known as one of the straightest arrows on Capitol Hill. In fact, it seems at times this unassuming man would just as soon be back home on his west-central Iowa farm. And you can be damned sure that if a hailstorm knocks out his soybeans, he'll drop what he's doing in Washington to fly home and replant.

He cares about the problems of his neighbors, who have made agriculture their lives. Ironically, this desire to look after his fellow farmers has thrown him into a vicious fight against the major packers whom the farmers depend upon to buy their livestock—particularly Iowa Beef, one of the most important names to livestock producers in Iowa. And not all farmers are sure Neal Smith is doing them any favor. Smith is involved in a lonely crusade to convince the nation that a few massive packers are in a position to monopolize the meat industry, to the detriment of farmers, small packers, and consumers. For his efforts the major packers and trade associations lambaste him, Lester Norton calls him a "demagogue" and worse in his *National Provisioner,* and even some of the livestock associations attack him. But Smith plods on. He's an entrenched congressman now, so he's relatively isolated from criticism, and he can take on an occasional unpopular cause. Besides, one of his greatest assets is patience. He knows change takes time, and he is willing to wait for results. Some of his assistants wish he would take a higher profile and push harder for reform. But they also know that when Smith finally does speak, his words carry weight on the Hill, and that may be more important than a few headlines. Smith has been through fights like this before, and he's confident that in time he'll get the job done.

The first time Smith came up against the meat industry was some twenty years ago, shortly after he was first elected to the House. As a farmer, he would from time to time attend cattle sales back in Iowa, and he noticed that when diseased cattle were put up on the auction block, the same buyers always stepped forward to bid on them. He discovered that these were the buyers for packing plants who had found a loophole in federal meat inspection laws. Meat that would be sold only within the state in which it was slaughtered did not have to comply with as rigorous inspection regulations back then, and some of these plants became the dumping grounds for what was known as "4-D meat"—dead, dying, diseased, and disabled. Smith introduced legislation in 1960 to outlaw the practice but it didn't get very far that year. The House Agriculture Committee refused to hold hearings on it, so it died. He reintroduced it the next year, and the next, and the next, all the way until 1967. The bill wasn't getting anywhere because it was vigorously opposed by all the major meat industry organizations and their powerful lobbyists. It was even opposed by the cattlemen's groups, who had been told by the packers that it could make it tougher for them to sell their animals. Smith took a lot of heat for continuing to push the bill, but finally, with the help of a strong consumer lobby, a new law resulted from his efforts. It was the

Wholesome Meat Act of 1967, which was hailed as one of the most important pieces of legislation to protect consumers since the original Meat Inspection Act was passed in 1906 following the revelations in *The Jungle.*

Smith has been behind other unpopular campaigns as well. Recognizing that futures trading would become volatile and controversial, he was an early backer of the formation of a Commodities Futures Trading Commission. And several years ago he recognized that small gas station owners might be squeezed out by the big oil companies, so he proposed legislation to protect them. But at the time, the small owners said they didn't want any help. Now they regret that decision. Since 1977, Smith has been after the meat industry again. He became chairman of the House Committee on Small Business, a rather innocuous committee that seldom talked about anything more exciting than the loans the Small Business Authority was handing out. Smith wanted to do better. He knew that only about 2 per cent of the small businesses in the country ever took out these loans anyway, so there had to be something more useful the committee could do. He decided that a more disturbing problem was that big business was squeezing out its small competitors. And the meat industry was one place where it looked as if the small businesses were in the most trouble. "I could see here is an industry that has not yet gone as far as the automobile industry and some of the others," he says. "It's not hopeless at this point, but it's headed that way, so that's the reason I picked it out." In Smith's mind, the meat industry had been saved from monopoly by the consent decree signed by the "big four" back in 1920. That decree opened up a closed industry to new competition. Now he fears a new "big four" is ready to take over.

Smith launched what would be a three-year-long investigation into "impediments" to the fair trading of meat. First he took on the Yellow Sheet, exposing its inaccuracies. From that part of the investigation he became a staunch backer of an electronic marketing system for the meat industry, which he feels is nearing reality.

Next he responded to pleas from truckers that they were

being extorted at supermarket loading docks when they tried to deliver shipments of meat. He discovered a practice known as "lumping," where drivers were forced to pay laborers fees ranging from $40 to $120 to unload their trucks. It's uncertain where the term "lumping" came from, but truckers knew if they didn't pay, either they or their rigs were likely to take some lumps from these thugs. One trucker told Smith's committee about how he was beaten when he tried to unload his truck without the help of lumpers at a Safeway depot in California. "One fellow came in and just took a swing at me and knocked me up against some produce there. I hit him back. At that time two more came in. They got me down. I just curled up in a ball. They kicked and beat on me until I was left laying there," he said. "I yelled for help until I lost my voice. I can recollect hearing my own echo across this vast warehouse and not a soul would come in to help me." When the trucker finally was able to get up, "the initial lumper, the one who swung the initial blow, he came in and said, 'Things have gone rough for you. If you think it is rough now, just call in the authorities, police officers.' I said, 'What do you mean?' He said, 'You call in the authorities and you will never make it to Fresno. We will kill you.' "

One maddening sidelight of the situation was that the Internal Revenue Service went after a few truckers who had tried to deduct the payments to lumpers as business expenses; the IRS ruled that the truckers should pay withholding tax on the "wages" they were paying the lumpers. Smith proposed legislation to safeguard truckers against lumping abuses, and it was eventually passed as part of a massive bill deregulating the trucking industry.

But the "impediment" that disturbs Smith the most, and that has led to the most controversy, is the potential domination of the meat industry by a few powerful packers. He has amassed stacks of dry economic studies dealing with such topics as "Estimates of Consumer Loss Due to Monopoly in the U.S. Food Manufacturing Industries," "The Relationship Between Structure and Performance in the Steer and Heifer Slaughter Industry," and "The Changing Structure of the Beef Packing Industry." Behind all the dense verbiage, Smith sees a distressing possibility: "We find that in central areas, conditions in the meat industry are ripe for large, predatory companies to almost invade a region and drive efficient competitors out of business."

Smith laid out his apprehensions in 1980 in a speech before the House. With his dry delivery and the complicated nature of his topic, it was not a rousing speech. But the facts were unsettling. "Nationally, the top four firms slaughtering steers and heifers accounted for about 32 per cent of the total in 1978; not a particularly high level of concentration," Smith said. "So what's the problem?" The problem, he explained, is that the national slaughter figures, the ones the major packers use to show how small they are and how nobody should be concerned about them, don't mean very much. As Smith points out, in the twenty-three states that account for virtually all marketing of fed cattle, the top four firms hold 66 per cent of the slaughter business. "What has happened over the last decade is that the large firms have concentrated at the source of the animals, driving out the competition." In addition, although there are still quite a few packers around, the twenty largest control 62 per cent of the business, so they already have much more power than their little brothers. "What cattle producers do not seem to realize is that in five or ten years there will be so few small and medium size packers left in business, the price of live animals will be determined totally by what the remaining oligopolists [the dominant packers] want to pay. When the crunch comes, the producers will share in the ultimate cost."

Equally disturbing to Smith is the trend toward what is known as "vertical integration." That means packers are no longer just packers: they are increasing their power by taking control of other parts of the chain that leads from farm to dinner table. For example, Iowa Beef has exclusive contracts with feedlots, which gives it increased control over the number of cattle it can buy and the price it will pay for them. And MBPXL, the second largest packer, is owned by the largest grain company in the country, which could give it control over cattle-feed prices, one of the most important variables in livestock prices. "The wave of conglomerate takeovers and vertical integration in the grain-livestock-meat packing complex is a telling sign of

monopoly profits to be made by those with economic power,"
Smith warns.

Where does all this lead? Smith is afraid it may lead to
control by the major packers extending from animals in the field
to the individual cuts of meat in the supermarkets. This last
step is known as "portion control," and the major packers are
already considering it. "This means the meat packer will take
charge of everything from killing the animals to consumer
packaging the meat for retail display. Portion-controlled meat
will come to the retail store just like boxes of breakfast cereal,
requiring no further processing." The dominant firms will then
be in a position "to control retailing and to force retailers to
display their products or even to take control and operate retail
meat shops in supermarkets." He points out that national brand
advertising is already a way of life for marketing poultry, pork
products, and processed meats. He says the advertising and the
brand names add to meat prices, but they don't add to the
quality of the meat. "If you doubt that nationally advertised
brand name beef is a realistic possibility because of the sixty
year history of unbranded fresh meat, then you would probably
say it could never happen in bananas. I give you Chiquita
bananas. Or if you say bananas are a special case, I give you
'Chiquita' lettuce—the United Brands Company attempt to
raise the price of lettuce through advertising—which was fore-
stalled at least in part by Federal Trade Commission action."

If this is allowed to happen with meat, it will cause a return
to the situation that existed in the first part of the century, when
the "big four" packers controlled the market and sold meat
under their own brand names. "Unfortunately, as the studies
show, the meat industry is returning to a state of concentrated
shared monopoly power and once again is on the verge of highly
advertised, needlessly differentiated national-brand marketing
of fresh meat which has no essential characteristics which can
be differentiated from the non-branded, non-advertised product. When this occurs, instead of the increased efficiencies
from boxing and portion control being passed back to the producer or on to the consumer, they will be wasted on needless
advertising and shared monopoly profits, resulting in losses for
both producers and consumers."

Unnamed in all of Smith's scenario is the company that seems to be leading the way toward this shared monopoly—Iowa Beef. And despite the cries from Iowa Beef officials, Smith adamantly maintains he is not out to get any one company. One of Smith's concerns when he made his speech was that even Iowa Beef might be ripe for acquisition by a well-financed conglomerate. And in August of 1981 he was proven right. Iowa Beef was acquired by Occidental Petroleum Corp. in an exchange of stock valued at approximately $800 million. Iowa Beef officials said the move could hasten its expansion. But Smith is also concerned about the power of second-place packer MBPXL, which is owned by the largest privately held corporation in the U.S., Cargill, Inc. This corporation has substantial grain holdings and other resources that could aid in MBPXL's expansion. Smith wants to make sure no one can take over the industry, and he has proposed legislation that would limit the opportunity for monopolization by prohibiting any one packer from taking more than a 25 per cent share of the market.

Smith draws a disturbing picture of the meat industry. And much of the meat industry doesn't want to accept it. Smith's charges, and the bills he has introduced to guard against this takeover by major packers, have been vigorously opposed by the major packers such as Iowa Beef, and by many of the smaller packers and farmers he is trying to help. Even the cattlemen's association for his home state came out against Smith's activities. "Many of these investigations and the introduction of bills are purely for political purposes and would not benefit the cattle industry," the Iowa Cattlemen's Association stated in 1979. Smith responded at that time that "they just are being a lackey for Iowa Beef." Smith is resigned to the opposition from people he is trying to help. It happened back in the 1960's in the fight for the Wholesome Meat Act, it's happening now, and it will happen in the future. "I'm accustomed to commodity organizations and their very, very small staffs," Smith says. "They don't have a capability of their own to do independent research and make these decisions." He knows they will rely on the major packers for information, and they will be wary of bucking these packers who buy their livestock. "They're sort of dependent upon the industry moguls, and I expect them to be led instead of leading the way for their own members."

Smith vows to continue his campaign until he wins his safeguards against monopolization. But this fight may be tougher than his earlier fights. Even he admits that the Pacific Northwest already may be too far along the road to domination by a few packers to be saved. And the western Plains may not be far behind. "It would be doubtful that area can be saved," he concedes. "Maybe the rest of the country can be."

However, the end of 1980 may have been an unfortunate turning point in his fight to save the meat industry. Smith fears that with the conservative swing that accompanied the election of Ronald Reagan it will be difficult to get his legislation approved. "I think it's got to happen sometime," he says, "but I'm not looking for it right now." As in the past, Smith is willing to wait as long as it takes to get the job done. But there has been another change that works against his efforts to save the meat industry. Smith's rising seniority allowed him to take over the chairmanship of a House appropriations subcommittee. But that meant he had to give up chairmanship of the Committee on Small Business, the committee most responsible for spurring efforts to reform the meat industry. Smith is still the ranking member of that committee, and he says he will follow through on his meat campaigns. But the investigatory role of that committee has most likely come to an end, and many reformers fear that without the push from that committee, the dominance of Iowa Beef and a few other packers will continue to grow unfettered.

Nick Wultich doesn't need this aggravation. He put in his time with the FBI as a white-collar-crime expert, and now he's supposed to be retired. But he's the kind of man who never will be. He's pushing sixty now, but he's still got that hard look of the G-man—from the white shirt and austere dark suit all the way down to the standard-issue black wing tips. He's a tall man, nearly bald, with a face somewhere between Hans Conried and Colonel Klink. When he speaks, it's in the staccato bursts of the stereotypical FBI man; in fact, it's a voice reminiscent of Eliot Ness. For more than three years, Wultich has been helping the

House Committee on Small Business investigate the meat industry. He's had his share of successes, and there are so many more abuses he'd love to dig into. "As an American, if I see something wrong, God damn it, I'm going to go after it," this nononsense investigator says. But he's frustrated now because his committee is going out of the meat business. As he sits at his desk in a sparsely furnished office—hardly more than a short corridor, actually—in House Annex Building No. 2, a dingy collection of offices that is a purgatory for bottom-rung bureaucrats, he is going through some documents on a pollution-control case that has nothing to do with meat. And he's not at all sure that his services as an investigator will be needed by the committee much longer.

Wultich won't talk much about what appears to be the end to the inquiry into the meat industry. He begs the question, saying only, "I'm just an Indian, not a chief." But it has to hurt that the investigation that Neal Smith pushed vigorously for three years is coming to an end with so many questions still unanswered. Wultich knows what needs to be probed and exposed. And he knows he could turn the meat industry upside down if he was given the chance.

Some people say Nick Wultich is the man they would least want to have mad at them. He's a hard-nosed investigator who is not ashamed to say he's doing a job for the good of his country and his government. "Hey, chief, as long as we're under the same flag, let's work together," he says. "I don't have an ax to grind." It's a line he uses often to coax reluctant sources to level with him. He's very direct, very blunt, and very determined to get to the bottom of things. He was one of the FBI agents who worked on the massive investigation of the first Russian grain deal, and in the past few years many meatmen have found out the hard way that he is not a man to mess with. Wultich was responsible for Smith's investigation into the failings of the Yellow Sheet, and he played an important role in the inquiries that followed.

When the committee won a historic court order allowing it to obtain the controversial Bagley Documents that had been kept secret by Iowa Beef, Wultich took the next flight to Sioux City. He spent two days and nights locked in an office poring over more than three thousand documents and picking out the ones the committee needed. It was quite a coup, because Wultich was in and out of Sioux City before Iowa Beef's attorneys had a chance to fight the order allowing the release of the documents; in fact, Wultich had gone before Iowa Beef even found out about the order.

And when Bagley was fired from his job with another packer within a week of testifying about his documents before Smith's committee, Wultich was back on a plane to Sioux City to find out if Iowa Beef had anything to do with forcing Bagley out of his job. Wultich remembers that confrontation well. As he tells it, he and a partner arrived at the Iowa Beef headquarters in Dakota City, a small town just outside of Sioux City, and demanded to see Iowa Beef president, Robert Peterson. They were ushered into his office, where Peterson was seated at his desk and one of his attorneys was standing off to the side. Wultich says he extended his hand to the attorney in greeting, but the attorney refused to shake. The reception was frosty all around; they weren't even offered a place to sit. So Wultich started in on Peterson. He wanted to know if there was any connection between the dismissal of Bagley and the fact that his employer, Dubuque Packing Co., did a lot of business with Iowa Beef. But before Peterson could answer, Wultich says, his attorney kept interrupting.

"I'm not talking to you," Wultich boomed at last. "If you have anything to say, say it to Peterson; you're his attorney, not mine."

"You can't talk to me like that," the attorney countered, but Wultich just bored in on Peterson. Wultich says he couldn't get an answer from Peterson, so he asked to talk to some other executives. "It doesn't matter to me," Peterson answered. Wultich named a specific man he wanted to talk to. "He's out of town," Peterson said. So Wultich named some more. "I don't want you to talk to them," Peterson said finally. So Wultich exchanged a few more words with him and then turned to leave. On his way out he made a point of bad-mouthing the attorney in tones loud enough for the office workers to hear. Wultich doesn't need this aggravation, and he's not about to let anyone push him around when he's on his country's business.

Those were heady times, and Wultich's unrelenting style helped the Smith committee force the meat industry to face up to a long list of serious problems. Now, unfortunately, those days are over. By 1980, Wultich wasn't out harassing the meat industry as much as before, and some people were starting to grumble that the Smith-committee investigation was losing its steam. One target of complaints was the special prosecutor who had been brought in to run the show, John Fitzgibbons. He was an aggressive young prosecutor who managed to rankle both the meat industry and his own staffers with the way he ran the investigation. Some critics contend he didn't give staffers such as Wultich a free enough hand in going after the industry. But others contend that a more compelling problem was that the Smith committee was simply coming up against its own limitations.

This had always been something of a quixotic crusade because in taking on the entire meat industry, the Committee on Small Business was really out of its depth. There are other committees and agencies with more direct responsibility over the meat industry, so there were some complaints in Washington that Smith and his staff were taking the committee into areas where it didn't belong. That may be true, but the sad fact is that Smith and his staffers found it necessary to mount their crusade because nobody else would.

By the end of 1980, Fitzgibbons was disillusioned as well, and he moved on to a job with the Justice Department. Looking back at the work of the Smith committee, he is frustrated by the failure of others to act on the serious problems the committee exposed. "My opinion is that nobody in the U.S. is enforcing the federal statutes, and everybody in the meat industry knows it," he says. "They all know they can get away with anything if they are willing to invest in good lawyers." He singles out the USDA, which has potent powers through antitrust laws and the Packers and Stockyards Act to police the industry. "They've got the tools, but they've not had the desire or ability to do anything. We've been awfully disappointed in their lack of aggressiveness. And when they do venture into court, the USDA attorneys are soundly licked by the industry attorneys."

Equally guilty is the House Agriculture Committee, specifically its Subcommittee on Livestock and Grains, which should have been addressing the problems Smith uncovered. "I think it's a disgrace that the members of that committee didn't have the interest and didn't have the guts to get into this," Fitzgibbons says. "The members and staff of that committee are the most unenthusiastic on the Hill. They only protect parochial interests. They're easily influenced by a variety of lobbyists."

That left Neal Smith to pull together a staff from his less powerful Committee on Small Business, and in so doing he came up against what Fitzgibbons calls the myth of the power of congressional committees. While Smith's committee could call before it all the witnesses it wanted to in an effort to get to the bottom of things, those witnesses didn't have to tell the committee anything. "They could just come in here, flip us the bird, and leave," Fitzgibbons complains. Except for extraordinary cases like Watergate, Congress rarely invokes its contempt powers, so there was little the Smith committee could do to force packers to tell the committee what it wanted to know. "The big companies refused to appear before us voluntarily. They preferred to stay on the sidelines and use their money and influence to attack Smith on a personal basis, with a degree of success. They scared a lot of congressmen away. It's surprising how much they can block on the Hill."

Now that the committee is ending its inquiry, Fitzgibbons is not optimistic about the chances for controlling the power of large packers such as Iowa Beef. Although he doesn't want to underestimate Smith's ability to keep legislation moving, he believes the only real hope for controlling the power of the major packers is through private litigation. He looks at the massive antitrust battle in Dallas by the cattlemen as maybe the last chance to stop the domination of the meat industry by Iowa Beef and a few other packers. Fitzgibbons fears that a few years from now he will strike up a conversation with someone who will look back at the work of such people as himself, Nick Wultich, and the rest of Neal Smith's staff and say, "You guys were right. We should have done something when we had the chance."

10

The Supermarket Meat Scandals

When the head meat-cutter was interviewed, I asked him if he thought the aforementioned steaks, which I had previously purchased, were "prime." The meat-cutter shook his head no. I then asked him if he would eat these steaks as prime. He said, "Maybe if they were run over by a truck a couple of times."

> —Signed statement of meat grader
> Amedio P. Fioravanti in
> Report of Investigation, Dominick's
> Finer Food Stores, Chicago, Illinois.
> U.S.D.A. Office of Inspector General
> General Investigative Report, File #CH-2436-2,
> p. 33, Feb. 15, 1979

The law offices of Kirkland and Ellis, a staid, conservative, establishment firm, begin on the fifty-ninth floor of the sleek, Italian marble-clad Standard Oil Building in Chicago, and they extend for four more floors up. This is one of the most respected and feared law firms in the country, representing corporate powers such as General Motors and Standard Oil, and a few smaller clients, such as the *National Provisioner*. Nearly two hundred attorneys work in these imposing offices, resplendent in rich wood and chrome. On March 28, 1979, two of the firm's sharp young attorneys, Sidney N. "Skip" Herman, a good-looking, stylishly dressed, businesslike man, and Kathleen Kelly Spear, a tall, attractive, serious woman, took their places in the fifty-ninth-floor conference room with its magnificent view of Lake Michigan, for the deposition of one Arlene Gitles, a named plaintiff in Reich *et al. v.* Dominick's Finer Foods. Skip Herman, a rising young star in the firm, handled the interrogation of the deponent, a thirty-seven-year-old woman who describes herself as a "typical suburban housewife."

Under Herman's pointed questioning, Arlene Gitles was forced to admit that on March 27, 1979, she entered the supermarket at Willow and Pfingsten roads in Glenview, Illinois, with her "partner in crime." That turns out to be Marcy, her two-year-old daughter. "I'm rarely without her," Gitles stated for the record. Herman demanded to know how much Gitles spent in the aforementioned supermarket. Gitles referred to her checkbook and responded, "$13.05." "The record will reflect," Herman added, "that the witness reached into her pocketbook and pulled out her checkbook and referred to a document." Under further probing, Gitles admitted, "I spent about 72 cents on apples. And I bought cucumbers, and I'm trying to think how much they were." She did not purchase any frozen foods or dairy products, but she did purchase some meat.

Q *What did you purchase in terms of nonfish meat?*
A *I purchased already cooked roast beef, precooked.*
Q *Do you remember how many pounds that beef was?*
A *Half a pound.*
Q *Exactly or approximately?*
A *Exactly.*

Gitles also admitted purchasing deli products, six packages of spaghetti, cheese, and toothpaste, and she exchanged a package of Fritos that she wasn't happy with.

During three and a half hours of questioning, Herman uncovered numerous other startling admissions.

Q *Does anyone in your household not eat meat?*
A *No, unfortunately.*
Q *Everyone in your household eats meat?*
A *Every single one, including the cat.*
Q *Do you feed the cat fresh beef?*
A *No.*

However, Gitles does feed the other members of her family fresh beef. "Becky, who is nine, likes rib steaks, and she also likes lamb chops, and she likes brisket. She is a good meat eater. Chuck has no preference," she said. In fact, "Chuck would have pizza for the rest of his life." As for Mr. Gitles, he has not "evidenced a particular preference," as Herman asked, but once in a great while he cooks meat on the grill. "Hamburgers. He cooks them rarely," Gitles said. "Sorry about that."

> Q *Have you ever purchased any prepackaged items, such as Carl Buddig beef, at Dominick's during the relevant time period?*
> A *Yes, I probably have. Yes.*
> Q *Have you ever purchased any sauerkraut at Dominick's during the relevant time period?*
> A *Sauerkraut? Good question. I might have, I don't know for sure.*

Gitles did not purchase smoked butts, smoked picnics, Jimmy Dean products, Oscar Mayer products, Bob Evans products, or Marvel frozen turkeys. She did buy Land O'Lakes turkeys, Mrs. Paul's products, Brilliant products, and Wakefield crab.

The mundane shopping habits of this suburban housewife were extremely important to the high-priced legal talent in the Kirkland and Ellis conference room that day. All of the questions were a necessary, if slightly ridiculous-sounding, part of the legal process. Dominick's Finer Foods, the second largest supermarket chain in the Chicago area, was the client of Kirkland and Ellis. And Arlene Gitles was charging Dominick's with mislabeling meat products—overcharging customers as much as thirty cents per pound. All this talk about Carl Buddig beef and sauerkraut and Marvel frozen turkeys was directed at a legal question of proof. Gitles' answers would help determine whether she and all the consumers of the Chicago area, whom she represented in a class action suit, deserved lower meat prices. About a year and a half after Arlene Gitles bared her shopping lists in this lengthy deposition, she strode up to the meat counter at her local Dominick's, trailed by reporters and television cameras. She was celebrating the first day of an historic rebate sale that resulted from her efforts. Under a court-approved settlement, Dominick's would return $355,000 to its customers through lower beef prices.

An old saying among supermarket executives goes: If you get the meat business, you'll get the food business. They know that Campbell's soup is the same at any store, but shoppers will keep coming back if the steaks are consistently good. Traditionally, the men who have managed the meat departments well have been the ones to move up in the supermarket corporate hierarchy. Meat represents the largest chunk of the food dollar, it's the largest portion of the supermarket advertising budget, and it's the product featured on special to get customers into the store. It's also a high-profit-margin product, with a markup in the neighborhood of 20 per cent. Still, supermarket executives lament that when they are blamed for high meat prices, they are taking a bum rap. Many of the forces driving up meat prices are beyond their control, they say, and supermarkets are the victims of the same inflationary pressures as everyone else, so there is little they can do about high prices.

But that's not how others see it. There have always been complaints about supermarkets short-weighting cuts, mislabeling cuts, misrepresenting grades, and otherwise trying to make their meat products seem better than they really are. In addition, the spread between the price ranchers are paid for their livestock and the price consumers pay for meat has increased dramatically since World War II, and there are serious questions about whether the increase in cost to the consumer is justified. Federal officials have pointed their fingers at supermarkets for selling meat at prices that have been at times "unjustifiably high," in the words of USDA economists. Presidents Carter, Ford, and Nixon all summoned food industry executives to the White House to "jawbone" them about soaring grocery prices. And meat has been a prime target. Some of the strongest charges came in the summer of 1979, when supermarket prices continued to rise even after farm prices dropped markedly. The USDA accused supermarkets of charging as much as 18.5 cents per pound more for meat than their market-ing costs justified. USDA economists said the overcharges began to moderate only after President Carter called food industry executives to the White House to complain. Another problem is that a few dominant chains have grown to the point where, because of the magnitude of their purchases, they set the price all supermarkets will pay for meat in some regions.

While supermarket executives vigorously deny these charges, the fact remains that the supermarket meat counter is where consumers must deal with all the problems of the meat industry. The concerns about grading, inspection, pricing, qual-ity, and healthfulness are all wrapped up with the cuts beneath those clear-plastic wrappers. At best, supermarkets pass on only the overcharges built into the bribery, price-fixing, and other forms of corruption in the chain that leads from ranch to dinner table. Unfortunately, the supermarkets often add some more. These additional problems range from simple matters such as butchers with their thumbs on the meat scales all the way up to supermarket executives wearing funny color-coded tags who have conspired to fix the price of meat.

One day in late July of 1978 a call came in to the Chicago office of the USDA meat-grading service from a young man who used to work at a supermarket in suburban Lincolnwood. He was calling because he was upset about what a friend who still worked at the store had just told him. This friend said he had seen the butchers at the store cutting the inked grade stamps that said USDA choice off cuts of beef. The butchers would then dip the meat into blood, squeeze-pack the meat in the plastic wrappers, and put the meat on the counter, marked USDA prime. The friend said he was sure the practice was company policy, because no employee would do anything like that on his own. The call was taken by an assistant to John Coplin, the longtime whistleblower who headed the grading service in Chicago. What followed was a series of events that prove individual consumers do have the power to make sure we all get what we pay for.

When John Coplin, the tall, gruff grader who had been exposing scandals across the country for nearly thirty years, was told of the call, he immediately went to work. He took the information to the USDA's Office of Inspector General in Chicago, and within days Coplin and the USDA agents began an investigation. On July 31, Coplin, his assistant Pat Fioravanti, and two USDA investigators made random visits to several stores operated by the supermarket chain mentioned by the caller, Dominick's Finer Foods. They proceeded to the meat counters to take a good hard look at the prime meats for sale. They did not like what they saw. After visiting the Dominick's in suburban Western Springs, Fioravanti filed this report: "I examined 36 packages of T-bone steaks which contained a package label identifying them as prime cuts. Fourteen of the package steaks that I examined had small to modest amount of marbling and should have been labeled 'USDA Choice.' Two of the packages that I examined were labeled prime, but should have been labeled 'USDA Good,' because they contained only a weak slight amount of marbling. There were no USDA grading marks on the product, but there were indications that the product had been trimmed thus removing the USDA grade mark." There was more. At that store, ten of twenty sirloin steaks marked prime should have been choice, and two more just good. At other stores, standing rib roasts, chuck roasts, porterhouse steaks, rib roasts, and more were all misgraded, in the opinion of these seasoned meat graders. In some cases, it wasn't even a matter of opinion: the USDA choice grade mark originally stamped on the meat when it was graded was still visible on some of the packages being sold as prime. In addition, there were cuts that weren't really what they were advertised to be; in one store, packages that were supposed to contain New York strip steaks actually contained less expensive club and strip steaks.

The USDA agents bought mislabeled meat at eight supermarkets in all, and the following day they went to the U.S. attorney's office in Chicago to discuss their findings. It was decided that more stores should be checked, so on August 2, Coplin, Fioravanti, and two more grading supervisors went out again with USDA investigators. They found more of the same. At this point, U.S. attorney Thomas Sullivan decided a concentrated raid was called for. Sullivan brought in eighty FBI agents—an unprecedented number of G-men for anything less than a full-scale assault on the Al Capone gang. On August 3 and 4, teams of FBI agents, graders, and USDA investigators blanketed the sixty-nine Dominick's stores in the Chicago area. They proceeded to the meat counters as before, but this time, when they found mislabeled meat, they confronted the startled store officials. Grading supervisor Fioravanti found mislabeled porterhouse and strip steaks at the Dominick's in suburban Glen Ellyn. When Fioravanti asked the head meat-cutter if he would eat the steaks as prime meat, he answered, "Maybe if they were run over by a truck a couple of times." When other employees at other stores were interviewed, they denied any knowledge of mislabeling, but in at least one store, meat-counter personnel were hurriedly removing prime meats from the counter by the time the federal agents returned from talking to the store managers.

It was a stunning raid, and when it was over the final scorecard read like this: Mislabeled meat was found at 62 of 69 Dominick's stores; of 270 packages of meat bought by the raiders, 23 contained meat branded USDA choice that Dominick's was selling as prime, 244 packages contained meat that in the opinion of the graders was lower in quality than Dominick's grade labels indicated, and three packages contained less expensive cuts of meat labeled as more expensive cuts.

Although the evidence sounds devastating, Dominick's contended that some of the charges were unfair. While large quantities of allegedly mislabeled meat were found at some stores, at others only a few cuts were challenged by the raiders. And Dominick's officials argued that many instances may have been either inadvertent mislabeling or no mislabeling at all. The officials pointed out that meat is graded in carcass form, so once the carcass is cut up, it's possible that some individual pieces from a prime carcass won't look like they should be prime. These officials complained that the graders on the raid were in effect second-guessing the original graders, and now Dominick's had no way to defend itself. In fact, USDA regulations technically prohibit the grading of retail cuts, and in the aftermath of the raid grading supervisor Coplin took some heat for authorizing his men to break the rules. Although the U.S.

attorney commended Coplin and his graders for helping make the raid a success, Coplin was reprimanded by his USDA superiors. The action irritated Coplin, who says the graders were well aware that they were operating in a sensitive area. But there could be no doubt the meat they picked out was misgraded. As he would later write in defending himself, "we did not even have to make any borderline decisions because the violations were so gross. In fact, we stayed away from any close decisions, we did not need them since there were so many violations. You see, it was like deciding whether the cow was black or white."

Still, there was enough uncertainty about the legal grounds for charging Dominick's with mislabeling based on the opinions of the graders that when Dominick's was formally charged, only twenty instances were cited. "In each of these instances the meat had been intentionally misbranded prime by Dominick's meat department employees at the time of its packaging," the firm admitted in a plea agreement resolving the case. Under the agreement, Dominick's pleaded guilty to overpricing the meat and it was fined the maximum—two hundred thousand dollars. The story of the raid, however, does not end here.

Arlene Gitles, a suburban housewife, and Betty Reich, a retired schoolteacher, both read the newspaper accounts of the Dominick's raid. They didn't know each other, but they shared a similar reaction to the raid because they had both stopped shopping at Dominick's after becoming dissatisfied with the quality of the meat. Gitles remembers complaining to the Dominick's butcher at least once. Reich remembers three or four occasions when she bought prime steaks and later found USDA choice stamp marks on them. "And I complained," Reich said. "However, as an individual, I couldn't do anything. I felt I couldn't do anything."

But as it turned out, she could. And she did. Within months of the Dominick's raid, Reich and Gitles were in the downtown law offices of Lowell Sachnoff, a nationally prominent antitrust lawyer. Both women had heard that there was the potential for filing a class action suit that might result in some sort of compensation for the consumers who had bought mislabeled meat at Dominick's. As Gitles' daughter Marcy crawled around the furniture, and as Reich, an inveterate ham radio operator, fiddled with her CB, one of Sachnoff's associates, Arnold Pagniucci, tried to explain the legal points and strategies involved in bringing suit against Dominick's. Pagniucci, a Chicago street-kid-made-good who looked like he'd be right at home on the Italian-dominated Dominick's payroll, spelled out how a suit could be brought on behalf of every Dominicks' meat customer in the entire Chicago area if these two women would agree to become the named plaintiffs in the suit. As a result of this meeting, Reich and Gitles decided to give it a try.

Fighting for consumer rights was not something new for Gitles. "Well, to go way back, I'd have to give full credit to my mother, who was a very wise and conservative shopper," she says. "I grew up with coupons all over the house. I was taught to be very careful with my money." When she and her husband, a former stand-up comic who became a psychotherapist, first moved to the Chicago area in 1969, she started keeping a list of businesses that offered good services. Soon her neighbors began to rely on her for the name of a plumber or a babysitter, or a clothing store, so she wrote up her recommendations in a booklet that she copied and gave out to her friends. Her consumer concerns were focused in the early seventies when, as a member of the National Council of Jewish Women, she attended a meeting organized by some women who wanted to start a consumer group. "I latched on to them. And ever since then I have been involved actively." Gitles became codirector of the Consumer Coalition, a loose-knit group of suburban women who began to tackle consumer issues. In 1977, Gitles testified at a Federal Trade Commission hearing on the problems with product warranties. In 1978 she testified before a congressional subcommittee about the dangers of credit-card abuse. That year she and the coalition also held informational meetings, passed out literature, met with supermarket officials, and campaigned for legislation to protect consumers against the Universal Products Code, the system of funny little lines and dots that eliminates the need for individual prices on supermarket products.

She first started getting interested in meat issues back in

1973 during the boycotts over high prices, although she didn't take an active role then. But three years later, when the USDA relaxed its grading standards, allowing lower-quality meat to qualify for the choice and prime grades, she and the coalition actively fought the change. Later, she took an interest in the problems with the meat industry's Yellow Sheet pricing system, and through her contacts on that issue she learned about the potential suit to recover damages from Dominick's.

Betty Reich had no formal contacts with consumer activism as Gitles did, but she had always been a public-spirited citizen, and she had always cared about her meat. Reich is a widowed former elementary-school teacher and guidance counselor. She has served as a school board member, a township board member, and a member of the township mental health commission. She's retired now, and her passion is ham radio. Her home is filled with expensive amateur radio equipment, and everywhere she goes she carries a CB, so she is always in touch with her far-flung radio contacts. She is also something of an expert on meat. She once did the meat buying for a small vacation resort, so she knows how to look for the proper marbling, and how to check the fat, the bone, the texture, and the color of meat to pick out the best cut. For herself, she buys only the top prime meats. On her shopping forays she usually buys about two weeks' worth of meat, mostly steaks. When she gets home, she picks out the one she will cook that night, and then she methodically unwraps and rewraps the rest for the freezer. It was after one of these trips that she first became concerned about Dominick's meat. Reich had a pile of about eight prime steaks all ready to be rewrapped for the freezer when she noticed that on some of the steaks the purple-inked grade stamps were still visible on the fat. They read USDA choice. Angrily, Reich took a knife and cut off the offending grade marks. During the next few months, the same thing happened a few more times. Once, she made a point of saving one of the mislabeled steaks to return to Dominick's, but it spoiled before she got around to it. Reich was disenchanted with Dominick's now, and soon she stopped shopping there entirely. But she remained upset about the mislabeling, and when she heard through a friend about the potential lawsuit, she decided to get involved. For Reich, it was a tougher decision than for Gitles. She was not an outgoing activist by any means. She preferred to stay at home, reaching out to her friends all over the world through her ham radio setup. Just taking the train downtown to meet with her attorney was an adventure for which she had to steel herself. But she felt strongly enough about the mislabeling to give her name to a suit on behalf of hundreds of thousands of consumers against the second largest supermarket chain in Chicago.

It's a rare person who will take the risks that go along with a class action suit. In representing an entire class of people who feel they have been wronged, the named plaintiffs agree to donate their time and subject themselves to intense questioning by attorneys on everything from their personal history to their personal finances to their shopping lists. If their suit is successful, they are entitled to nothing more than anyone else in the class, even though they did all the work. And if they lose, they are responsible for all the costs of depositions, legal notices, and other expenses rung up by the attorneys on both sides. Even after accepting these conditions, the plaintiffs must prepare themselves for what can be a complicated, drawn-out battle. By nature, class action suits are rather unwieldy. Since they are brought on behalf of large numbers of injured parties— sometimes thousands or even millions—they can be administrative nightmares. The legal procedures for class actions are still somewhat uncharted, so attorneys can drag them out for years. Then, if the case is won or a settlement is reached, compensating the large throngs of injured parties can be extremely difficult; in fact, compensating every individual is virtually impossible. Often, administrative costs and attorneys' fees can eat up the majority of money that is to be doled out. For all these reasons, class action suits are still relatively rare.

But they can be extremely effective. In the suit brought by Gitles and Reich, a strategy was developed to get around many of the problems with class actions. Their attorneys would push for a settlement calling for a rebate sale, during which Dominick's would sell beef at reduced prices to compensate shoppers for the alleged mislabeling. Such a settlement would not reach everyone who had bought meat during the three-year period the suit charged mislabeling had occurred, but it would reach a significant number of the shoppers. In addition, it would not be subject to the large administrative and accounting costs that cut into many class action settlements.

The suit of Betty Reich and Arlene Gitles, "on behalf of themselves and others similarly situated," was filed on September 6, 1978. But the usual lengthy battle did not follow. Instead, the response of Dominick's to the suit was as remarkable as the efforts of the two women. Dominick's moved quickly to resolve the dispute, and within two years a settlement was worked out that was hailed by the plaintiffs, the defendant, and the court as comprehensive, innovative, and fair. Under the terms of the settlement, Dominick's did not admit any liability for mislabeling, but it nevertheless agreed to hold a four-week rebate sale. During that time, prime meat would be sold at a twenty-cent-per-pound discount, and for two of the four weeks choice beef would be sold at a ten-cent-per-pound discount. The sale was supposed to return approximately $280,000 to consumers and, in addition, Dominick's agreed to spend $17,000 on a consumer education program to teach meat buyers how to judge the grades of beef. All along, Dominick's had contended that much of the mislabeling was inadvertent, so a final provision of the settlement called for Dominick's to institute new procedures to eliminate inadvertent mislabeling and confusion between prime and choice meats at the meat counter. As it turned out, the rebate sale was more successful than anyone had anticipated, and a total of $355,000 was actually returned to consumers through the sale.

It was notable that Dominick's agreed to nearly all of the demands of Gitles and Reich, even though it could have used the considerable legal power of Kirkland and Ellis to fight the charges and possibly disprove them during a long and costly court battle. But when the settlement was presented to the judge, Dominick's attorney Skip Herman made it clear Dominick's did not intend to operate that way. "As Your Honor knows, the settlement of a case usually does not involve the defendant coming up with 100 per cent of the requested amount," Herman told Judge Richard L. Curry. "As the plaintiffs' counsel has stated to the court, we are so doing today, and

I think the reason for that should be stated. Dominick's is a customer oriented organization. We deal with customers' problems and complaints all of the time. We always try to work them out. Indeed, we have dealt with one of the Plaintiffs in this case, Mrs. Gitles, in the past and helped her out of various problems that she has brought to our attention in the past. We view this case as a class of people with a problem, and we are happy to return any money that people believe should be returned to them. . . ."

Dominick's chairman of the board, Dominick DiMatteo, Jr., also praised the settlement, saying, "It's fair to everyone concerned." He added, "We are also relieved that a lengthy court battle has been averted. I am confident that our revised policies and procedures will preclude any more inadvertent mislabeling."

Arlene Gitles and Betty Reich each had different ways of showing their satisfaction with the settlement. Gitles, the activist, celebrated by filling her shopping cart with meat that first day of the rebate sale, as reporters and television cameras recorded the scene. Reich was much more subdued. She had gone out for a drink with attorneys to celebrate when the settlement was approved by the court, and that was good enough for her. She didn't even make a trip down to her local Dominick's the first day of the sale. In their own ways, both women were able to take pride in proving just how much of a difference individual consumers can make.

Regrettably, the problems uncovered in the Dominick's raid are nothing new in the supermarket industry. Fresh meat, with no brand name and no standard packaging direct from the factory, is easy to tamper with. Mislabeling and fudging the weights of individual cuts are practices that have gone on for years. Even the names of meat cuts can be a problem. Supermarkets have been known to sell such enticing products as "His 'N Hers Steaks," or "Paradise Roasts" whose only distinguishing qualities are their price tags, which are sometimes as much as a dollar more than the same cuts with more mundane names. That's no longer as much of a problem as it used to be, thanks to the efforts of the National Livestock and Meat Board. This industry organization has devised a standardized system for identifying meat cuts, trimming the list of names for individual beef, pork, lamb, and veal cuts from more than a thousand to a more manageable 314. However, that still leaves a lot of names and a lot of opportunity for deception, and supermarkets are not bound by the standardized names anyway. A related problem is that many supermarkets are moving away from selling USDA-graded meat. Instead, they sell leaner, ungraded meat under house-brand names such as "Bonded" or "Supreme Cut" that tell the shopper absolutely nothing about the quality of the meat. Some stores are even devious enough to come up with such names as "Butcher's Choice" or "Gourmet Choice" that might be confused with USDA choice by unwary shoppers. All of these names mask the fact that while the meat isn't unhealthful, it is not of high enough quality to be graded choice, the grade most consumers prefer. The supermarkets pay less for this meat, yet they sell it to consumers at prices comparable to those for choice meat—sometimes even more.

Even when supermarkets are trying to do an honest job, they are susceptible to being duped by packers. Packers have been known to switch carcasses, delivering lower-quality carcasses than the ones the supermarket buyer picked out in the cooler. Packers also have to be watched to make sure they don't short-weight carcasses or provide "hot beef"—meat that has not been chilled properly so it is still heavy with blood and moisture that will only end up draining on the butcher room floor or soaking the bottoms of the packages at the meat counter. All of this and more can be helped along when supermarket buyers are on the take, accepting gifts and money from packers in return for looking the other way when the packer tries to slip something by.

As consumer awareness and consumer-protection programs continue to grow, many of these tricks become harder to pull off. But they still happen. In one distressing instance, the very people who were supposed to be the watchdogs guarding against these problems were found to be on the take. During the past few years the New York City Department of Consumer Affairs has been praised for its fight against supermarket deception. It regularly sends out press releases heralding the work of its special investigatory unit. And when violations are found, the department works out innovative settlements that often call for the offender to repay consumers by selling meat at cost for a specified period of time. But in November of 1980, confidence in the unit was shattered. All seven investigators were indicted on charges of taking bribes from 57 supermarket officials and 13 firms. Brooklyn district attorney Eugene Gold said that during a two-year investigation, approximately 180 bribes totaling $7605 were documented. The bribes, ranging from $5 to $500, were allegedly given in exchange for overlooking violations including short-weighting, selling meat with excess fat, and false advertising.

Unfortunately, the problems at the supermarket level extend far beyond individual cuts that are not what they're supposed to be. The power of the major supermarket chains has grown to the point where some critics fear these giants can control the price of virtually every piece of meat sold in this country. Allegations have been made that through price-fixing, conspiracy, and monopoly power these giants inflate the cost of meat to consumers while shortchanging the farmers and ranchers who raise livestock. These are abuses that may have the most devastating impact on consumers, yet it is not consumer groups who are investigating them. If these charges are proven, it will be the result of the efforts of a few solitary cattlemen who have dared to bite the hands that feed them.

For cattlemen, complaining about how little they are paid for their livestock has become a way of life. It is an unfortunate fact that in recent years cattlemen have been able to make a profit on their animals in only about one year out of every four or five. They know there are many complex reasons for the ups and downs in livestock prices, but they gripe that they end up seeing too many downs, even when consumers are screaming about meat prices that only seem to go up. Some of these cattlemen blame the major packers and supermarket chains for their plight. They fear that these giants have the power to dictate prices, both at the farm level and at the retail level. But most cattlemen have been afraid to do anything about their fears because, after all, they need the good will of the packers and supermarkets if they expect to get any kind of decent price for their livestock. In fact, many are in awe of the major powers and end up believing whatever these giants tell them. A few cattlemen, however, have dared to take on the giants. They have mounted lonely individual campaigns that have raised extremely disturbing questions about the power of a few dominant packers and supermarket chains. If consumers have any hope for controlling skyrocketing meat prices, they'd better heed the warnings of these few courageous cattlemen.

One of the first crusaders was Courtenay C. Davis of the Y Cross Ranch in Horse Creek, Wyoming. Davis was a city boy with a law degree who in the early 1940's decided he felt more at home on the range, so he bought himself a ranch in southeastern Wyoming. As far back as the fifties he began to see an unsettling trend in the prices he was paid for his cattle. After the Korean War, the demand for beef and the price of beef began to rise steadily. But the price he and other cattlemen were paid for their livestock didn't follow along. Davis looked into the whole structure of the food industry to find out why. What he discovered was that competition was slowly disappearing from the supermarket industry. After World War II, the developing supermarket chains started to force out the smaller grocery stores. With fewer small stores, there were fewer buyers for livestock. And the remaining buyers—the supermarket chains—had more leverage because of their size. Not only that, but these chains started a trend toward "centralized buying": instead of purchasing meat on a store-by-store basis, the decisions were made from one centralized office, further concentrating the market power. Davis also saw the trend toward "formula trading" based on the Yellow Sheet, the system whereby traders agreed to accept the price printed in the Yellow Sheet rather than haggle among themselves, which was another tactic that reduced genuine competition. And finally, Davis saw that the price spread between what cattlemen were paid for their livestock and what consumers paid for meat was increasing as the power of the supermarket chains increased; that meant that even as retail prices kept going up, cattlemen couldn't count on receiving better prices; in some instances, livestock prices even went down. What all this means is that consumers and cattlemen, who are often played off against each other, are not really enemies; they are both victims of the powers in between.

Davis spread his message in speeches throughout the Plains in the late fifties and early sixties, and in 1964 he even went to Washington to testify at a congressional hearing on livestock prices. That trip prompted a flurry of activity when an assistant to President Johnson gave the President an outline of Davis's charges. In fact, it wasn't long before Johnson signed a bill forming a National Commission on Food Marketing to investigate the buying practices of chain stores. But nothing much came of the commission, so Davis was forced to continue the campaign on his own. By now other cattlemen were starting to complain about the same problems, and they were all starting to reach the conclusion that if they were ever going to accomplish anything, they would have to file some sort of suit. In 1967, a prominent San Jose, California, attorney named James F. Boccardo began to interview the disgruntled cattlemen such as Davis. At a meeting in Denver he told Davis and a few others that the way to go after the supermarket chains was to file an antitrust suit against them. By midsummer, about 200 cattlemen had agreed to enter into legal action.

On January 17, 1968, a suit was filed that became known as Bray v. Safeway. In the next decade, this suit would become famous and infamous on a number of levels. To some people it is clear proof that the dominant supermarket chains gouge consumers and shortchange cattlemen, but to others it is nothing more than a curious aberration that is best forgotten. The case name is legal shorthand for an action in which Irvin Bray, a King City, California, cattleman, and five other cattlemen sued Safeway, Kroger, and the Great Atlantic & Pacific Tea Co. (A&P), the three largest supermarket chains at the time. The charge was that these chains had conspired by a variety of means to fix the price of beef. Davis was not a plaintiff in this suit for a number of technical reasons, but the suit was only a first step in a campaign that was eventually supposed to result in suits on behalf of Davis and other cattlemen throughout the West and the Plains.

Cattlemen such as Davis were enthusiastic that they might finally expose the sins of the supermarkets, and they were even more enthusiastic when Boccardo brought in one of the most fearsome antitrust lawyers in the country to handle the case: Joseph L. Alioto. Alioto's presence added to the stature of the case, but Alioto was about to be elected mayor of San Francisco, so the case was eventually turned over to his son Joey. The younger Alioto was a tough, ambitious lawyer in his own right, and when the case finally came to trial his courtroom performance was, by all accounts, brilliant. But it wasn't until 1974 that the trial began, and in the meantime two of the defendants, Safeway and Kroger, agreed to out-of-court settlements. By paying a combined total of eighty-five thousand dollars, these two chains were dropped from the suit without admitting any liability. A&P, however, turned down settlement offers and chose to fight the cattlemen in court.

What followed was a virtuoso performance by Joey Alioto in a trial that spanned eight weeks, producing 3698 pages of transcript. When it was done, the jury deliberated just two days before returning to the courtroom and handing the court clerk its verdict. "The jury finds in favor of the plaintiffs in the amount of ten thousand, nine hundred—" the clerk read. After all the years the cattlemen had fought for their cause, ten thousand dollars was a real disappointment. But then the clerk corrected himself: the actual amount was ten *million,* nine hundred four thousand, and twenty-seven dollars. It was a shocking amount. In coming up with its multimillion-dollar damage award the jury had ruled that the cattlemen had been cheated out of twenty cents per pound on all the meat they had produced between 1964 and 1967. In addition, antitrust awards are tripled for punitive effect, so A&P was actually being socked for $32,712,081.

This was the vindication C. C. Davis and other cattlemen had been seeking for so many years. This decision laid out all the ploys used by the major supermarket chains to control meat prices. Judge Oliver J. Carter, in his order affirming the jury's verdict, stated that "there was sufficient proof that the conspirators had not only the ability to artificially depress meat prices, but in fact did dictate to the packer and the cattleman the price that would be paid for beef. The result was a 'funnel' effect; the beef produced by the plaintiffs had to be

distributed through the retail market yet, because of the conspirators' pervasive dominance in the market, the prices the
plaintiffs received were prices dictated by the retailers. The
result of the conspirators' influence in the meat industry was a
market wide depression of wholesale beef prices."

Carter reviewed the tools used to fix prices. First was the
size of the chains. A&P was then the single largest purchaser of
carcass beef in the country. Although its share of the market
was only 7 to 8 per cent nationally, the combined market power
of A&P and other chains was enough to control prices. The suit
charged A&P conspired with Safeway, Kroger, and several
additional chains, although Safeway and Kroger had been
dropped from the suit and the others were never formally
charged. A second tool was centralized buying. "There was
sufficient evidence to support the conclusion that not only A&P
but Safeway and Kroger as well, maintained a buying system
whereby beef purchases could be made for the entire chain from
one centralized location," Carter wrote. "The purchases were
made on a national level and enabled the company to select the
price it would pay for beef. Local stores within the chain were
allowed only a small amount of flexibility in purchasing beef
from sources other than the main office."

Another tool was the Yellow Sheet, which Alioto had
argued was used by the chains to keep themselves informed of
prices, to calculate prices, and communicate to other stores
amounts paid. Carter ruled that "the Yellow Sheet is a further
example of an otherwise legitimate endeavor that may be
manipulated to exploit an illegal design." In addition, it was
"another tool available to the defendant and the co-conspirators
that would facilitate the regulation of beef prices." There were
more tools, such as the fact that the major chains bought their
meat on different days, so they each had a stronger impact on
the market when they bought, and they sometimes coordinated
the specials they offered. In addition, packers testified at the
trial that meat prices were dictated by the chains.

Carter concluded, "Perhaps the most persuasive evidence
presented by the plaintiffs was that concerning the economic
effects of the alleged conspiracy." Alioto had presented expert
witnesses who argued that in a free market, the prices received

by the cattlemen should rise as the demand for beef exceeded supply. But that was not happening. "At the time that the price received by the cattleman for his beef was paradoxically dropping or leveling off in face of increasing consumption, the gross profit margin of the retailer (i.e., the difference between the price at which the retailer sold the beef and the price he paid for it) was greatly increasing. It thus appears that the retailer was able to take advantage of the high consumption by selling his beef at higher prices and increasing the difference between the prices he paid and the price he received," Carter said.

To a judge's legal mind, that may have been the most persuasive evidence. But to many who have reviewed the case, there was another factor that had more impact on the jury. Throughout the trial, Alioto had called forward an imposing array of expert witnesses testifying to economic theories, interpreting statistical data, and explaining how the standard principles of supply and demand seemed to be malfunctioning in the meat industry. The evidence was dry, technical, and highly complex. But Alioto had one piece of evidence that wasn't complex at all.

Alioto pointed out that A&P was a member of the National Association of Food Chains. This was a trade association for supermarkets, but an exclusive one; only the larger chains were allowed to join. The members were the largest purchasers of carcass beef in the United States, and Alioto charged that the association, through its periodic meetings, provided a forum for the supermarkets to clandestinely fix meat prices and profit margins. As Judge Carter stated in his review of the case, "One of the most significant aspects of the plaintiffs' case concerned the aura of secrecy surrounding NAFC meat discussions. The meeting topics, agenda, and minutes were labeled confidential and were generally unavailable. Meeting participants were identified, not by name or company, but by color-coded badges; anonymity was assured by the association." During the trial, A&P's attorneys scoffed at Alioto's contention that there was anything conspiratorial about these meetings, or that they were shrouded in secrecy and deceit. They described the discussions of prices by the supermarket representatives as "innocuous," and they said the color-coded badges were only used to encourage individuals to speak freely. And in any event, when A&P's chief meat buyer, Robert Carpenter, took the stand, he denied ever attending these meetings, so how could he be involved in any kind of conspiracy?

The testimony of this meat buyer may have been the key to the trial. When Carpenter denied meeting with the competition, Alioto confronted him with a photograph taken at a National Association of Food Chains meeting in Denver; it showed Carpenter sitting there with his cohorts, wearing his color-coded badge just like the rest. "And why do they give themselves color designations and number designations—grown men?" Alioto demanded. "What for? Not for fun. They are not playing games, these people. This is a big game. It involves meat; they know it involves every American's life, whether he's a rancher or consumer or whatever he is. It is big money, and it's big stakes, and they are going in there under color cover or number cover, and they are not doing it for fun."

This was the smoking gun attorneys pray for in the absence of an outright confession. And this, along with Alioto's mesmerizing courtroom performance that pulled together dry economic theories and disconnected pieces of evidence for a persuasive story of conspiracy and price fixing, may well have won him the trial. As Judge Carter noted, "As usual in cases such as this, there exists no proof of formal agreement between A&P and the co-conspirators; the plaintiffs' case is undoubtedly circumstantial. Yet, the law contemplates that seldom will direct proof of a conspiracy be available."

Still, in the years since the verdict was announced it has become a topic of heated debate in the legal community. Although Judge Carter defended the decision, some critics contend that the jury was swayed not by the evidence, but by an Academy Award-caliber courtroom performance by Alioto. The U.S. Justice Department criticized the decision in a scathing sixty-page memorandum. The memo states that the verdict, which some people accept as "prima facie proof of a massive price-fixing conspiracy among the nation's leading food retailers," is in reality "a shell with nothing of substance behind it." However, others argue that the Justice Department should have been addressing the issues raised in the Bray case all along, and this is nothing more than a "cover your ass" memo to justify the department's inaction. In any event, the Justice Department has been reluctant to build additional cases using the evidence brought out in the Bray case.

If the decision itself was controversial, so was its aftermath. A&P knew it could be devastated by the verdict because in addition to the $32 million it was ordered to pay, the firm was now fair game for similar suits that could be filed by cattlemen throughout the country. So A&P attorneys sought out Alioto to find out if there was still a chance for some sort of settlement. After all, A&P was appealing the decision, so there was the chance that a higher court would overturn the verdict and leave the cattlemen with nothing. If A&P could reach a settlement, even one for several million dollars, it could come out ahead. It would not have to pay the full amount of the damage award and, more importantly, if the Bray verdict were vacated other cattlemen would not be able to rely on the decision as proof in additional suits that could potentially have wrecked the corporation.

It was at this point that the historic Bray decision began to fall apart. Alioto started working out a settlement but, as C. C. Davis would later claim, Alioto seemed to be looking out more for himself than for the two hundred cattlemen whose concerns had started the campaign that led to the Bray case. After all, these cattlemen were waiting for suits to be filed on their own behalf. In fact Davis, the Wyoming rancher who had been at his crusade for more than twenty-five years, now feared that victory was slipping away. And when Davis realized the full implications of the settlement Alioto ultimately worked out, Davis decided that his only recourse was to turn against the very man who had won the case he had been championing for so long. Davis filed a malpractice suit against Joey Alioto, his father, and the family law firm. And on June 5, 1980, a jury awarded Davis an astounding $3.55 million in damages. The jury determined that in handling what had been hailed as one of the greatest antitrust victories in years, the Aliotos had also been guilty of negligence, had intentionally misrepresented and concealed information, and had breached their fiduciary duty to Davis. The award was later reduced by the judge to $880,000, and the Aliotos are appealing the verdict.

Davis's attorney told the jury in the malpractice case that the Aliotos "sold Davis down the river, without notice, and became independently wealthy in the process." Joey Alioto had worked out a settlement that obligated A&P to pay the still-sizable sum of $9 million. But the settlement also vacated the Bray decision, taking away the right of other cattlemen not named in the Bray suit to rely on it as proof in future suits; now they would have to prove everything all over again. In addition, the settlement slashed the amount of money to be paid the cattlemen, but not the multimillion-dollar attorneys' fees.* An unfortunate problem with high stakes antitrust cases is that they often end up being taken over by the attorneys. They become matters by and for attorneys, with the original clients often forgotten. There are indications that the Bray case turned out to be just that type of case. When James Boccardo, the lawyer who had first gotten the cattlemen together, heard about the terms of the settlement Alioto had worked out, he complained to Alioto. He was concerned about the way Alioto was proposing to "cavalierly" given away the cattlemen's money, but Boccardo was also concerned that he wasn't getting his share. As Ehud Yonay would write in a disturbing examination of the aftermath of the Bray case in *New West* magazine, the fighting between attorneys became nearly as vicious as anything in the trial. Yonay concluded: "When it came right down to it, the greatest beef antitrust case of the century boiled down to bickering over money among attorneys."

The Bray decision, which had already been tainted by charges that it rested on a dubious factual base, was now further tarnished. And the cattlemen who had been grumbling about their low prices and how they couldn't do anything about them were still grumbling. Now they had good reason to believe a

---

*Trial testimony quoted in "Former SF Mayor, Son Lose Case Stemming From '68 Price Fix Suit," *Supermarket News*, June 16, 1980; "Alioto Cited For Malpractice In $3.55 Million Judgment," The *New York Times*, June 7, 1980; and "Bonanza! Or How a Persistent Wyoming Rancher Won the Largest Legal Malpractice Victory on Record, Against All Odds and Against the Sharpest Antitrust Lawyers in the Business: Mayor Joe & Little Joe Alioto," by Ehud Yonay, *New West* magazine, Sept. 8, 1980, pp. 17–27.

conspiracy existed that was hurting both themselves and consumers, but they had no court decision to back up their claims.
By the time C. C. Davis had won his malpractice suit, he was
seventy-nine years old, too old to mount another drive. It would
be up to younger people to see if anyone could ever expose the
power of the supermarkets.

In the years following the Bray verdict, others would begin
to independently corroborate much of the evidence in the Bray
case. One of them was California state senator John Garamendi,
a rising political figure in the state, who first came upon some of
the concerns during hearings he conducted on retailing in 1976.
A former meat-packer testified at that time that Safeway, the
largest supermarket chain on the West Coast, in effect set the
price of meat for the entire region. As the packer, Bob Minch,
told it, Safeway made its meat purchases every Wednesday, and
because of the magnitude of those purchases, its "buying impact would be so great that the trend would be set and the word
would be out before nightfall, not only to every packer, but to
every feedlot. So in the West every Wednesday night or Thurs-
day morning, the word is 'What did Safeway do?' From that
indication, there is a sigh of relief or of anguish as to what is
going to happen next week." The smaller chains ended up
paying a price based on what Safeway had paid. The only way
the packers could try to blunt this power was through price-
fixing—as was proven in the 1978 price-fixing case against
thirteen of the leading Southern California packers. The Bray
case had established that the power of the supermarkets fil-
tered all the way down to the cattlemen. If a cattleman asked a
western packer on a Monday what the price of meat was, he
would be told to wait until Wednesday when Safeway made its
purchases.

The implication to Garamendi was that Safeway on the
West Coast, and other packers in other parts of the country,
were setting the price of meat—whether they wanted to or not—
because their purchases were so large. In a follow-up hearing in
1977, Garamendi further backed the concerns about the power
of supermarkets over consumers and cattlemen, stating that the
"massive increases in economic concentration place giant food

retailers in a dominant position where, as the largest buyers of wholesale beef, they can influence the wholesale price of beef." In fact, Garamendi said, "I am fearful that the large retailers have used this kind of marketing power to manipulate the price of beef. In other words, the rules of supply and demand, traditional economics, are not followed and no longer apply. Instead, we have substituted rules that we might call Safeway-A&P-Kroger rules."

However, the concerns about dominating the market can no longer be directed only at the supermarkets; the major meatpackers have grown to the point where they may have the ability to control the supply of meat. If there are Safeway-A&P-Kroger rules, there may also be Iowa Beef-MBPXL-Spencer rules. The combined power of the supermarkets and the packers is awesome. And it is the latest target of cattlemen upset about meat prices. There is a collection of cases being fought in federal court in Dallas that may make people forget about the Bray case. In fact, this assault on the powers of the meat industry has the potential for the largest antitrust award in the nation's history.

While C. C. Davis was coming to the end of his long and ultimately disappointing crusade, another cattleman was just starting his. And he may be the man responsible for bringing the vindication Davis sought for all these years. He is Glenn Freie, the short, barrel-chested, sandy-haired farmer from Latimer, Iowa, who heads the Meat Price Investigators Association. Freie is the man who calls himself "just an old country boy," but who spends much of his time lobbying senators and representatives and other government officials, and conferring with some of the most high-powered attorneys in the country. He is the man who is charging that the major supermarkets and the major packers are part of a massive conspiracy that cheats both cattlemen and consumers.

Freie's campaign had begun at about the time the Bray verdict was making headlines. And there would be a lot of similarities in the campaign he mounted and the one Davis had begun some twenty years earlier. As Freie recalls in one of his standard governmental presentations,* "In early 1975, a group of Iowa cattlemen, including myself, became disturbed by the extended depressed price that cattlemen were receiving for their cattle. We simply could not understand the way the cattle market was working. All that we knew was that we were losing a lot of money. We started talking to other cattlemen around the state of Iowa, and eventually in March of 1975, about one hundred and twenty met together in Des Moines to discuss our common problems. We decided to put our money where our mouths were." The cattlemen formed the Meat Price Investigators Association, and they hired one of the nation's toughest antitrust lawyers, Lex Hawkins. He is an attorney with a fearsome courtroom demeanor and a track record for winning multi-million-dollar verdicts who conducts his business from a historic English Tudor mansion in Des Moines.

"First of all," Freie continues, "we went to Washington, D.C., and talked with the Justice Department, the FTC, the Department of Agriculture, Packers and Stockyards Administration, and various committees of Congress who were then, or had been recently, generally investigating the food marketing system. What we found then was that for one reason or another no one was really interested in getting behind the problem. We also concluded that there must have been a great fear of disease in Washington then, because none of the various government groups had talked to any of the others—none of them knew what any of the others were doing. . . . The stark reality in 1975 for Meat Price Investigators Association was that if we were going to get behind the beef marketing system in the United States and find out where the problems were, we were going to have to do it alone. So we put our lawyers on airplanes and told them not to come back until they could tell us something that made sense." Freie went along too, logging more than two hundred thousand miles that first year. He and his attorneys were building evidence, lining up experts, and signing up supporters for their campaign. By the end of 1975, some five

---

*Testimony before House Subcommittee on Livestock and Grains, October 4, 1977, p. 166.

hundred cattlemen were behind Meat Price Investigators Association, and it was time to go to court. They filed suits charging the eighteen largest supermarket chains, the four largest packing companies, and the Yellow Sheet with conspiracy to violate antitrust laws. During the next few years these suits would be consolidated with more than a dozen similar suits by other cattlemen throughout the country—individuals with names such as Noah Tipton, James Guy Campbell and Di-Ann Campbell, and groups such as the Sagebrush Cattlefeeders, the Rawhide Cattlefeeders, and the Triple S Cattle Co.—into one massive antitrust case being handled in federal court in Dallas.

Included are a broad range of charges which, if proven, would call for a total overhaul of the American meat industry. As one of the suits charges, since at least 1963 the defendants have conspired to "fix, stabilize, and maintain at uniform, non-competitive, and artificially low prices" the amount cattlemen are paid for beef. They have conspired to "charge noncompetitive and artificially high prices for fresh, frozen, and processed beef sold at retail to consumers, which had the effect of reducing beef consumption." Also included are charges that the supermarkets "eliminate price competition for fresh, frozen, and processed beef by employing a system of price leadership whereby Safeway on the West Coast and A&P on the East Coast and other coconspirators at other times and places set prices by accepting bids from packers one day in advance of all other retail food chains who thereafter follow the prices established by the dominant firms." The Yellow Sheet is manipulated by the coconspirators, and it is "a device to communicate the price paid in the different areas of the United States and thereby stabilizes the prices throughout the United States." Another of the suits includes charges that the packers divide territories to restrict the market, agree to purchase livestock on certain days of the week when the price will be fixed low, and manipulate the commodities futures market to depress the price of live cattle.

The suits are built on many of the allegations in the Bray case, but they go far beyond it. They are bolstered by additional economic studies and factual evidence, including the controversial documents of Hughes Bagley, the former Iowa Beef executive who filled several beef boxes with company papers when he left the firm. Sources close to the case say these documents alone may contain more potent evidence than anything revealed in the Bray case. "The complexity of what we're doing is just so much greater than what they [the Bray case attorneys] ever did," Freie claims.

The charges are undeniably serious, and those who are familiar with the cases say some of the evidence is devastating. But no one aside from the participants knows for sure. While these suits may be the most damaging litigation ever mounted against the powers of the meat industry, they also may be the most mysterious. They have generated little publicity, largely because all but the most innocuous documents have been placed under protective orders, so no one can be sure exactly how much damning information is on file. What is clear is that the legal battling has been savage. Every procedural issue has been fought as if the entire litigation hinged on it, and numerous issues have been carried all the way to the Supreme Court. Some of the attorneys have sued each other for alleged ethical violations, which is usually a sign of personal vindictiveness. It is also a sign that the stakes are uncommonly high.

The legal process has been further muddied by a disastrous Supreme Court decision in an unrelated case that has made the cases against the supermarkets tougher to pursue. The decision, known as Illinois Brick, totally turned around antitrust laws, and it has hamstrung numerous suits by consumers and suppliers against dominant corporations. The ruling prohibits suits by "indirect purchasers," so it could have meant that the cattlemen could only sue the packers who bought their livestock, not the supermarkets who bought meat from the packers. In fact, some of the suits against the supermarkets were actually dismissed, but they were later reinstated when the cattlemen's attorneys found an exemption from the ruling. Still, the cases against the supermarkets may be tougher to prove. When Glenn Freie has not been pushing his lawsuits, he has been working in Washington with Ted Kennedy to pass legislation that would once again allow suits by indirect purchasers.

All of the legal battling has drawn out the cases considerably, and it still could be years before all of the cases are resolved. "I'll be very frank," Freie warns, "we're going to be very tough to deal with. We think we're in the driver's seat, and we have the hard evidence, and we just ain't going to let them get by."

For now, there is only Freie's word, and many are skeptical. His fellow farmers have not exactly jumped to his defense. In fact, many farmers' and cattlemen's groups actually oppose his efforts. They say he is needlessly antagonizing the people they all must depend upon to sell their livestock. And they find his talk about a massive conspiracy little short of ridiculous. But Freie sees another reason for their opposition. In his mind, the major farm organizations "have interwoven themselves in business deals and so forth with the large corporate interests and they can no longer speak out for the people they're supposed to be representing." And beyond that, farmers generally do not have a sufficient amount of information to truly understand what's going on. "I just wonder if you really took a test out of all the producers in the United States today, whether 30 per cent would be able to fully understand and tell you what's going on in the marketplace," Freie says. "I'm not saying I'd have been any different, but because of what I've been through, I understand."

The Dallas litigation remains an ominous presence that has everyone in the meat industry edgy. If the charges are ever proven, the Yellow Sheet would almost certainly be forced out of business, the supermarkets and packers could be crippled by astronomical damage awards, and the federal government could be forced to step in and break up the dominant supermarkets and packers. The cases could prove that every time we buy a piece of meat we are paying a nickel or dime per pound more than we should, while the farmer who raised the livestock is getting a dime or a quarter less than he should. Glenn Freie has a haunting assessment to keep in mind every time we wheel our shopping carts up to the meat counter: "This is a very, very crooked business."

11

Conclusion—
Prime Rip

Nothing is black or white in the meat industry. We're all just different shades of gray. It's a tough business.

—Anonymous meatman

These are not happy times for the American consumer. A trip to the supermarket has become a task to be approached with dread as food prices continue to rise relentlessly. And for the past few years meat prices have been one of the items leading the way. Families accustomed to putting meat on the table every day are finding that the cost is now beyond their means. And some cuts of beef have become true luxury items.

The reasons for high prices are undeniably complex, but the standard justifications ignore one of the main problems: corruption. One of the favorite rationalizations cited by meat industry groups is a mysterious force known as the "cattle cycle." This is a confusing pattern of rising and falling prices that is tied to the number of animals cattlemen are raising. When meat prices are high, cattlemen expand their herds to cash in on the good fortune. But as more cattle are produced and the supply of meat increases, prices fall. So cattlemen cut back their herds to avoid losing money. Then they wait for prices to turn up again before starting to raise more animals. The process is complicated by the fact that it takes a year and a half to two and a half years to raise a steer, so the effects of high or low prices linger while the cattlemen try to adjust. This roller coaster continues for ten to thirteen years, with herd sizes bottoming out and prices reaching their peak at the very end.

The latest cycle has just reached its end, which, according to the meat industry groups, explains today's high prices. And it is surely part of the problem. Although cattlemen, packers, and supermarkets routinely try to blame each other for high prices, there can be no denying that cattlemen have been taking a beating in recent years. They are finally making some money now, but the nation's general inflationary problems, coupled with disastrous droughts and other agricultural problems in recent years, have made cattlemen reluctant to start what is supposed to be the inevitable process of expanding their herds again. As a result, prices will remain high through at least the mid-eighties.

The cattle cycle is a ready excuse used by the meat industry to explain away complaints about continuing high prices. Unfortunately, the cattle cycle has nothing to do with many of the problems that are running up meat prices. It has nothing to do with packers who bribe meat graders so that meat can be sold for twenty to thirty cents per pound more than it's worth. It has nothing to do with price-fixing scandals that have cost shoppers an estimated ten cents per pound. It has nothing to do with military meat scandals that have included such outrageous abuses as packers charging $2.40 per pound extra for beef knuckle cut to look like top sirloin. And it has nothing to do with the fact that a growing number of supermarkets are selling leaner ungraded meat that costs the supermarket less to buy, but is sold to consumers for as much as or more than USDA choice meat—giving the supermarkets twenty cents per pound or more in extra profit. These abuses happen all the time in one part of the country or another.

Then there are the problems that affect us all, no matter where we live. There is the archaic formula-trading system based on the work of Lester Norton's handful of aging Yellow Sheet reporters. There is the massive market power of the major packers and supermarket chains. There is the healthy markup, usually around 20 per cent, that supermarkets add to meat prices while complaining that they are a low-profit-margin business. And there is the ever-widening price spread between what farmers are paid for their livestock and what consumers pay for meat, which the USDA alleges has resulted in overcharges to consumers of as much as 18.5 cents per pound. These factors affect the price of virtually every piece of meat Americans buy, but calculating how much they cost us on a regular basis is extremely frustrating.

A famous Roald Dahl short story adapted by Alfred Hitchcock tells of a woman who murders her husband with a frozen leg of lamb and then invites his policeman colleagues over to eat up the murder weapon. The prime rip facing American consumers leaves us in a similar position. We are hit over the head with high meat prices, but then we proceed to consume the evidence. The cattle purchased Monday are slaughtered Wednesday, and the meat is in our stomachs by Saturday night. The money for all this changes hands quickly, and the accounting for who got what and why is sketchy at best. But as pieced together from assessments by government, industry, and consumer-movement sources, the total overcharges to the American consumer from all the problems of the American meat industry may run as high as 15 to 20 per cent on a regular basis. That's maybe thirty cents per pound on hamburger, and as much as five or six dollars total on a good-sized roast. Even when the vaunted cattle cycle starts to bring meat prices down, these prime rips will remain.

Who is responsible? The greatest villain may be the USDA. The USDA has vast powers to make sure the meat industry provides wholesome products at fair prices. Yet it has done a disgraceful job of using those powers. The revolving door that connects the USDA and the meat industry has for too long fostered a mentality that finds some reforms impossible to even consider because "the industry won't accept" them. Too many officials know they will draw their paychecks whether or not they choose to deal with the serious problems facing the meat industry. It is left up to outsiders, such as Meat Price Investigators Association attorney Lex Hawkins, who has his million-dollar law office to support, to find the incentive to tackle abuses that should be taken care of by the USDA.

President Reagan is bent on reducing the bureaucracy, and the USDA is certainly overburdened with do-nothing paper shufflers. But those who remain must be forced to do their jobs. In recent years the USDA has allowed the industry's pricing system to deteriorate to the point where there can be little faith that the prices we pay bear any relation to the real value of the meat; it has watched while a few packers have grown to the point where they can dominate the market; and it has been unable to come to grips with the corruption and incompetence among its own employees, let alone in the meat industry. While attacking the increasing burden of government regulation has become fashionable, asking the USDA to keep a close eye on the meat industry is not asking for more regulation; it is merely asking the USDA to do the job it is supposed to do with the tools it has had for many years. To ask for less regulation of the meat industry is to ask for a return to the conditions of those carefree days before Upton Sinclair wrote *The Jungle.*

Blame also lies with the entire character of the meat industry. There can be no doubt that this is a tough business. No matter how much new technology is developed, and no matter how nicely meat is packaged, the central facts of the meat business cannot be changed. This is an industry built around noisy, foul-smelling animals whose fate is to have an eight-inch-long pin fired into their foreheads at point-blank range. Their blood and guts will spill forth on the killing floor, and their carcasses will be stripped and carved and chopped during a process that, although it is governed by "humane slaughter" laws, can be nothing other than gross and brutal. The men who decide to put up with the realities of the meat business are by nature tough men. They are defensive about their industry and about critics who attack their practices while eating their finished products. Some of them have become hardened to accept a certain level of corruption as a way of life. "Nothing is black or white in the meat industry," says one source in the packing industry. "We're all just different shades of gray. It's a tough business."

But it is also a business that is made up of a collection of disparate elements, from cattlemen to feedlot operators to small packers to meat wholesalers to meat processors to giant packers. What's good for one element of the industry is not necessarily good for the rest. Unfortunately, a sort of bunker mentality prevails, and few in the industry are willing to speak about the abuses of others. They all tend to meekly follow the party line established by the major packers and major trade associations, even though it is becoming increasingly clear that the powers of the industry no longer have the best interests of the rest of the industry at heart.

The timidity of the bulk of the meat industry is particularly disturbing because the meat industry is uniquely an industry where individuals can still have a startling impact. This is the second largest manufacturing and processing industry in the nation, but it is still in many ways unsophisticated. The whole industry can be transformed by individuals with guts, determination, and fresh ideas. Currier Holman can build a company such as Iowa Beef that dominates the entire industry inside of twenty years. Lester Norton can build a one-page newsletter of meat prices into a force so powerful that the sale of meat would literally halt if it failed to publish one day. Bill Albanos can devise an electronic marketing system that may be on the verge of revolutionizing the pricing of meat. And equally important, men such as John Coplin can blow the whistle and bring down scandals anywhere in the country. Glenn Freie can strike the fear of God in the dominant packers and supermarkets by relentlessly pursuing his charges of a massive conspiracy. And individual consumers such as Arlene Gitles, Betty Reich, and Frank Hogya have the power to force the meat industry to pay up for some of the prime rips that are costing consumers billions of dollars each year.

Afterword

When retired Navy CPO Frank Hogya came to the office of San Diego attorney Bill Bauer one day in 1976 with his gripes about the "crap" he was seeing at the meat counters of the San Diego Navy commissaries, he set in motion a series of events that helped uncover widespread corruption in the California meat industry. He also set in motion the events that led to this book.

The law clerk who was given the opportunity to look into the charges of this eccentric man whose hobby was meat was coauthor George Schultz. From that initial inquiry, Schultz went on to become a national consumer spokesman on the problems of the meat industry, as well as a partner in Bauer's law firm. He assisted Dan Rather and his *60 Minutes* team on their investigation of the meat industry and he helped handle the consumer suits against San Diego meat packers and against the Chicago supermarket chain described in these pages. The actual planning of *Prime Rip* began in 1978 when Wayne Swanson, a childhood friend, agreed to quit his job as a newspaper reporter in Chicago, and move to San Diego to begin working on the project. Together, we have devoted the past three years to gathering our evidence and writing *Prime Rip.*

We have chosen to tell the story of meat industry corruption through the experiences of the actual people who have shaped the industry—for better and for worse—because we feel strongly that these people are as important as the problems we have exposed. Too often, American consumers tend to assume we are helpless at the hands of faceless, impersonal industries that are just too big to fight. But our work on *Prime Rip* has proven to us that strong-willed individuals can have a remarkable

242

impact on the industry that is responsible for taking the largest chunk of the consumer food dollar.

In researching this book we have talked to hundreds of people on all sides of the issues. Although we have not always agreed with their positions, and although we have written unfavorably of some of these people, we have come away with a deep respect for the determination of *all* of them to survive in an extremely tough business. We are grateful for the perspectives they have given us on the problems facing the American meat industry. We have tried to name in *Prime Rip* as many of these men and women who have affected the industry as possible, leaving out mainly a few "Meat Throats" whose contributions were important, but who must remain nameless.

We particularly wish to thank the California Public Interest Research Group (CalPIRG) for its help in bringing the problems of the meat industry to the attention of consumers. Numerous CalPIRG members donated their time to conduct surveys, produce studies, and back legislation aimed at safeguarding the rights of consumers.

We also wish to thank Pat Pestka and Monica Bonilla, without whose assistance this manuscript could not have been prepared.

This book is written in the hope that such people as Frank Hogya, John Coplin, and all the others we have described will continue to make the effort to know a rump from a stump, so all consumers will benefit.

Index